Apache CXF Web Service Development

Develop and deploy SOAP and RESTful Web Services

Naveen Balani

Rajeev Hathi

BIRMINGHAM - MUMBAI

Apache CXF Web Service Development

First published: December 2009

Production Reference: 2291209

Published by Packt Publishing Ltd.
32 Lincoln Road
Olton
Birmingham, B27 6PA, UK.

ISBN 978-1-847195-40-1

www.packtpub.com

Cover Image by Vinayak Chittar (vinayak.chittar@gmail.com)

Credits

Authors
Naveen Balani
Rajeev Hathi

Reviewer
Brett Porter

Acquisition Editor
Usha Iyer

Development Editor
Reshma Sundaresan

Technical Editor
Shadab N Khan

Copy Editor
Leonard D'silva

Indexer
Hemangini Bari

Editorial Team Leader
Akshara Aware

Project Team Leader
Priya Mukherji

Project Coordinator
Ashwin Shetty

Proofreader
Kevin McGowan

Graphics
Nilesh R. Mohite

Production Coordinator
Adline Swetha Jesuthas

Cover Work
Adline Swetha Jesuthas

About the Authors

Naveen Balani works as a Software Architect with IBM India Software Labs (ISL). He leads the design and development activities for WebSphere Business Services Fabric product out of ISL Mumbai. He has over nine years of industrial experience and has architected and implemented large scale enterprise solutions.

Naveen Balani likes to research upcoming technologies and is a Master Author with IBM developerWorks having written over 60 plus publications, on topics such as Web services, ESB, JMS, SOA, architectures, open source frameworks, semantic Web, J2ME, pervasive computing, Spring, Ajax, and various IBM products. He started working with web services way back in 2001 and proposed the first MVC web services-based pattern (`http://www.ibm.com/developerworks/library/ws-mvc/`) in 2002.

Naveen Balani's articles on Spring Series (`http://www.ibm.com/developerworks/web/library/wa-spring1/`) were rated as the top articles in the last 10 years for developerWorks web architecture zone. He has co-authored books on Spring framework (`http://www.wrox.com/WileyCDA/WroxTitle/Beginning-Spring-Framework-2.productCd-047010161X.html`) and Multiple IBM Redbooks on WebSphere Business Services Fabric and BPM 6.2 Product deployments. You can reach him on his website—`http://soaweb.co.in`

I would like to thank my wonderful wife, Sonia, for her love and patience and her endless support in spending many hours sitting beside me, reviewing my work and providing valuable inputs.

I would also like to thank my parents for their support and encouragement in all my endeavors.

And last but not least, to my good friend and co-author Rajeev Hathi.

Rajeev Hathi is a J2EE Consultant and Developer living in Mumbai, India. He grew up in a joint Hindu family and pursued his primary education in the field of Economics and Commerce. His hobbies are watching sports and listening to rock music. His favorite bands are Pink Floyd and Dire Straits.

Rajeev has written several articles for IBM developerWorks portal. His major contributions are in the fields of Java, web service, and DB2. He developed an interest in computers after pursuing a diploma in Advanced Systems Management at NIIT (National Institute of Information Technology).

Rajeev has been working on J2EE-based projects for more than ten years now. He has worked with several companies offering software services and conducted various knowledge sessions on Java and J2EE. He has attained several Java-based certifications such as SCJP, SCWCD, SCBCD, and SCEA. He, along with the co-author Naveen Balani, has initiated a portal `http://soaweb.co.in` which aims to provide online consulting on the subject of web services.

A book is often the product of many hands. To start with I'd like to thank Usha Iyer, an Acquisition Editor with Packt Publishing, for having enough faith in my writing skills and abilities. My special thanks to the Packt Publishing team in making enormous efforts to make this book a reality. A good book cannot be made better without a constructive review and feedback and the reviewers equally contributed to the whole writing process.

I owe thanks to my wonderful and lovely friend, Sunita, who instilled in me enough confidence and zest to make my writing look effortless. I owe thanks and gratitude to my family members who have supported and encouraged my writing efforts day and night. And last but not least, without my co-author and amazing friend Naveen Balani, this project would not have been achievable.

Finally, I would like to dedicate this book to my late parents and late sister without their blessings, this project would have just remained a mere thought.

About the Reviewer

Brett Porter is a software developer from Sydney, Australia, with a passion for development tooling, and automation. Seeking a more standardized and reproducible solution to organize, build, and deploy a number of software projects across teams, he discovered an early beta of Maven 1.0 in 2003, and has since been heavily involved in the development of the project. Brett is a Director and a Member of the Apache Software Foundation. He is a member of the Apache Maven Project Management Committee, and has conducted presentations and training on Maven and related tooling at several conferences and events. He founded the **Archiva project** in 2005.

Brett is the co-author of *Apache Maven 2: Effective Implementation*, published by Packt Publishing in 2009. He was also the co-author of *Better Builds with Maven*, the first book to be written about the Maven 2.0 release in 2005, and has been involved in reviewing *Maven: A Developer's Notebook and Java Power Tools.*

My thanks goes to everyone involved at the Apache Software Foundation, and all those that contribute to and use the software. You make projects such as CXF and the many others possible.

I'd also like to thank my wife Laura and my young daughter Samantha, who could afford to spare me the extra hours to review this book, so soon after having written my own!

Table of Contents

Preface

Apache CXF is an open source services framework that makes web service development easy, simplified, and standard based. CXF provides many features such as frontend programming, support for different transports and data bindings, support for different protocols, and other advanced concepts like Features and Invokers. It also provides a programming model to build and deploy RESTful services.

The focus of the book is to provide readers with comprehensive details on how to use the CXF framework for web services development. The book begins by giving us an overview of CXF features and architecture. Each feature is explained in a separate chapter, each of which covers well defined practical illustrations using real world examples. This helps developers to easily understand the CXF API. Each chapter provides hands on examples and provides step-by-step instructions to develop, deploy, and execute the code.

What this book covers

The book is about the CXF service development framework. The book covers two of the most widely used approaches, for web services development, SOAP and REST. Each chapter in the book provides hands on examples, where we look in detail at how to use the various CXF features in detail to develop web services in a step-by-step fashion.

Chapter 1: *Getting Familiar with CXF* revisits web service concepts and provides an introduction to CXF framework and its usage, and prepares the CXF environment for the following chapters. By the end of this chapter the reader will be able to understand the core concepts of CXF.

Chapter 2: *Developing a Web Service with CXF* focuses on getting the reader quickly started with the CXF framework by developing a simple web service and running it under the Tomcat container.

By the end of this chapter the reader will be able to develop a simple web service using CXF.

Chapter 3: *Working with CXF Frontends* illustrates the use of different frontends, like JAX-WS and CXF simple fronted API, and shows how to apply code-first and contract-first development approaches for developing web services. We will look at how to create dynamic web service clients, the use of web service context, and how to work directly with XML messages using CXF Provide and Dispatch implementation.

By the end of this chapter the reader will be able to apply different frontends to develop a web service.

Chapter 4: *Learning about Service Transports* explains basic transport protocols for a service and shows you how to configure HTTP, HTTP(s), JMS, and Local protocol for web services communication. You will get introduced to the concept of HTTP conduit, which enables the client program to apply policies or properties to HTTP and HTTPs protocols, and how to generate a crypto key and a key store for HTTPs based service communication. You will learn how to use JMS protocol for web services communication and how to facilitate web services message exchange using CXF Local service transport.

By the end of this chapter the reader will be able develop services with different transports

Chapter 5: *Implementing Advanced Features* will explain advanced concepts using CXF Features, Interceptors, and Invokers, and how to integrate these concepts in existing applications.

By the end of this chapter the reader will be able develop services with features like Interceptors and Invokers

Chapter 6: *Developing RESTful Services with CXF* explains the concept of REST technology and JAX-RS specifications, how CXF realizes the JAX-RS specification, and demonstrates additional features for developing enterprise RESTful services. We will look at how to design, develop, and unit test the RESTful Service by taking a real world example using CXF JAX-RS implementation.

By the end of this chapter the reader will be able to design, develop, and unit test the RESTful service

Chapter 7: *Deploying RESTful Services with CXF* will explain how to deploy REST services in a container like Tomcat using Spring configuration, and how to test out the various operations exposed by the RESTFul application using CXF RESTful client API using a web service development tool. We will look at how to enable exception handling, JSON message support, and logging support for RESTful applications using CXF framework.

By the end of this chapter the reader would be able utilize various CXF features for developing RESTful services and how to leverage Spring configuration for deploying RESTful service in the tomcat container.

Chapter 8: *Working with CXF Tools* will explain some of the commonly used CXF tools that assist us in web services development. We will look at how to invoke a real world .NET service over the internet using a Java client and JavaScript, create web service implementation from WSDL files, generate WSDL files from web service implementation, and validate the WSDL file for compliance.

By the end of this chapter the reader will be able to use different CXF tools to develop a service.

Appendix A deals with how to set up the CXF environment, provides details on how the source code for each chapter is organized, and shows how to run the source code examples using the ANT tool and Maven Tool.

Appendix B provides an explanation of the basics of the Spring framework and IoC concepts, along with an end-to-end example which utilizes Spring IoC concepts.

By the end of this Appendix chapter the reader will have a good understanding of Spring capabilities used in the context of CXF web services development in this book.

What you need for this book

You will need the following software to be installed before running the code example:

- Java 5 or higher. Apache CXF requires JDK 5 or a later version. JDK 5 can be downloaded from the following site: `http://java.sun.com/j2se/1.5.0/download.jsp`
- Tomcat 6.0 or higher. There is no strict requirement for Tomcat for CXF. In fact, any servlet container that supports Java 5 or higher can be used with CXF. For our illustrations, we will use Tomcat as our servlet container. Tomcat version 6.0 can be downloaded from the following site: `http://tomcat.apache.org/download-60.cgi`

- Apache Ant 1.7.1 or higher. Ant will be used to build and deploy the code. The build utility can be downloaded from the site: `http://ant.apache.org/bindownload.cgi`
- CXF binary distribution 2.2.3 or latest. CXF binary distribution can be downloaded from the site: `http://cxf.apache.org/download.html.`
- Maven 2.x or higher, if you plan to use Maven instead of ANT for running the code examples. Maven can be downloaded from the site `http://maven.apache.org/`

Refer to Appendix A for more details on how to set up the environment for running the code examples.

Who this book is for

This book is for developers who want to design and develop SOAP and RESTful services using Apache CXF framework, and leverage various CXF features for service development. It is ideal for developers who have some experience in Java application development as well as some basic knowledge of web services, but it covers some of the basic fundamentals of web services and REST to get you acquainted with these technologies before using these concepts to develop services using the CXF framework.

Conventions

In this book, you will find a number of styles of text that distinguish between different kinds of information. Here are some examples of these styles, and an explanation of their meaning.

Code words in text are shown as follows: " You need to specify the `<http:address>` element for sending messages in an HTTP format. "

A block of code is set as follows:

```
import javax.jws.WebService;

@WebService
public interface OrderProcess {
    String processOrder(Order order);
}
```

When we wish to draw your attention to a particular part of a code block, the relevant lines or items are set in bold:

```
<import resource="classpath:META-INF/cxf/cxf.xml" />
<import resource="classpath:META-INF/cxf/cxf-extension-soap.xml" />
<import resource="classpath:META-INF/cxf/cxf-servlet.xml" />
<jaxws:endpoint id="orderProcess" implementor="demo.order.
OrderProcessImpl" address="/OrderProcess" />
```

Any command-line input or output is written as follows:

```
set ACTIVEMQ_HOME = C:\apache-activemq-5.2.0
set ACTIVEMQ_VERSION = 5.2.0
```

New terms and **important words** are shown in bold. Words that you see on the screen, in menus or dialog boxes for example, appear in the text like this: "Click the **Add To Firefox** button. A pop-up screen will appear, as shown in the next screenshot. Click on the **install** button."

Warnings or important notes appear in a box like this.

Reader feedback

Feedback from our readers is always welcome. Let us know what you think about this book—what you liked or may have disliked. Reader feedback is important for us to develop titles that you really get the most out of.

To send us general feedback, simply send an email to `feedback@packtpub.com`, and mention the book title via the subject of your message.

If there is a book that you need and would like to see us publish, please send us a note in the **SUGGEST A TITLE** form on `www.packtpub.com` or email `suggest@packtpub.com`.

If there is a topic that you have expertise in and you are interested in either writing or contributing to a book on, see our author guide on `www.packtpub.com/authors`.

Customer support

Now that you are the proud owner of a Packt book, we have a number of things to help you to get the most from your purchase.

> **Downloading the example code for the book**
>
> Visit `http://www.packtpub.com/files/code/5401_Code.zip` to directly download the example code.
>
> The downloadable files contain instructions on how to use them.

Errata

Although we have taken every care to ensure the accuracy of our content, mistakes do happen. If you find a mistake in one of our books—maybe a mistake in the text or the code—we would be grateful if you would report this to us. By doing so, you can save other readers from frustration, and help us to improve subsequent versions of this book. If you find any errata, please report them by visiting `http://www.packtpub.com/support`, selecting your book, clicking on the **let us know** link, and entering the details of your errata. Once your errata are verified, your submission will be accepted and the errata added to any list of existing errata. Any existing errata can be viewed by selecting your title from `http://www.packtpub.com/support`.

Piracy

Piracy of copyright material on the Internet is an ongoing problem across all media. At Packt, we take the protection of our copyright and licenses very seriously. If you come across any illegal copies of our works, in any form, on the Internet, please provide us with the location address or web site name immediately so that we can pursue a remedy.

Please contact us at `copyright@packtpub.com` with a link to the suspected pirated material.

We appreciate your help in protecting our authors, and our ability to bring you valuable content.

Questions

You can contact us at `questions@packtpub.com` if you are having a problem with any aspect of the book, and we will do our best to address it.

1
Getting Familiar with CXF

We often require real world systems and applications to integrate with each other. Application integration is one of the critical areas that you need to focus on during application development, if your application involves integrating with third party or external systems. Alternatively, depending on your requirements, you may want other systems to access your application. Let's take an example of a credit card company providing services to guarantee payments made by consumers. These services are available over the Web, and consumers or applications, such as an online shopping application, or an airline firm that accepts credit cards as payment for its services, uses the credit card payment service for a consumer's payments. Since the credit card services can be accessed by any application client such as a web browser or a **WAP (Wireless Application Protocol**) enabled phone, and developed using any programming language, there is a need for a standard-based communication where the services offered can be used by any application, irrespective of any underlying technology. This is where web services come into play, and to simplify the design and development of web services, you have the option of using various web service frameworks. Apache CXF is one such leading standard-based web services framework whose goal is to simplify web services development.

In order to get started with the CXF framework, you first need to understand the concepts behind web services, the technology, and the standards that make up web service and features provided by the CXF framework. This chapter will cover these core concepts.

Specifically, in this chapter we will cover the following topics:

- The core technology standards and concepts behind web services
- Approaches for web services development
- Overview of Apache CXF framework
- Features provided by Apache CXF framework
- Setting up Apache CXF environment

Web service technology standards

Before you look at the concept behind web services you need to understand the core technology standards that make up web services. Covering all the concepts and standards associated with web services is a vast topic in itself. In this chapter we attempt to cover the relevant web service standards and information used in the context of this book to get you acquainted with the technologies for developing web services using CXF. Some of the concepts will be explained in greater detail during the course of this book.

XML

XML stands for **Extensible Markup Language**. XML is a markup language that specifies or describes the format of the data to be exchanged between two parties. The data is significantly structured as tags or elements in a hierarchical order. A user can create his/her own tag to represent structured information. XML has become the de facto standard for representing structured information. Some of the important standard technologies associated with an XML document are listed below:

- XML namespace—an XML namespace is a standard for providing uniquely named elements and attributes in an XML document. The XML namespace concept is similar to package definitions in Java, which provide conflict resolution of class names based on package declarations. A namespace is declared using the reserved XML attribute `xmlns`, the value of which must be a **URI (Uniform Resource Identifier)** reference, for example, `xmlns=http://www.w3.org/1999/xhtml` or using a prefix `xmlns:xhtml=http://www.w3.org/1999/xhtml`.
- XML schema—XML schema provides a means of defining the structure, content, and semantics of XML documents. The XML Schema data model includes the vocabulary (element and attribute names), the content model (relationships and structure), and data types. An example of XML Schema describing address information is provided below:

```
<xs:schema
 xmlns:xs="http://www.w3.org/2001/XMLSchema">
 <xs:element name="address" type="Address"/>
 <xs:complexType name="Address">
  <xs:sequence>
   <xs:element name="addressLine1" type="xs:string"/>
   <xs:element name="addressLine2" type="xs:string"/>
   <xs:element name="city" type="xs:string"/>
   <xs:element name="state" type="xs:string"/>
   <xs:element name="country" type="xs:string"/>
```

```
    </xs:sequence>
  </xs:complexType>
</xs:schema>
```

In the above example, `xs` represents the namespace of the XML Schema. The `address` represents an element whose type is `Address`. The `Address type` in turn is represented as `complexType` (similar to a Java bean `Address` class which stores address information), which is comprised of elements "`addressLine1`", "`addressLine2`", "`city`", "`state`", and "`country`" with data type as `string`. The code listing below provides a valid Address XML document based on the above Address XML schema. The Address XML Schema provides validation for the following XML document:

```
<address xmlns:xsi="http://www.w3.org/2001/XMLSchema-instance"
  xsi:noNamespaceSchemaLocation="address.xsd">
  <addressLine1>1501 ACity</addressLine1>
  <addressLine2>UCity</addressLine2>
  <city>SFO</city>
  <state>CA</state>
  <country>US</country>
</address>
```

SOAP (Simple Object Access Protocol)

SOAP is a protocol for exchanging XML-based messages over a network, typically using HTTP protocol. The SOAP message format is comprised of a SOAP Envelope which encloses all request information. The SOAP Envelope, in turn, is then made up of optional headers and a body. The headers optionally contain context related information, such as security or transaction, while the body contains actual payload or application data.

The following listing provides a sample SOAP message format containing address information:

```
<?xml version="1.0"?>
<soapenv:Envelope xmlns:soapenv="http://schemas.xmlsoap.org/soap/
envelope/"
xmlns:ns1="http://apress.com/beginjava6/address"
xmlns:xsd="http://www.w3.org/2001/XMLSchema">
<soapenv:Header></soapenv:Header>
<soapenv:Body>
<ns1:Address>
<ns1:addressLine1>1501ACity</ns1:addressLine1>
<ns1:addressLine2>UCity</ns1:addressLine2>
<ns1:city>SFO</ns1:city>
```

```
<ns1:state>CA</ns1:state>
<ns1:country>US</ns1:country>
</ns1:Address>
</soapenv:Body>
</soapenv:Envelope>
```

WSDL (Web Services Description language)

WSDL is a standard-based XML language used to describe web services. Under WSDL, a web service is described as a set of communication endpoints that are capable of exchanging messages. These communication endpoints are called **ports**.

An endpoint is comprised of two parts:

- The first part is the abstract definitions of operations (similar to methods in Java) provided by the services and messages (input and output parameter types for methods) which are needed to invoke the service. The set of abstract operation definitions is referred to as port type.
- The second part is the concrete binding of those abstract definitions of operations to concrete network protocol, where the service is located, and message format for the service.

The WSDL binding describes how the service is bound to a messaging protocol, particularly the SOAP messaging protocol. Typically, the WSDL files would be created using the tool provided by the web service framework. The following block of code shows a listing of Address Verification WSDL, which uses the Address XML schema. Please refer to the inline comments for an explanation of the elements in the below WSDL file:

```
<?xml version='1.0' encoding='UTF-8'?><wsdl:definitions name="Addr
essVerifyProcessImplService" targetNamespace="http://order.demo/"
xmlns:ns1="http://schemas.xmlsoap.org/soap/http" xmlns:soap="http://
schemas.xmlsoap.org/wsdl/soap/" xmlns:tns="http://order.demo/"
xmlns:wsdl="http://schemas.xmlsoap.org/wsdl/" xmlns:xsd="http://www.
w3.org/2001/XMLSchema">
<wsdl:types>
<!-- Schema definition for Address element. This serves as the input
message format for invoking the Address verification service. -->
<xs:schema attributeFormDefault="unqualified" elementFormDefault="unqu
alified" targetNamespace="http://order.demo/" xmlns:tns="http://order.
demo/" xmlns:xs="http://www.w3.org/2001/XMLSchema">
<xs:element name="Address" type="tns:address" />
<xs:element name="verifyAddress" type="tns:verifyAddress" />
<xs:element name="verifyAddressResponse" type="tns:verifyAddressRespo
nse" />
```

```
<xs:complexType name="verifyAddress">
<xs:sequence>
<xs:element minOccurs="0" name="arg0" type="tns:address" />
</xs:sequence>
</xs:complexType>
<xs:complexType name="address">
<xs:sequence>
<xs:element minOccurs="0" name="addressLine1" type="xs:string" />
<xs:element minOccurs="0" name="addressLine2" type="xs:string" />
<xs:element minOccurs="0" name="city" type="xs:string" />
<xs:element minOccurs="0" name="country" type="xs:string" />
<xs:element minOccurs="0" name="state" type="xs:string" />
</xs:sequence>
</xs:complexType>
<xs:complexType name="verifyAddressResponse">
<xs:sequence>
<xs:element minOccurs="0" name="return" type="xs:string" />
</xs:sequence>
</xs:complexType>
</xs:schema>
  </wsdl:types>
  <!-- Specifies the Messages for Address Verification Service. -->
  <wsdl:message name="verifyAddressResponse">
    <wsdl:part element="tns:verifyAddressResponse" name="parameters">
    </wsdl:part>
  </wsdl:message>
  <wsdl:message name="verifyAddress">
    <wsdl:part element="tns:verifyAddress" name="parameters">
    </wsdl:part>
  </wsdl:message>
    <!-- Specifies the Operations for Verify Address service. -->
  <wsdl:portType name="AddressVerifyProcess">
    <wsdl:operation name="verifyAddress">
      <wsdl:input message="tns:verifyAddress" name="verifyAddress">
    </wsdl:input>
      <wsdl:output message="tns:verifyAddressResponse"
      name="verifyAddressResponse">
    </wsdl:output>
    </wsdl:operation>
  </wsdl:portType>
  <!-- Specifies the SOAP Binding for Verify Address Process. -->
  <wsdl:binding name="AddressVerifyProcessImplServiceSoapBinding"
  type="tns:AddressVerifyProcess">
```

```
    <soap:binding style="document" transport=
    "http://schemas.xmlsoap.org/soap/http" />
    <wsdl:operation name="verifyAddress">
      <soap:operation soapAction="" style="document" />
      <wsdl:input name="verifyAddress">
        <soap:body use="literal" />
      </wsdl:input>
      <wsdl:output name="verifyAddressResponse">
        <soap:body use="literal" />
      </wsdl:output>
    </wsdl:operation>
  </wsdl:binding>
    <!-- Service definition for Verify Address . -->
    <!-- The soap location specifies the URL where the address verify
service is located. -->
  <wsdl:service name="AddressVerifyProcessImplService">
  <wsdl:port binding="tns:AddressVerifyProcessImplServiceSoapBinding"
  name="AddressVerifyProcessImplPort">
      <soap:address location="http://localhost:9000/
      AddressVerifyProcess" />
    </wsdl:port>
  </wsdl:service>
</wsdl:definitions>
```

In Chapter 8 you will look at how to use the various CXF tools for web services development and format of WSDL files in detail.

REST (Representational State Transfer)

REST (**Representational State Transfer**) is neither a technology nor a standard; it's an architectural style—a set of guidelines for exposing resources over the Web. The REST architecture style is related to a resource, which is a representation identified by a Uniform Resource Indicator (URI), for example, `http://cxf.soaweb.co.in/mybook`. The resource can be any piece of information such as a book, order, customer, employee, and so on. The client queries or updates the resource through the URI and, therefore, influences a state change in its representation. All resources share a uniform interface for the transfer of state between client and resource.

The World Wide Web is a classic example built on the REST architecture style. As implemented on the World Wide Web, URIs identify the resources (`http://amazon.com/mybook`), and HTTP is the protocol by which resources are accessed. HTTP provides a uniform interface and set of methods to manipulate the resource. A client program, like a web browser, can access, update, add, or remove a Web resource through URI using various HTTP methods, like GET and POST, thereby changing its representational state.

In Chapter 6 and 7 you will look at the REST concepts in detail and how to develop web services using the REST architecture style (also termed RESTful Web Services).

Service Registry

Service Registry provides a mechanism to look up web services. Traditionally, there was UDDI specification that defined the standards on registering and discovering a web service, but it lacked enterprise-wide adoption. Enterprises started shipping their own version of Service Registry, providing enterprise capabilities like service versioning, service classifications, and life cycle management.

Introducing web services

There are many different definitions available for a web service. The World Wide Web Consortium (**W3C**) defines a web service as follows:

> *A Web service is a software system identified by a URI whose public interfaces and bindings are defined and described using XML (specifically WSDL). Its definition can be discovered by other software systems. These systems may then interact with the web service in a manner prescribed by its definition, using XML-based messages conveyed by Internet protocols.*

Simply, put web service is a software component that provides a business function as a service over the web that can be accessed through a URL. Web services are next generation web applications, modules, or components that can be thought of as a service provided over the web. Traditionally, we had static HTML pages as web content, which evolved into more dynamic full featured web applications providing business functionality and rich GUI features to the end user. A web service component is one step ahead of this web paradigm and provides only business service, usually in the form of raw XML data that can be digested by virtually all client systems. The GUI and business functionality are well separated. A web service can be thought of as a self contained, self describing, modular application that can be published, located, and invoked across the web.

The greatest benefit that web services provide is interoperability. Web services can be ported on any platform and can be written in different programming languages. Similarly, the client accessing the web service can be an application written in a different language and running on a different platform than that of a service itself.

Approaches for web service development

Two of the most widely used approaches for developing web services are SOAP (Simple Object Access Protocol) and the REST (Representational State Transfer) architecture style. In depth details on developing SOAP-based web services are provided in Chapters 2-5, while Chapters 6 and 7 are dedicated to RESTful web service development.

A web service involves three types of roles—a service consumer, a service provider, and an optional service registry. The following diagram shows the interaction between the service provider, the service consumer, and the service registry:

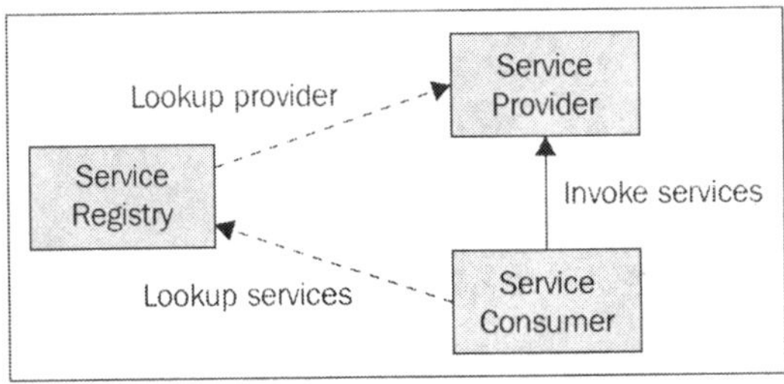

The service providers furnish the services over the web and respond to web service requests. The service consumer consumes the services offered by the service provider. In SOAP-based web services, the service provider publishes the contract (WSDL file) of the service over the web where a consumer can access it directly or by looking up a service registry. The service consumer usually generates a web service client code from a WSDL file using the tools offered by the web service framework to interact with the web service. In the next chapter you will look at how to create web service clients from a WSDL file.

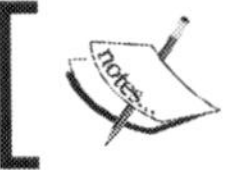

[In Chapter 8 you will look at how to use various CXF tools for web service development.]

With RESTful Web Services there is no formal contract between the service provider and the service consumer. The service requestor needs to know the format of the message, for instance, XML or **JSON (Java Script Object Notation)**, and operations supported by the service provider. The service provider exposes the set of operations using standard HTTP methods like GET or POST. The service requestor invokes one of the methods defined for the resources using the URI over the HTTP protocol.

The choice of adopting SOAP rather than REST depends on your application's requirements. If your requirement consists of transmitting and receiving simple XML messages, then you would probably go with RESTful Web Services. However, if your requirement consists of various contracts to be defined and negotiated between the provider and consumer such as using a **WSDL (Web Service Description Language)** file and adhering to various web services specifications (WS Specifications) such as web service security for enterprise adoption, then SOAP-based web services is the right option. If you are developing SOAP-based services, then you also need to be aware of SOAP communication styles.

Web service SOAP communication styles

The web service SOAP communication style plays a significant role in communicating SOAP XML messages between the service provider and the service consumer. There exist two types of SOAP message styles, **Document** and **RPC**. The SOAP message styles are defined in a WSDL document as SOAP binding. A SOAP binding can have either an encoded use or a literal use. Encoding as the term implies, the message would be encoded using some format, while literal specifies plain text messages without any encoding logic.

Document style, as the name suggests, deals with XML documents as payloads which adhere to well defined contracts, typically created using XML schema definitions. The XML schema format specifies the contract for business messages being exchanged between web service provider and consumer, which the consumers can call and adhere to. The XML schema defines the request and response message format between the service provider and the service consumer. Document literal style is the preferred way of web service communication for achieving interoperability.

RPC (Remote Procedure Call) style, on the other hand, indicates that the SOAP body contains an XML representation of a method. In order to serialize method parameters into the SOAP message so it can be deserialized back by any web service implementation, the SOAP specification defines a standard set of encoding rules. As RPC is traditionally used in conjunction with SOAP encoding rules, the combination is referred to as RPC/encoded. You also have an RPC/literal communication style model where you don't have any encoding formats, but the messages are still limited to RPC method-based communication, where messages can't be validated as they are not tied to any XML Schema definition. You should probably avoid developing RPC style web services as it has a lot of interoperability issues.

There are lot of specifications designed for SOAP-based web services. These web service specifications are designed for interoperable protocols for Security, Reliable Messaging, Management, and Transactions in loosely coupled systems. The specifications are built on top of the core XML and SOAP standards.

Apache CXF

Apache CXF is an open source web service framework that provides an easy to use, standard-based programming model for developing web services. Web services can be implemented using different application protocols like SOAP, XML, JSON, RESTful HTTP, and support various transport protocols like HTTP or JMS (Java Message Service).

History of CXF

Exactly what does CXF stand for? Apache CXF is the product of two projects, Celtix and XFire, hence the name **CXF.** Celtix, an open source Java-based Enterprise Service Bus (ESB) project, is a product of ObjectWeb consortia that delivers open source middleware solutions. The project was sponsored by IONA. On the other hand, XFire, a Java-based SOAP framework, is an open source project from Codehaus. Both Celtix and XFire, while in their initial versions, had many things in common and therefore the developers of both projects decided to bring out the best of both worlds and planned a better 2.0 version of Celtix and XFire. The communities of both these projects entered incubation at the Apache Software foundation to develop version 2.0. It took about 20 months at the Apache incubator before CXF finally rolled out. CXF is now formally known as Apache CXF which concentrates on delivering an open source web service framework. The framework which had its first release as v2.0, is now evolved as v2.2, with bug fixes, and the addition of new features.

Why CXF?

Picking up a framework is always a challenging task. There are many web service frameworks available today. Historically, there was Axis 1 which evolved into Axis 2, providing better flexibility and enhanced support for web service standards. Other widely used web service frameworks are GlassFish Metro, Glue, JBossWS, and so on. Every web services framework aims to provide a robust infrastructure for the developer to conveniently build, deploy, and publish the web services. So which one is the better framework? That's a million dollar question!

We choose CXF rather than other web service frameworks as it supports all the leading web service standards and provides a simplified programming model for developing SOAP and RESTful-based web services, along with options for various other application protocols. CXF provides a flexible deployment model for implementing web services. More specifically, we choose CXF as it provides the following capabilities.

Support for web service standards

Web service standards define the norms of a web service implementation with respect to its interoperability. The standards ensure that a web service is accessed independently of the client platform.

The framework provides the following web service standards support:

- **Java API for XML Web Services** (**JAX-WS**)
- SOAP
- **Web Services Description Language** (**WSDL**)
- **Message Transmission Optimization Mechanism** (**MTOM**)
- WS-Basic Profile
- WS-Addressing
- WS-Policy
- WS-ReliableMessaging
- WS-Security

One of the most important web services technologies is JAX-WS. JAX-WS is a specification designed to simplify the construction of primarily SOAP-based web services and web service clients in Java. JAX-WS also includes the **Java Architecture for XML Binding** (**JAXB**) and **SOAP with Attachments API for Java** (**SAAJ**).

JAXB offers data binding capabilities by providing a convenient way to map XML schema to a representation in Java code. The JAXB shields the conversion of XML schema messages in SOAP messages to Java code without having the developers see the XML and SOAP parsing. The JAXB specification defines the binding between Java and XML schema. SAAJ provides a standard way of dealing with XML attachments contained in a SOAP message. CXF provides support for a complete JAX-WS stack. We will look at how to use the JAX-WS standards while developing web services in the next chapter.

The WS-Addressing, WS-Policy, WS-ReliableMessaging, and WS-Security are all part of the web services specification aimed to bring in consistency in various areas of web services. For instance, WS-Security specification is about how integrity and confidentiality can be enforced on web services using a standard method.

The WS-I Basic Profile is a specification from the **Web Services Interoperability industry consortium** (**WS-I**), which provides a reasonable set of rules and guidelines that are best suited for achieving web services interoperability. The rules and specifications are applied to a WSDL file, as the said file serves as the contract between service provider and service consumer in SOAP-based web services. Adhering to WS-I basic profiles ensures that your services can interoperate between different platforms.

Support for POJO (Plain Old Java Object)

POJOs are Plain Old Java Objects that don't implement any infrastructure framework-specific interfaces such as JMS or EJB interfaces. Using the POJO programming model simplifies testing and keeps things simple. POJO makes it easier to integrate with other frameworks like Spring, which provides various services such as transactions, and conforms to POJO in a standardized way. Throughout the book we have used POJO to demonstrate the CXF capabilities. CXF implements the JAX-WS and JAX-RS (Java API for RESTful services) specification, which provides a set of annotations to convert POJOs as SOAP and RESTful web services.

Frontend programming APIs

CXF frontends are programming APIs that can be used to develop web services and web service clients. CXF supports two types of frontends, namely standard-based JAX-WS, and simple frontend. These CXF frontends provide simple to use APIs to expose POJOs as web services and create web service clients. In Chapter 3, we will look at how to use the frontend programming APIs for developing web services.

Tools support

CXF provides different tools for conversion between JavaBeans, web services, and WSDL. These tools assist developers in generating web service clients like Java and JavaScript from WSDL or generating a WSDL file from a service implementation. CXF provides support for Maven and Ant integration for build and dependency management. Some of the tools supported are as follows:

- Java to web service
- Java to WSDL
- WSDL to Java
- WSDL to JavaScript
- WSDL to Service
- WSDL to SOAP
- WSDL to XML
- WSDL Validator
- XSD to WSDL

In Chapter 8, we will look at some of the commonly used CXF tools which assist in web service development.

Support for RESTful services

CXF supports the concept of RESTful (Representational State Transfer) services and the JAX-RS specification which specifies the semantics to create web services according to the REST architectural style. JAX-RS specification does not provide any details on RESTful clients. CXF goes a step further and provides various options to create clients that can interact with the JAX-RS web service. CXF also supports **Java Script Object Notation (JSON)** data format which is a widely used format developing Web 2.0-based applications. In Chapters 6 and 7, we will look at these concepts in detail and how they are used for designing and developing RESTful web services.

Support for different transports and bindings

Data binding is the key for all web service development. Data binding means mapping between Java objects and message formats which have been exposed by the service's implementation, for instance XML or **JSON** (**Java Script Object Notation**). SOAP-based web services would use XML as the data format, while RESTful services have a choice of using XML or JSON as the data format. CXF provides data binding components that transparently handle the mapping for you. CXF also supports **Java Architecture for XML Binding** (**JAXB**) and AEGIS data binding apart from SOAP and HTTP protocol binding. CXF supports different kinds of transport protocols such as HTTP, HTTP(s), JMS, and CXF Local protocol that allow service-to-service communication within the single Java Virtual Machine (JVM).

All of the transport protocols are explained in the context of web service development in Chapter 4.

Support for non-XML binding

CXF supports non-XML bindings such as **JavaScript Object Notation** (**JSON**) and **Common Object Request Broker Architecture** (**CORBA**). It also supports the **Java Business Integration** (**JBI**) architectures and **Service Component Architectures** (**SCAs**). Non-XML binding provides more choices for integration with existing infrastructure which support these formats. In Chapter 7 we will look at how to add JSON support for RESTful web services.

Ease of use

The framework is developed with a mission to provide a robust infrastructure for web services development and to ease the development process. CXF provides first class integration support with Spring framework, where a POJO exposed as web services through CXF framework can leverage the services offered by the Spring framework. For instance, transaction capabilities can be applied declaratively to POJO web services through the Spring transaction infrastructure support. Using the Spring framework simplifies the overall configuration of web services and eases deployment through XML-based configuration files. You will look at how CXF provides Spring configuration support, which eases configuration and deployment while developing web services.

Flexible deployment

CXF offers a flexible deployment model where services can be developed and unit tested in a standalone environment, and promoted for deployment in an application server environment. Web services developed with CXF can be deployed with light weight containers like Tomcat and also J2EE-based containers such as Websphere, Weblogic, JBoss, Geronimo, and JOnAS. It can also be deployed in the two tier client/server environment. CXF provides integration with a **Service Component Architecture** (**SCA**) container like Tuscany. It also supports **Java Business Integration** (**JBI**) integration with a web service deployed as a service engine in JBI containers such as ServiceMix, OpenESB, and Petals.

Setting up the environment

In this section we will set up the CXF environment for running the code examples. We will be using the ANT tool throughout the book for building and running the code examples.

For ANT users

You will have to download and install the following software before setting up the environment. The book illustrates the setup process in a Windows environment. The same can be emulated in a Unix-based environment with ease:

- Java 5 or higher. Apache CXF requires JDK 5 or a later version. JDK 5 can be downloaded from the following website: `http://java.sun.com/j2se/1.5.0/download.jsp`.
- Tomcat 6.0 or higher. There is no strict requirement for Tomcat for CXF. In fact, any servlet container that supports Java 5 or higher can be used with CXF. For our illustrations, we will use Tomcat as our servlet container. Tomcat version 6.0 can be downloaded from the following website: `http://tomcat.apache.org/download-60.cgi`.
- Apache Ant 1.7.1 or higher. Ant will be used to build and deploy the code. The build utility can be downloaded from the site: `http://ant.apache.org/bindownload.cgi`.
- CXF binary distribution 2.2.3. CXF binary distribution can be downloaded from the website: `http://cxf.apache.org/download.html`.

Once the above list of software is installed, we go about setting up the following environment variables:

Environment Variable	Description
JAVA_HOME	Set this to point to the JDK 1.5 installation root folder, for example C:\jdk1.5.0_12.
CATALINA_HOME	Set this to point to the Tomcat installation root folder, for example C:\Program Files\Tomcat 6.0.
ANT_HOME	Set this to point to the ANT installation root folder, for example C:\apache-ant-1.7.1.
CXF_HOME	Set this to point to the CXF installation root folder, for example C:\apache-cxf-2.2.3.
PATH	Set this to point to the above respective 'HOME'/ bin folder, for example %JAVA_HOME%\bin. Make sure that you do not overwrite the existing PATH variable content. You will need to add to the existing PATH.

The environment setup can also be automated using batch script. The script might look like the following:

```
@echo off
rem ---------------------------------------------------------------
rem CXF Environment Setup script
rem ---------------------------------------------------------------
set JAVA_HOME=C:\jdk1.5.0_12
set CATALINA_HOME=C:\Program Files\Tomcat 6.0
set ANT_HOME=C:\apache-ant-1.7.1
set CXF_HOME=C:\apache-cxf-2.2.3
set PATH=%PATH%;%JAVA_HOME%\bin;%CATALINA_HOME%\bin;%ANT_HOME%\
bin;%CXF_HOME%\bin
rem ---------------------------------------------------------------
```

For Maven users

Apache CXF also supports a Maven-based build and installation. For readers using Maven 2 for developing their applications, the CXF artifacts can be accessed from the Maven central repository itself. The complete release is available at the following location:

```
http://repo1.maven.org/maven2/
```

The following POM dependencies need to be declared to build CXF code using Maven:

```
<properties>
  <cxf.version>2.2.1</cxf.version>
</properties>

<dependencies>
   <dependency>
      <groupId>org.apache.cxf</groupId>
      <artifactId>cxf-rt-frontend-jaxws</artifactId>
      <version>${cxf.version}</version>
   </dependency>
   <dependency>
      <groupId>org.apache.cxf</groupId>
      <artifactId>cxf-rt-transports-http</artifactId>
      <version>${cxf.version}</version>
   </dependency>
   <dependency>
            <groupId>org.apache.cxf</groupId>
            <artifactId>cxf-rt-transports-http-jetty</artifactId>
            <version>${cxf.version}</version>
    </dependency>
</dependencies>
```

In each chapter we have developed the source code from scratch along with Ant build files to build and run the code. If you are interested in running the examples directly without developing it from scratch, the entire source code is available at the Packt website (`www.packtpub.com/files/code/5401_Code.zip`). The appendix chapter *Getting Ready with the Code Examples* provides detailed instructions on how to download the source code from the Packt site. If you plan to use Maven, relevant `pom.xml` files are provided with the source code download. Refer to the *Using Maven for Build management* section in the *Getting Ready with the Code Examples* appendix chapter on how to use Maven to build the examples.

Summary

In this chapter we introduced some of the basic concepts of web services and technology standards that are relevant in the context of the book to get you acquainted with these technologies before using these concepts for services development using CXF. We went through the two of the most widely used approaches for web services development, namely, SOAP-based web services and RESTful web services.

We looked at the Apache CXF framework, its history, and went through the various standards and features offered by the CXF framework for web services development. The Apache CXF provides a robust framework that makes web service development easy, simplified, and standard-based. Finally, we looked at how to set up the CXF environment for both Ant and Maven users.

2

Developing a Web Service with CXF

The first chapter provided an introduction to web services and CXF framework. We looked at the features supported by the CXF framework and how to set up the CXF environment. This chapter will focus on programming web service with CXF. CXF provides a robust programming model that offers simple and convenient APIs for web service development. The chapter will focus on illustrating a simple web service development using CXF and Spring-based configurations. The chapter will also talk about the architecture of CXF.

Before we examine CXF-based web service development, we will review the example application that will be illustrated throughout the book. The example application will be called **Order Processing Application**. The book will demonstrate the same application to communicate different concepts and features of CXF so that the reader can have a better understanding of CXF as a whole. This chapter will focus on the following topics:

- Overview of a sample Order Processing Application
- CXF-based web service development with Spring
- Insight into CXF architecture

The Order Processing Application

The objective of the Order Processing Application is to process a customer order. The order process functionality will generate the customer order, thereby making the order valid and approved. A typical scenario will be a customer making an order request to buy a particular item. The purchase department will receive the order request from the customer and prepare a formal purchase order. The purchase order will hold the details of the customer, the name of the item to be purchased, the quantity, and the price. Once the order is prepared, it will be sent to the Order Processing department for the necessary approval. If the order is valid and approved, then the department will generate the unique order ID and send it back to the Purchase department. The Purchase department will communicate the order ID back to the customer.

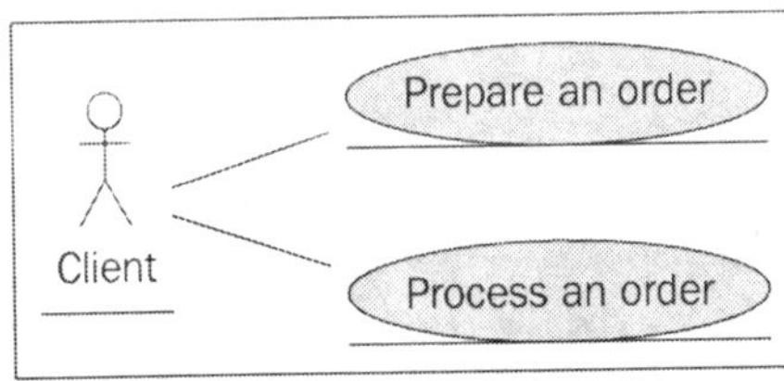

For simplicity, we will look at the following use cases:

- Prepare an order
- Process the order

The client application will prepare an order and send it to the server application through a business method call. The server application will contain a web service that will process the order and generate a unique order ID. The generation of the unique order ID will signify order approval.

In real world applications a unique order ID is always accompanied by the date the order was approved. However, in this example we chose to keep it simple by only generating order ID.

Developing a service

Let's look specifically at how to create an Order Processing Web Service and then register it as a Spring bean using a JAX-WS frontend.

In Chapter 3 you will learn about the JAX-WS frontend. The chapter will also cover a brief discussion on JAX-WS. The Sun-based JAX-WS specification can be found at the following URL:

`http://jcp.org/aboutJava/communityprocess/final/jsr224/index.html`

JAX-WS frontend offers two ways of developing a web service—Code-first and Contract-first. We will use the *Code-first* approach, that is, we will first create a Java class and convert this into a web service component. The first set of tasks will be to create server-side components.

In web service terminology, Code-first is termed as the Bottoms Up approach, and Contract-first is referred to as the Top Down approach.

To achieve this, we typically perform the following steps:

- Create a **Service Endpoint Interface** (**SEI**) and define a business method to be used with the web service.
- Create the implementation class and annotate it as a web service.
- Create `beans.xml` and define the service class as a Spring bean using a JAX-WS frontend.

Creating a Service Endpoint Interface (SEI)

Let's first create the SEI for our Order Processing Application. We will name our SEI `OrderProcess`. The following code illustrates the `OrderProcess` SEI:

```
package demo.order;
import javax.jws.WebService;
@WebService
public interface OrderProcess {
@WebMethod
String processOrder(Order order);
}
```

As you can see from the preceding code, we created a Service Endpoint Interface named `OrderProcess`. The SEI is just like any other Java interface. It defines an abstract business method `processOrder`. The method takes an Order bean as a parameter and returns an order ID String value. The goal of the `processOrder` method is to process the order placed by the customer and return the unique order ID.

One significant thing to observe is the `@WebService` annotation. The annotation is placed right above the interface definition. It signifies that this interface is not an ordinary interface but a web service interface. This interface is known as **Service Endpoint Interface** and will have a business method exposed as a service method to be invoked by the client.

The `@WebService` annotation is part of the JAX-WS annotation library. JAX-WS provides a library of annotations to turn Plain Old Java classes into web services and specifies detailed mapping from a service defined in WSDL to the Java classes that will implement that service. The `javax.jws.WebService` annotation also comes with attributes that completely define a web service. For the moment we will ignore these attributes and proceed with our development.

The `javax.jws.@WebMethod` annotation is optional and is used for customizing the web service operation. The `@WebMethod` annotation provides the operation name and the action elements which are used to customize the `name` attribute of the operation and the SOAP action element in the WSDL document.

The following code shows the `Order` class:

```
package demo.order;

import javax.xml.bind.annotation.XmlRootElement;

@XmlRootElement(name = "Order")
public class Order {

    private String customerID;
    private String itemID;
    private int qty;
    private double price;

    // Contructor
    public Order() {
    }

    public String getCustomerID() {
        return customerID;
    }

    public void setCustomerID(String customerID) {
        this.customerID = customerID;
    }
```

```
        public String getItemID() {
            return itemID;
        }

        public void setItemID(String itemID) {
            this.itemID = itemID;
        }

        public int getQty() {
            return qty;
        }

        public void setQty(int qty) {
            this.qty = qty;
        }

        public double getPrice() {
            return price;
        }

        public void setPrice(double price) {
            this.price = price;
        }
    }
```

As you can see, we have added an `@XmlRootElement` annotation to the `Order` class. The `@XmlRootElement` is part of the **Java Architecture for XML Binding (JAXB)** annotation library. JAXB provides data binding capabilities by providing a convenient way to map XML schema to a representation in Java code. The JAXB shields the conversion of XML schema messages in SOAP messages to Java code without having the developers know about XML and SOAP parsing. CXF uses JAXB as the default data binding component.

The `@XmlRootElement` annotations associated with `Order` class map the `Order` class to the XML root element. The attributes contained within the `Order` object by default are mapped to `@XmlElement`. The `@XmlElement` annotations are used to define elements within the XML. The `@XmlRootElement` and `@XmlElement` annotations allow you to customize the namespace and name of the XML element. If no customizations are provided, then the JAXB runtime by default would use the same name of attribute for the XML element. CXF handles this mapping of Java objects to XML.

Developing a service implementation class

We will now develop the implementation class that will realize our `OrderProcess` SEI. We will name this implementation class `OrderProcessImpl`. The following code illustrates the service implementation class `OrderProcessImpl`:

```
@WebService
public class OrderProcessImpl implements OrderProcess {

    public String processOrder(Order order) {
      String orderID = validate(order);
        return orderID;
    }
   /**
    * Validates the order and returns the order ID
   **/
    private String validate(Order order) {
      String custID = order.getCustomerID();
      String itemID = order.getItemID();
      int qty = order.getQty();
      double price = order.getPrice();
      if (custID != null && itemID != null && !custID.equals("")
                          && !itemID.equals("") && qty > 0
                          && price > 0.0) {
          return "ORD1234";
      }
      return null;
    }
}
```

As we can see from the preceding code, our implementation class `OrderProcessImpl` is pretty straightforward. It also has `@WebService` annotation defined above the class declaration. The class `OrderProcessImpl` implements `OrderProcess` SEI. The class implements the `processOrder` method. The `processOrder` method checks for the validity of the order by invoking the `validate` method. The `validate` method checks whether the `Order` bean has all the relevant properties valid and not null.

It is recommended that developers explicitly implement OrderProcess SEI, though it may not be necessary. This can minimize coding errors by ensuring that the methods are implemented as defined.

Next we will look at how to publish the OrderProcess JAX-WS web service using Sping configuration.

Spring-based server bean

What makes CXF the obvious choice as a web service framework is its use of Spring-based configuration files to publish web service endpoints. It is the use of such configuration files that makes the development of web service convenient and easy with CXF.

Please refer to the *Getting Started with Spring framework* appendix chapter to understand the concept of Inversion of Control, **AOP** (**Aspect oriented program**), and features provided by the Spring framework using a sample use case.

Spring provides a lightweight container which works on the concept of **Inversion of Control** (**IoC**) or **Dependency Injection** (**DI**) architecture; it does so through the implementation of a configuration file that defines Java beans and its dependencies. By using Spring you can abstract and wire all the class dependencies in a single configuration file. The configuration file is often referred to as an Application Context or Bean Context file.

We will create a server side Spring-based configuration file and name it as `beans.xml`. The following code illustrates the `beans.xml` configuration file:

```
<beans xmlns="http://www.springframework.org/schema/beans"
    xmlns:xsi="http://www.w3.org/2001/XMLSchema-instance"
    xmlns:jaxws="http://cxf.apache.org/jaxws"
    xsi:schemaLocation="
http://www.springframework.org/schema/beans
http://www.springframework.org/schema/beans/spring-beans.xsd
http://cxf.apache.org/jaxws http://cxf.apache.org/schemas/jaxws.xsd">

    <import resource="classpath:META-INF/cxf/cxf.xml" />
    <import resource="classpath:META-INF/cxf/cxf-extension-soap.xml" />
    <import resource="classpath:META-INF/cxf/cxf-servlet.xml" />

    <jaxws:endpoint
      id="orderProcess"
      implementor="demo.order.OrderProcessImpl"
      address="/OrderProcess" />

</beans>
```

Let's examine the previous code and understand what it really means. It first defines the necessary namespaces. It then defines a series of `<import>` statements. It imports `cxf.xml`, `cxf-extension-soap.xml`, and `cxf-servlet.xml`. These files are Spring-based configuration files that define core components of CXF. They are used to kick start CXF runtime and load the necessary infrastructure objects such as WSDL manager, conduit manager, destination factory manager, and so on.

The `<jaxws:endpoint>` element in the `beans.xml` file specifies the `OrderProcess` web service as a JAX-WS endpoint. The element is defined with the following three attributes:

- `id`—specifies a unique identifier for a bean. In this case, `jaxws:endpoint` is a bean, and the `id` name is `orderProcess`.
- `implementor`—specifies the actual web service implementation class. In this case, our implementor class is `OrderProcessImpl`.
- `address`—specifies the URL address where the endpoint is to be published. The URL address must to be relative to the web context. For our example, the endpoint will be published using the relative path `/OrderProcess`.

The `<jaxws:endpoint>` element signifies that the CXF internally uses JAX-WS frontend to publish the web service. This element definition provides a short and convenient way to publish a web service. A developer need not have to write any Java class to publish a web service.

Developing a client

In the previous section we discussed and illustrated how to develop and publish a web service. We now have the server-side code that publishes our `OrderProcess` web service. The next set of tasks will be to create the client-side code that will consume or invoke our `OrderProcess` web service. To achieve this, we will perform the following steps:

- Develop the `client-beans.xml` to define the client factory class as a Spring bean using JAX-WS frontend
- Develop a client Java application to invoke the web service

Developing a Spring-based client bean

We will create a client-side Spring-based configuration file and name it as `client-beans.xml`. The following code illustrates the `client-beans.xml` configuration file:

```
<beans xmlns="http://www.springframework.org/schema/beans"
   xmlns:xsi="http://www.w3.org/2001/XMLSchema-instance"
   xmlns:jaxws="http://cxf.apache.org/jaxws"
   xsi:schemaLocation="
http://www.springframework.org/schema/beans
http://www.springframework.org/schema/beans/spring-beans.xsd
http://cxf.apache.org/jaxws http://cxf.apache.org/schemas/jaxws.xsd">
<jaxws:client id="orderClient" serviceClass=
                "demo.order.OrderProcess" address=
                "http://localhost:8080/orderapp/OrderProcess" />
</beans>
```

The `<jaxws:client>` element in the `client-beans.xml` file specifies the client bean using JAX-WS frontend. The element is defined with the following three attributes:

- `id`—specifies a unique identifier for a bean. In this case, `jaxws:client` is a bean and the `id` name is `orderClient`. The bean will represent an SEI.
- `serviceClass`—specifies the web service SEI. In this case our SEI class is `OrderProcess`.
- `address`—specifies the URL address where the endpoint is published. In this case the endpoint is published at the URL address: `http://localhost:8080/orderapp/OrderProcess`.

`<jaxws:client>` signifies the client bean that represents an `OrderProcess` SEI. The client application will make use of this SEI to invoke the web service. Again, CXF internally uses JAX-WS frontend to define this client-side component.

Developing web service client code

We will now create a standalone Java class to invoke our `OrderProcess` web service. The following code illustrates the client invocation of a web service method:

```
public final class Client {
    public Client() {
    }
    public static void main(String args[]) throws Exception {
        // START SNIPPET: client
        ClassPathXmlApplicationContext context
```

```
            = new ClassPathXmlApplicationContext(new String[]
                  {"demo/order/client/client-beans.xml"});

          OrderProcess client = (OrderProcess) context.
                                getBean("orderClient");

        // Populate the Order bean
        Order order = new Order();
        order.setCustomerID("C001");
        order.setItemID("I001");
        order.setQty(100);
        order.setPrice(200.00);
          String orderID = client.processOrder(order);
          String message = (orderID == null) ?
                            "Order not approved" : "Order approved;
                             order ID is " + orderID;
          System.out.println(message);
          System.exit(0);
```

As you can see from the above code, we have the `main` method that first loads the `client-beans.xml` configuration file. It uses the Spring application context component `ClassPathXmlApplicationContext` to load the configuration file. The context component's `getBean` method is passed the bean ID `orderClient`. This method will return the `OrderProcess` SEI component. Using the SEI, we then invoke the web service method `processOrder`. One thing to observe here is that the client always uses the interface to invoke a web service method. The `processOrder` method takes the `Order` bean as a parameter. The following code depicts the `Order` bean:

```
public class Order {

   private String customerID;
   private String itemID;
   private int qty;
   private double price;

   // Contructor
   public Order() {
   }

   // Getter and setter methods for the above declared properties
}
```

The above `Order` bean is populated with the valid values and passed to the `processOrder` method. The method will then process the order and return the unique order ID.

We have now finished developing server and client side components. To summarize, we created the `OrderProcess` service endpoint interface and the implementation class. We then created server and client-side Spring-based configuration files and finally we created the client application. The relevant components are developed and we are all set to run or execute our code. But before we do that, you will have to create one final component that will integrate Spring and CXF.

We need to wire Spring and CXF through `web.xml`. The following code illustrates the `web.xml` file:

```
<web-app>
   <context-param>
      <param-name>contextConfigLocation</param-name>
      <param-value>WEB-INF/beans.xml</param-value>
   </context-param>

   <listener>
      <listener-class>
         org.springframework.web.context.ContextLoaderListener
      </listener-class>
   </listener>

   <servlet>
      <servlet-name>CXFServlet</servlet-name>
      <display-name>CXF Servlet</display-name>
      <servlet-class>
         org.apache.cxf.transport.servlet.CXFServlet
      </servlet-class>
      <load-on-startup>1</load-on-startup>
   </servlet>

   <servlet-mapping>
      <servlet-name>CXFServlet</servlet-name>
      <url-pattern>/*</url-pattern>
   </servlet-mapping>
</web-app>
```

Let's go through the above piece of code. The `web.xml`, as we know, is the web application configuration file that defines a servlet and its properties. The file defines `CXFServlet`, which acts as a front runner component that initiates the CXF environment. It defines the `listener` class `ContextLoaderListener`, which is responsible for loading the server-side configuration file `beans.xml`. So upon the web server startup, the order process web service endpoint will be registered and published.

Running the program

The source code and build file for the chapter is available in the `Chapter2/orderapp` folder of the downloaded source code.

Before running the program, we will organize the code so far developed in the appropriate folder structure. You can create the folder structure, as shown in the following screenshot, and put the components in the respective sub folders

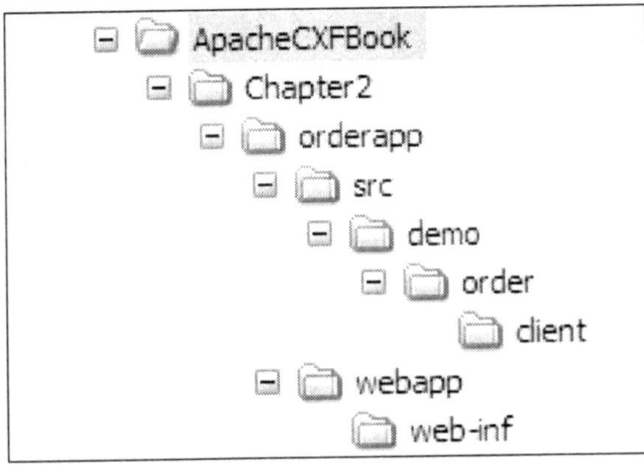

The developed code will go into the following:

- The Java code will go into the respective package folders
- The `beans.xml` and `web.xml` will go into the `webapp\WEB-INF` folder
- The `client-beans.xml` file will go into the `demo\order\client` folder

Once the code is organized, we will go about building and deploying it in the Tomcat server. It will typically involve three steps:

- Building the code
- Deploying the code
- Executing the code

Building the code

Building the code means compiling the source Java code. We will use the ANT tool to do this. The ANT file is provided in `Chapter2\orderapp` folder. The following code illustrates the sample `build.xml` build script:

```
<?xml version="1.0" encoding="UTF-8"?>
<project name="CXF Chapter2 example" default="build" basedir=".">
   <import file="common_build.xml"/>
    <target name="client" description=
                 "run demo client" depends="build">
        <property name="param" value=""/>
        <cxfrun classname="demo.order.client.Client" />
    </target>
    <target name="server" description=
                 "run demo server" depends="build">
        <cxfrun classname="demo.spring.servlet.Server"/>
    </target>
    <property name="cxf.war.file.name" value="orderapp"/>
      <target name="war" depends="build">
     <cxfwar filename="${cxf.war.file.name}.war" webxml=
                      "webapp/WEB-INF/web.xml" />
    </target>
</project>
```

Alongside `build.xml`, you will also find `common_build.xml` in the same folder. The `common_buid.xml` refers to `CATALINA_HOME` environment variable to find location of tomcat installation. Please make sure that you have set up the environment variables as mentioned in Appendix A. Open the command prompt window, go to `C:\orderapp` folder and run the **ant** command. It will build the code and put the class files under the newly created `build` folder. The following figure shows the output generated upon running the `ant` command.

```
C:\orderapp>ant
Buildfile: build.xml
    [mkdir] Created dir: C:\orderapp\build

maybe.generate.code:

compile:
    [mkdir] Created dir: C:\orderapp\build\classes
    [mkdir] Created dir: C:\orderapp\build\src
    [javac] Compiling 4 source files to C:\orderapp\build\classes
     [copy] Copying 1 file to C:\orderapp\build\classes

build:

BUILD SUCCESSFUL
Total time: 17 seconds
```

Deploying the code

Having built the code, we will deploy it. Deployment effectively means building and moving the code archive to the server deploy path. We will be using the Tomcat web container to deploy and run the application. To deploy our built code, navigate to `project root` folder, and enter the following command:

```
ant deploy
```

This will build the WAR file and put it under the Tomcat server `webapp` path. For example, if you have installed the Tomcat under the root folder, then the WAR will be deployed to `/Tomcat/webapp` folder.

Executing the code

Following code deployment, we are all set to run the Order Process Application. You will execute the Java client program `Client.java` to invoke the Order Process web service. The program will invoke the `processOrder` method that will generate the order ID if the specified order is approved. Before running the client program, we need to start the Tomcat web server. There are several ways of starting the Tomcat server depending on the Tomcat version that is installed. Once the server is started, you need to run the client program by giving the following command at the command prompt window:

```
ant client
```

As you can see above, we are using Ant to run the client program. Upon executing this command, it will generate the following output:

```
C:\orderapp>ant client
Buildfile: build.xml

maybe.generate.code:

compile:

build:

client:
     [java] Order approved; order ID is ORD1234

BUILD SUCCESSFUL
Total time: 52 seconds
```

Thus we have successfully executed the order processing web service.

CXF architecture

The architecture of CXF is built upon the following components:

- Bus
- Frontend
- Messaging and Interceptors
- Service Model
- Data bindings
- Protocol bindings
- Transport

The following figure shows the overall architecture:

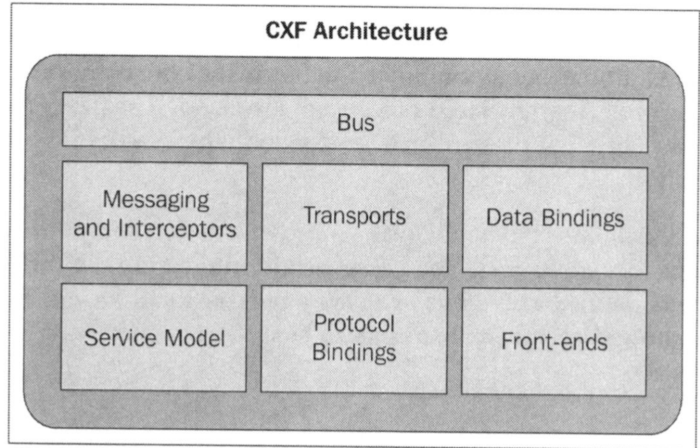

Bus

Bus is the backbone of the CXF architecture. The CXF bus is comprised of a Spring-based configuration file, namely, `cxf.xml` which is loaded upon servlet initialization through `SpringBusFactory`. It defines a common context for all the endpoints. It wires all the runtime infrastructure components and provides a common application context. The `SpringBusFactory` scans and loads the relevant configuration files in the `META-INF/cxf` directory placed in the classpath and accordingly builds the application context. It builds the application context from the following files:

- `META-INF/cxf/cxf.xml`
- `META-INF/cxf/cxf-extension.xml`
- `META-INF/cxf/cxf-property-editors.xml`

The XML file is part of the installation bundle's core CXF library JAR. Now, we know that CXF internally uses Spring for its configuration. The following XML fragment shows the bus definition in the `cxf.xml` file.

```
<bean id="cxf" class="org.apache.cxf.bus.CXFBusImpl" />
```

The core bus component is `CXFBusImpl`. The class acts more as an interceptor provider for incoming and outgoing requests to a web service endpoint. These interceptors, once defined, are available to all the endpoints in that context. The `cxf.xml` file also defines other infrastructure components such as `BindingFactoryManager`, `ConduitFactoryManager`, and so on. These components are made available as bus extensions. One can access these infrastructure objects using the `getExtension` method. These infrastructure components are registered so as to get and update various service endpoint level parameters such as service binding, transport protocol, conduits, and so on.

CXF bus architecture can be overridden, but one must apply caution when overriding the default bus behavior. Since the bus is the core component that loads the CXF runtime, many shared objects are also loaded as part of this runtime. You want to make sure that these objects are loaded when overriding the existing bus implementation.

You can extend the default bus to include your own custom components or service objects such as factory managers. You can also add interceptors to the bus bean. These interceptors defined at the bus level are available to all the endpoints. The following code shows how to create a custom bus:

```
SpringBeanFactory.createBus("mycxf.xml")
```

`SpringBeanFactory` class is used to create a bus. You can complement or overwrite the bean definitions that the original `cxf.xml` file would use. For the CXF to load the `mycxf.xml` file, it has to be in the classpath or you can use a factory method to load the file. The following code illustrates the use of interceptors at the bus level:

```
<bean id="cxf" class="org.apache.cxf.bus.spring.SpringBusImpl">
    <property name="outInterceptors">
           <list>
              <ref bean="myLoggingInterceptor"/>
           </list>
        </property>
</bean>
<bean id="myLogHandler" class="org.mycompany.com.cxf.logging.
                                LoggingInterceptor">

    ...
</bean>
```

The preceding bus definition adds the logging interceptor that will perform logging for all outgoing messages.

Frontend

CXF provides the concept of frontend modeling, which lets you create web services using different frontend APIs. The APIs let you create a web service using simple factory beans and JAX-WS implementation. It also lets you create dynamic web service clients. The primary frontend supported by CXF is JAX-WS. We will look at how to use the Frontend programming model in the next chapter.

JAX-WS

JAX-WS is a specification that establishes the semantics to develop, publish, and consume web services. JAX-WS simplifies web service development. It defines Java-based APIs that ease the development and deployment of web services. The specification supports WS-Basic Profile 1.1 that addresses web service interoperability. It effectively means a web service can be invoked or consumed by a client written in any language. JAX-WS also defines standards such as **JAXB** and **SAAJ**. CXF provides support for complete JAX-WS stack.

JAXB provides data binding capabilities by providing a convenient way to map XML schema to a representation in Java code. The JAXB shields the conversion of XML schema messages in SOAP messages to Java code without the developers seeing XML and SOAP parsing. JAXB specification defines the binding between Java and XML Schema. SAAJ provides a standard way of dealing with XML attachments contained in a SOAP message.

JAX-WS also speeds up web service development by providing a library of annotations to turn Plain Old Java classes into web services and specifies a detailed mapping from a service defined in WSDL to the Java classes that will implement that service. Any complex types defined in WSDL are mapped into Java classes following the mapping defined by the JAXB specification.

As discussed earlier, two approaches for web service development exist: Code-First and Contract-First. With JAX-WS, you can perform web service development using one of the said approaches, depending on the nature of the application.

With the Code-first approach, you start by developing a Java class and interface and annotating the same as a web service. The approach is particularly useful where Java implementations are already available and you need to expose implementations as services.

You typically create a **Service Endpoint Interface** (**SEI**) that defines the service methods and the implementation class that implements the SEI methods. The consumer of a web service uses SEI to invoke the service functions. The SEI directly corresponds to a `wsdl:portType` element. The methods defined by SEI correspond to the `wsdl:operation` element.

```
@WebService
public interface OrderProcess {
    String processOrder(Order order);
}
```

JAX-WS makes use of annotations to convert an SEI or a Java class to a web service. In the above example, the `@WebService` annotation defined above the interface declaration signifies an interface as a web service interface or Service Endpoint Interface.

In the Contract-first approach, you start with the existing WSDL contract, and generate Java class to implement the service. The advantage is that you are sure about what to expose as a service since you define the appropriate WSDL Contract-first. Again the contract definitions can be made consistent with respect to data types so that it can be easily converted in Java objects without any portability issue. In Chapter 3 we will look at how to develop web services using both these approaches.

WSDL contains different elements that can be directly mapped to a Java class that implements the service. For example, the `wsdl:portType` element is directly mapped to SEI, type elements are mapped to Java class types through the use of **Java Architecture of XML Binding** (**JAXB**), and the `wsdl:service` element is mapped to a Java class that is used by a consumer to access the web service.

The `WSDL2Java` tool can be used to generate a web service from WSDL. It has various options to generate SEI and the implementation web service class. As a developer, you need to provide the method implementation for the generated class. If the WSDL includes custom XML Schema types, then the same is converted into its equivalent Java class.

In Chapter 8 you will learn about CXF tools. The chapter will also cover a brief discussion on the *wsdl2java* tool.

Simple frontend

Apart from JAX-WS frontend, CXF also supports what is known as 'simple frontend'. The simple frontend provides simple components or Java classes that use reflection to build and publish web services. It is simple because we do not use any annotation to create web services. In JAX-WS, we have to annotate a Java class to denote it as a web service and use tools to convert between a Java object and WSDL. The simple frontend uses factory components to create a service and the client. It does so by using Java reflection API. In Chapter 3 we will look at how to develop simple frontend web services.

The following code shows a web service created using simple frontend:

```
// Build and publish the service
OrderProcessImpl orderProcessImpl = new OrderProcessImpl();
ServerFactoryBean svrFactory = new ServerFactoryBean();
svrFactory.setServiceClass(OrderProcess.class);
svrFactory.setAddress("http://localhost:8080/OrderProcess");
svrFactory.setServiceBean(orderProcessImpl);
svrFactory.create();
```

Messaging and Interceptors

One of the important elements of CXF architecture is the Interceptor components. Interceptors are components that intercept the messages exchanged or passed between web service clients and server components. In CXF, this is implemented through the concept of Interceptor chains. The concept of Interceptor chaining is the core functionality of CXF runtime.

The interceptors act on the messages which are sent and received from the web service and are processed in chains. Each interceptor in a chain is configurable, and the user has the ability to control its execution.

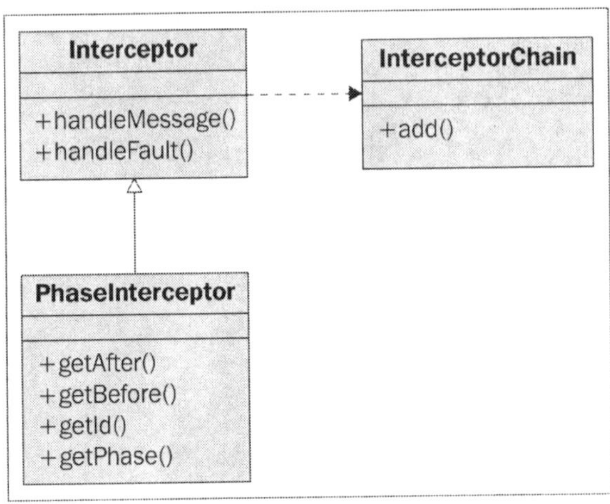

The core of the framework is the Interceptor interface. It defines two abstract methods—`handleMessage` and `handleFault`. Each of the methods takes the object of type `Message` as a parameter. A developer implements the `handleMessage` to process or act upon the message. The `handleFault` method is implemented to handle the error condition. Interceptors are usually processed in chains with every interceptor in the chain performing some processing on the message in sequence, and the chain moves forward. Whenever an error condition arises, a `handleFault` method is invoked on each interceptor, and the chain unwinds or moves backwards.

Interceptors are often organized or grouped into phases. Interceptors providing common functionality can be grouped into one phase. Each phase performs specific message processing. Each phase is then added to the interceptor chain. The chain, therefore, is a list of ordered interceptor phases. The chain can be created for both inbound and outbound messages. A typical web service endpoint will have three interceptor chains:

- Inbound messages chain
- Outbound messages chain
- Error messages chain

There are built-in interceptors such as logging, security, and so on, and the developers can also choose to create custom interceptors.

In Chapter 5 we will learn about working with CXF advanced features. The chapter will mainly focus on Interceptors.

Service model

The **Service model**, in a true sense, models your service. It is a framework of components that represents a service in a WSDL-like model. It provides functionality to create various WSDL elements such as operations, bindings, endpoints, schema, and so on. The following figure shows the various components that form the Service model:

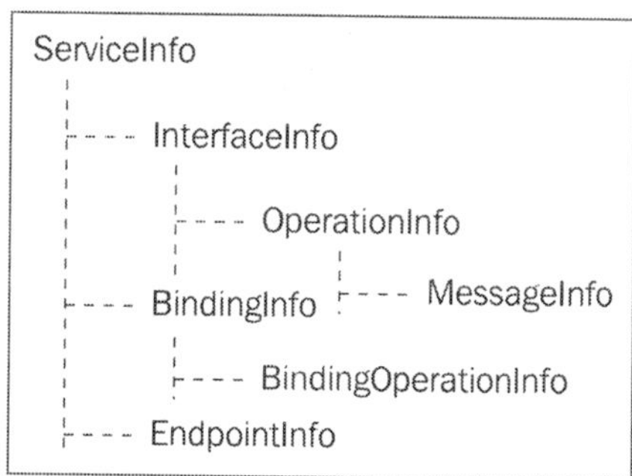

The components of the Service model can be used to create a service. As you can see from the above figure, the service model's primary component is **ServiceInfo** which aggregates other related components that make up the complete service model. **ServiceInfo** is comprised of the following components that more or less represent WSDL elements:

- **InterfaceInfo**
- **OperationInfo**
- **MessageInfo**
- **BindingInfo**
- **EndpointInfo**

A web service is usually created using one of the frontends offered by CXF. It can be either constructed from a Java class or from a WSDL.

CXF frontends internally use the service model to create web services. For example, by using a simple frontend, we can create, publish, and consume web services through factory components such as `ServerFactoryBean` and `ClientProxyFactoryBean`. These factory classes internally use the service model of CXF.

Data binding

Data binding is the key for any web service development. Data binding means mapping between Java objects and XML elements. As we know, with web service, messages are exchanged as XML artifacts. So there has to be some way to convert these XML into Java objects and vice versa for the application to process as service and client. Data binding components perform this mapping for you. CXF supports two types of data binding components—**JAXB** and **Aegis**. CXF uses JAXB as the default data binding component. As a developer, you have the choice of specifying the binding discipline through a configuration file or API. If no binding is specified, then JAXB is taken as a default binding discipline. The latest version of CXF uses JAXB 2.1. JAXB uses annotations to define the mapping between Java objects and XML. The following code illustrates the use of JAXB annotations:

```
@XmlRootElement(name="processOrder", namespace=" http://localhost/
                          orderprocess")
@XmlAccessorType(XmlAccessType.FIELD)
@XmlType(name="processOrder", namespace=
              " http://localhost/orderprocess")
public class OrderProcess {
    @XmlElement(name="arg0", namespace="")
    private order.Order arg0;
   //Gettter and Setter
....
}
```

As shown in the previous code, the `@Xml` specific annotations represents the JAXB metadata that is used by JAXB to map Java classes to XML schema constructs. For example, the `@XmlType` annotation specifies that the `OrderProcess` class will be mapped to complex XSD element type '`processOrder`' that contains an element '`arg0`' of type '`Order`' bean.

CXF also supports the Aegis data binding component to map between Java objects and XML. Aegis allows developers to gain control of data binding through its flexible mapping system. You do not have to rely on annotations to devise the mapping. Your Java code is clean and simple POJO.

Aegis also supports some annotations that can be used to devise binding. Some of the annotations that can be used with Aegis are:

- XmlAttribute
- XmlElement
- XmlParamType
- XmlReturnType
- XmlType

In Aegis, you define the data mapping in a file called `<MyJavaObject>.aegis.xml`, where `MyJavaObject` is the object that you are trying to map with XML. Aegis reads this XML to perform the necessary binding. Aegis also uses reflection to derive the mapping between Java object and XML. The following code fragment shows the sample Aegis mapping file:

```
<?xml version="1.0" encoding="UTF-8"?>
<mappings>
    <mapping name="HelloWorld">
        <method name="sayHi">
            <parameter index="0" mappedName=
                                "greeting" nillable='false' />
        </method>
    </mapping>
</mappings>
```

The above XML fragment states that a string parameter of a method named `sayHi` of the bean `HelloWorld` should be mapped to a name as `greeting`.

You can configure your web service to use Aegis data binding as follows:

```
<jaxws:endpoint id="orderProcess" implementor="demo.order.
OrderProcessImpl" address="/OrderProcess" >
   <jaxws:dataBinding>
    <bean class="org.apache.cxf.aegis.databinding.AegisDatabinding" />
   </jaxws:dataBinding>
</jaxws:endpoint>
```

Protocol binding

Bindings bind the web service's messages with the protocol-specific format. The messages, in web service terminology, are nothing but an operation with input and output parameters. The message defined in the web service component is called a logical message. The logical message used by a service component is mapped or bound to a physical data format used by endpoints in the physical world. It lays down rules as to how the logical messages will be mapped to an actual payload sent over the wire or network.

Bindings are directly related to port types in a WSDL artifact. Port types define operations and input and output parameters which are abstract in nature. They define the logical message, whereas binding translates this logical message into actual payload data defined by the underlying protocol. The following WSDL portion shows the sample binding details:

```
<wsdl:binding name="OrderProcessImplServiceSoapBinding"
              type="tns:OrderProcess">
   <soap:binding style="document" transport=
                       "http://schemas.xmlsoap.org/soap/http" />
   <wsdl:operation name="processOrder">
      <soap:operation soapAction="" style="document" />
      <wsdl:input name="processOrder">
         <soap:body use="literal" />
      </wsdl:input>
      <wsdl:output name="processOrderResponse">
         <soap:body use="literal" />
      </wsdl:output>
     </wsdl:operation>
</wsdl:binding>
```

As you can see from the above sample binding fragment, it is defined using the `<binding>` element. This element has two attributes, namely, `name` and `type`. The `name` attribute identifies the binding, and the `type` attribute maps it with the port type. The `name` attribute of the binding element is used to associate with the endpoint. The child elements of the `<binding>` parent element define the actual mapping of the messages with the protocol format. In the previous case, the communication protocol used is SOAP 1.1.

CXF supports the following binding protocols:

- SOAP 1.1
- SOAP 1.2
- CORBA
- Pure XML

Transports

Transport defines the high-level routing protocol to transmit the messages over the wire. Transport protocols are associated with the endpoints. One endpoint can communicate with another using a specific transport protocol. Transport details are nothing but networking details. Service endpoints are a physical representation of a service interface. Endpoints are composed of binding and networking details. In a WSDL artifact, transport details are specified as part of the `<port>` element. The port element is a child of the service element. The WSDL portion following shows the sample transport details:

```
<wsdl:service name="OrderProcessImplService">
   <wsdl:port binding="tns:OrderProcessImplServiceSoapBinding"
              name="OrderProcessImplPort">
      <soap:address location="http://localhost:8080/orderapp/
                              OrderProcess" />
   </wsdl:port>
</wsdl:service>
```

As you see from the above XML fragment, transport details are specified as part of the service element. The service element has one child element as port element. The port element maps to binding as defined by the binding element and provides details of the transport. The previous example shows SOAP as binding protocol and HTTP as a transport protocol. In Chapter 4, the various transport protocols are explained in the context of web services development.

CXF supports the following transports for its endpoints:

- HTTP
- CORBA
- JMS
- Local

Summary

The chapter started by describing the Order Processing Application and we saw how to develop a web service with CXF and Spring-based configuration. CXF's seamless integration with Spring makes it extremely easy and convenient to build and publish a web service. We also saw how to build, deploy, and execute a web service using ANT and Tomcat. The chapter later described the CXF architecture, which is built upon the core components. These components lay down the foundation for building web services.

3

Working with CXF Frontends

CXF frontends are programming APIs that can be used to develop and publish web services. CXF supports two types of frontends, JAX-WS and simple frontend. This chapter will provide a more detailed explanation of the JAX-WS frontend. We will also look at how to build a web service using simple frontend API. The chapter will focus on developing SOAP-based web services using two types of frontends:

- JAX-WS frontend
- Simple frontend

Using JAX-WS frontend, we will look at the following:

- Web service development using the Code-first development approach
- Web service development using the contract-first development approach
- Building a dynamic client or consumer
- Provider and Dispatch based implementation
- Understanding web service context

JAX-WS frontend

CXF supports the JAX-WS 2.0 API specification provided by **Java Community Process (JCP)**. JAX-WS is a formal specification by JCP that defines APIs to build, develop, and deploy web services. CXF provides its own JAX-WS implementation adhering to JAX-WS specification standards. The CXF JAX-WS frontend provides different APIs to build different kinds of web services. Apart from providing standard WSDL-based development, it also provides APIs to build XML-based services in the form of Provider and Dispatch interfaces.

There are two ways or approaches for developing JAX-WS SOAP-based web services—Code-first development and contract-first development. In Code-first development, as the name suggests, you start off with the code and then convert it into WSDL. Code-first development is typically used where the input and output objects format of the implementation methods is simpler, and you want to quickly expose them as web services. Code-first development is much simpler as you start off with Java objects without worrying about how the WSDL and XSD would be generated which could lead to issues where Java objects can't be mapped to XML elements the way you had intended. Note that based on the input and output format of the implementation method, tools like CXF Java2WSDL would generate contracts, including XSD formats, for you. For instance, you can't expose a Map or Collection as an output message format as there is no standard way to map this to an XML schema, and this could lead to interoperability issues.

In Contract-first development the developer builds the web service from an existing WSDL artifact. Contract-first development is typically used when you already have an XML schema defining the input and output message format for the web service operations, or you want to gain finer control of how the XML is being mapped to Java objects. Contract-first development requires you to be well versed in XSD and WSDL contracts as you start modeling contracts using these constructs. If you are creating services based on industry standards, you would probably start off with Contract-first development as the industry message formats are typically available as XML Schema.

If you are familiar with both these approaches and know how the objects are mapped to XML, you can go with code-first development. CXF supports both these approaches and provides support for various Data binding mechanisms which help you to map Java objects to XML.

We will start off with the code-first development approach.

Code-first development

In this section, we will start by developing a Java class and convert it into a service class by annotating it. You can carry out web service development using the following steps:

- Creating **Service Endpoint Interface (SEI)**
- Adding Java annotations
- Publishing the service
- Developing a consumer
- Running the Code-first example

Creating Service Endpoint Interface (SEI)

Service Endpoint Interface is a Java interface that defines a business method to be exposed as a service method. The service method is implemented by a service class. An SEI can be modeled by using two different approaches:

- Building an SEI component from scratch
- Converting existing business functionality into service-based components

The first approach is to build an SEI component from scratch, that is, develop a whole new web service without any existing code or WSDL contract. It is recommended that you start by writing the service interface and then creating the service implementation class. Writing the service interface is always good practice as it gives a proper client side view of your service methods. The implementation class can then implement the methods defined in the interface.

The second approach is to take the existing business functionality and convert it into service-based components. Most of the time you have business logic already developed and you want to expose them as service methods. You can achieve this by developing an SEI and defining only those business methods that you want to expose as a service method, and then make the existing Java code implement that SEI. The other approach commonly used is to create Wrapper SEI and an implementation class, which would use the existing implementation classes to carry out the functionality.

We will start off by creating an SEI component from scratch. We start by developing an `OrderProcess` SEI and implementing it. The following code illustrates the `OrderProcess` SEI:

```
package demo.order;

public interface OrderProcess {
    String processOrder(Order order);
}
```

The above code, as you can see, is a simple POJO interface. It defines one abstract method `processOrder` that takes an `Order` bean as a parameter. The `OrderProcessImpl` implementation class implements the `processOrder` method, and this method will be exposed later as a web service method.

We will now implement the interface by providing the business logic to the interface method. You will write the `OrderProcessImpl` class that will implement the `OrderProcess` SEI. The following code illustrates the `OrderProcessImpl` class:

```
package demo.order;

public class OrderProcessImpl implements OrderProcess {

    public String processOrder(Order order) {
      System.out.println("Processing order...");
      String orderID = validate(order);
        return orderID;
    }
. . .
```

The above code is a simple POJO implementation class that implements the `processOrder` method. The method simply verifies the order and returns a unique order ID. For simplicity, we return a static order ID as part of our implementation. In the next section we will convert the SEI and implementation class into web service components by annotating them.

Adding Java annotations

Web service annotations are added to a Java class to expose it as a service component. JAX-WS uses Java 5 annotations, provided by the Web Services Metadata for the **Java Platform specification (JSR-181)** to convert a component to a web service. The annotations are simply markups that can be used to define a specific context for a particular component or a method. Each annotation is supported by one or more of the attributes or properties of that context. In this section we will add annotations to our `OrderProcess` SEI and the implementation class and convert them into a service component. In this section we will cover the following web service annotations:

- `javax.jws.WebService`
- `javax.jws.soap.SOAPBinding`

javax.jws.WebService

A Java component can be converted into a service by adding a `@WebService` annotation. This annotation has to be defined both in SEI and the implementation class. The `@WebService` annotation is defined by the `javax.jws.WebService` interface.

The `@WebService` annotation supports the following attributes:

Attribute	Description
`Name`	Indicates the name of the service interface. It is directly mapped to a name attribute of the `<wsdl:portType>` element in WSDL document. If the attribute is not provided, then the name of the service interface is taken as default.
`targetNamespace`	It holds the namespace where the service is defined. If no namespace is provided, then the package name is taken as default.
`serviceName`	The name of the published service object. It directly maps to a name attribute of `wsdl:service` element in WSDL document. The default value is the name of the service implementation class.
`wsdlLocation`	It indicates the location of WSDL document in the form of URL.
`endpointInterface`	This attribute is used by the service implementation class. It specifies the fully qualified name of the service interface which will be implemented by the service implementation class.
`portName`	It indicates the name of the endpoint where the service is published. It directly maps to a `name` attribute of the `<wsdl:port>` element in the WSDL document.

Let's annotate our `OrderProcess` SEI and `OrderProcessImpl` implementation class. The following code illustrates the use of `@WebService` annotation:

```
package demo.order;
import javax.jws.WebService;
@WebService
public interface OrderProcess {
    String processOrder(Order order);
}
```

The `@WebService` annotation is declared directly above the interface or class declaration. It annotates the class or interface as a web service class or interface. In the above code, the `OrderProcess` interface is defined as a web service interface by annotating it with `@WebService` annotation.

Let's look at the `OrderProcessImpl` implementation class.

The following code shows the annotated `OrderProcessImpl` implementation class:

```
package demo.order;

import javax.jws.WebService;

@WebService(serviceName="OrderProcessService",
portName="OrderProcessPort")

public class OrderProcessImpl implements OrderProcess {

    public String processOrder(Order order) {
      System.out.println("Processing order...");
      String orderID = validate(order);
        return orderID;
    }
 . . .
```

As with SEI, you define the `@WebService` above the class declaration. You will define two attributes—`serviceName` and `portName`. The `serviceName` attribute is defined with the value as `OrderProcessService`. The service name is used by the consumer to obtain the remote interface stub for invoking the service method. The port name signifies the endpoint name. The service endpoint is also called as a service port where the service is published. The name here is `OrderProcessPort`.

There are many other optional annotations that can be used alongside `@WebService` to fully describe a web service. Other annotations add finer level details to the service. It is always recommended that you make use of these annotations to describe your web service, so that the generated WSDL document has more specific details as specified by these annotations. If you do not use these optional annotations, then the WSDL is generated with default conventions, as discussed in previous table.

javax.jws.soap.SOAPBinding

The `@SOAPBinding` annotation is defined by the `javax.jws.soap.SOAPBinding` interface. The annotation is used if you want to specify SOAP binding for your service.

The annotation supports the following attributes:

Attribute	Description	Default
`Style`	Indicates the style of the SOAP message. The attribute supports two styles, namely, `Style.DOCUMENT` and `Style.RPC`.	The default is `DOCUMENT`.
`Use`	The attribute determines how the SOAP message is to be formatted during serialization. It supports two values, namely, `Use.LITERAL` and `Use.ENCODED`	The default is `LITERAL`.
`parameterStyle`	Indicates how the SOAP messages are to be used. The message can be either wrapped, that is, operation parameters are wrapped as child elements inside an element in the SOAP body, or it can be unwrapped as different individual elements. It supports two values, namely `ParameterStyle.BARE` and `ParameterStyle.WRAPPED`.	The default is `WRAPPED`.

The SOAP Binding plays an important role in web service communication. Let's look at two styles of SOAP Binding in greater detail.

RPC versus Document style

The web service SOAP communication style plays an important role in communicating SOAP XML messages between service provider and consumer. There are two SOAP message styles, **Document** and **RPC**. The SOAP message styles are defined in WSDL document as SOAP binding. A SOAP binding can have an encoded use or a literal use. Encoding, as the term implies the message would be encoded using some format, while literal specifies plain text messages without any encoding logic.

Document style, as the name suggests, deals with XML documents as payloads which adhere to well defined contracts, typically created using XML Schema definitions. The XML schema format specifies the contract of the service messages invoked by consumers. The XML Schema defines the request and response message format between service provider and service consumer which can be validated by service consumer or service provider. Document literal style is the preferred way for web service communication to achieve interoperability.

RPC (Remote Procedure Call) style, on the other hand, indicates that the SOAP body contains an XML representation of a method. In order to serialize method parameters into the SOAP message so that it can be deserialized back by any web service implementation, the SOAP specification defines a standard set of encoding rules. As RPC is traditionally used in conjunction with the SOAP encoding rules, the combination is referred to as RPC/encoded. You also have an RPC/literal communication style model where you don't have any encoding formats, but still the messages are limited to RPC method-based communication, where messages can't be validated as they are not tied to any XML schema definition. You should probably avoid developing RPC style web services as they have a lot of interoperability issues.

The following code illustrates the use of the `@SOAPBinding` annotation:

```
@WebService(name="OrderProcess")
@SOAPBinding(parameterSyle=ParameterStyle.BARE)
public interface OrderProcess {
    String processOrder(Order order);
}
```

javax.jws.WebMethod

The `@WebMethod` annotation is defined by the `javax.jws.WebMethod` interface. The annotation is used for customizing web service operation. The `@WebMethod` provides the operation `name` and `action` attributes which are used to customize the `name` attribute of the `<wsdl:operation>` element and the `soapAction` attribute of the `<soap:operation>` element in the WSDL document. The `@WebMethod` annotation is placed just above the service method declaration.

The `@WebMethod` annotation supports the following attributes:

Attribute	Description
`Name`	Indicates the name of the service method. It directly maps to the name attribute of the `<wsdl:operation>` element in the WSDL document. The default value is the name of the method.
`Action`	It indicates the SOAP action for the SOAP operation. It directly maps to a `soapAction` attribute of the `<soap:operation>` element. The default value is a blank string.
`Exclude`	It determines whether the method will be a web service or a non-service method. The default value is `false`.

The following code snippet illustrates the use of the `@WebMethod` annotation:

```
@WebMethod (name="processOrder")

public String processOrder(Order order) {
. . .
```

JAX-WS web service annotations support a host of other annotations like `@RequestWrapper`, `@ResponseWrapper`, `@Oneway`, and so on. Some of these will be explained during the course of this chapter.

Publishing the service

Publishing the service means registering the service component on the server and making it available to the consumer through the endpoint URL. You will publish the `OrderProcess` web service on a particular endpoint URL. The endpoint URL in this case will be `http://localhost:8080/OrderProcess`. You will develop a server component that will publish your `OrderProcess` service. For this example, we will use the lightweight web server provided by Java 5 to publish our service. CXF provides its own standalone server utility, `JaxWsServerFactoryBean` to publish the web service, which will be used in Chapter 5.

The following code illustrates the server code:

```
import javax.xml.ws.Endpoint;

public class Server {

    protected Server() throws Exception {
        System.out.println(«Starting Server»);
        OrderProcessImpl orderProcessImpl = new OrderProcessImpl();
        String address = «http://localhost:8080/OrderProcess»;
        Endpoint.publish(address, orderProcessImpl);
    }
   public static void main(String[] args) {
      new Server();
      Thread.sleep(50000);
      System.exit(0);
   }
}
```

The static method of publishing the `Endpoint` class provides a convenient way to publish and test the JAX-WS web service. The method takes the endpoint URL address and an object of `OrderProcessImpl` class as a parameter. The endpoint address is where the `OrderProcess` service will be published. The `publish` method creates a lightweight web server at the URL `http://localhost:8080/OrderProcess` and deploys the service to that location. The lightweight web server runs in the JVM for a minute and automatically exits. One can view the WSDL contract of the service by adding the following URL to a web browser

```
http://localhost:8080/OrderProcess?wsdl
```

Developing a consumer

The consumer of the web service invokes the service method to get the required result. In this section we will develop a `Client` class that will look up our `OrderProcess` service and invoke its `processOrder` method. The following code illustrates the service consumer component:

```
public class Client {

    private static final QName SERVICE_NAME =
    new QName("http://order.demo/", "OrderProcessService");
    private static final QName PORT_NAME =
    new QName("http://order.demo/", "OrderProcessPort");

    private static final String WSDL_LOCATION =
    "http://localhost:8080/OrderProcess?wsdl";

    public static void main(String args[]) throws Exception {
        URL wsdlURL = new URL(WSDL_LOCATION);
        Service service = Service.create(wsdlURL, SERVICE_NAME);
        OrderProcess port = service.getPort(PORT_NAME,
        OrderProcess.class);

      Order order = new Order();
      order.setCustomerID("C001");
      order.setItemID("I001");
      order.setPrice(100.00);
      order.setQty(20);
        String result = port.processOrder(order);
        System.out.println("The order ID is " + result);

    }

}
```

The client code performs the following:

1. It first constructs the WSDL URL. The WSDL URL is `http://localhost:8080/OrderProcess?wsdl`. The URL signifies the location of WSDL document.

> Before running the client program, you can validate that the service is available by invoking the above WSDL URL. If you are able to see the WSDL, then it means that the `OrderProcess` service was published successfully.

2. It then creates the `Service` object. The `Service` object is created using the static `create` method. The method takes the WSDL URL and service name as the parameter. The service name `OrderProcessService` is a `QName` and is mapped to the `<wsdl:service>` element in the WSDL document. The `<wsdl:service>` element defines the service endpoints.
3. Using the `Service` object, you obtain the SEI stub proxy component by calling the `getPort` method. The `getPort` method takes the port name and SEI class as the parameters. The port name `OrderProcessPort` is a `QName` and is mapped to the `<wsdl:port>` element in the WSDL document. The SEI class is `OrderProcess`.
4. The proxy component is then used to invoke the service method `processOrder`. Before invoking the method, you have to populate the `Order` bean and pass it to the `processOrder` method. The method is called on the server, and it returns the order ID.

Running the Code-first example

We will use the ANT tool to build and execute the code. The source code and build file for the chapter is available in the `Chapter3/codefirst` folder of the downloaded source code. Navigate to the `Chapter3/codefirst` folder, and run the following command on the command prompt:

- `ant build`

  This will build the source code.
- `ant server`

  This will run the `Server` class and publish the Order Process web service to the location `http://localhost:8080`.

- Open a new command prompt and run the client. Doing this will invoke the service.

  ```
  ant client
  ```

  Upon the running the client, you will see the following output:

  ```
  INFO: Creating Service {http://order.demo/}OrderProcessImplService
  from WSDL: http://localhost:8080/OrderProcess?wsdl
  The order ID is ORD1234
  ```

  The output shows the generated order ID.

  On the console, where the server is running, you will see the following output, denoting that an order has been processed:

  Processed order...ORD1234

Contract-first development

In Contract-first development, the developer builds the web service from an existing WSDL artifact. One can use the CXF `wsdl2java` tool to generate relevant server and client-side components from the existing WSDL document. The generated server-side service implementation class can then be used to add or implement the business method. To build the Contract-first JAX-WS web service, go through the following steps:

1. Generating service components
2. Implementing the service method
3. Publishing the web service
4. Developing a client

We will first build the service provider component from the given WSDL. We will make use of the WSDL below to generate service components. The WSDL is created using earlier examples. Please refer to inline comments for explanation of important tags in a WSDL file.

```
<?xml version='1.0' encoding='UTF-8'?>
<wsdl:definitions name="OrderProcessService" targetNamespace="http://
order.demo/" xmlns:ns1="http://schemas.xmlsoap.org/soap/http" xmlns:
soap="http://schemas.xmlsoap.org/wsdl/soap/" xmlns:tns="http://
order.demo/" xmlns:wsdl="http://schemas.xmlsoap.org/wsdl/" xmlns:
xsd="http://www.w3.org/2001/XMLSchema">
   <wsdl:types>
      <xs:schema attributeFormDefault="unqualified" elementFormDefault
="unqualified" targetNamespace="http://order.demo/" xmlns:tns="http://
order.demo/" xmlns:xs="http://www.w3.org/2001/XMLSchema">
```

```
        <!-- XSD Schema for Input and Output operations -->
        <xs:element name="processOrder" type="tns:processOrder" />
        <xs:element name="processOrderResponse" type="tns:
        processOrderResponse" />
         <xs:complexType name="processOrder">
           <xs:sequence>
              <xs:element minOccurs="0" name="arg0"
              type="tns:order" />
           </xs:sequence>
        </xs:complexType>
        <!-- Complex order type elemnets i.e maps to Order Bean -->
        <xs:complexType name="order">
           <xs:sequence>
              <xs:element minOccurs="0" name="customerID"
              type="xs:string" />
              <xs:element minOccurs="0" name="itemID"
              type="xs:string" />
              <xs:element name="price" type="xs:double" />
              <xs:element name="qty" type="xs:int" />
           </xs:sequence>
        </xs:complexType>
        <xs:complexType name="processOrderResponse">
            <xs:sequence>
           <xs:element minOccurs="0" name="return"
           type="xs:string" />
           </xs:sequence>
        </xs:complexType>
     </xs:schema>
  </wsdl:types>
  <!-- Message formats for request and response -->
  <wsdl:message name="processOrderResponse">
     <wsdl:part element="tns:processOrderResponse" name="parameters">
     </wsdl:part>
  </wsdl:message>
  <wsdl:message name="processOrder">
     <wsdl:part element="tns:processOrder" name="parameters">
     </wsdl:part>
  </wsdl:message>
  <!-- Port type and operations for processOrder operation -->
  <wsdl:portType name="OrderProcess">
     <wsdl:operation name="processOrder">
        <wsdl:input message="tns:processOrder" name="processOrder">
        </wsdl:input>
        <wsdl:output message="tns:processOrderResponse"
        name="processOrderResponse">
```

```
          </wsdl:output>
       </wsdl:operation>
    </wsdl:portType>
    <!-- WSDL Binding definition for Order Process-->
    <wsdl:binding name="OrderProcessServiceSoapBinding"
    type="tns:OrderProcess">
       <soap:binding style="document" transport=
       "http://schemas.xmlsoap.org/soap/http" />
       <wsdl:operation name="processOrder">
          <!-- SOAP Binding style -->
          <soap:operation soapAction="" style="document" />
          <wsdl:input name="processOrder">
             <soap:body use="literal" />
          </wsdl:input>
          <wsdl:output name="processOrderResponse">
             <soap:body use="literal" />
          </wsdl:output>
       </wsdl:operation>
    </wsdl:binding>
    <!-- WSDL service definition-->
    <wsdl:service name="OrderProcessService">
       <wsdl:port binding="tns:OrderProcessServiceSoapBinding"
       name="OrderProcessPort">
          <!--soap address location for orderprocess web service-->
          <soap:address location="http://localhost:8080/OrderProcess" />
       </wsdl:port>
    </wsdl:service>
 </wsdl:definitions>
```

Generating service components

Just as we created the WSDL from a web service, here we will create a web service from a WSDL. The elements that define the service in the WSDL document can be mapped to a Java service component using JAX-WS. The following table shows some of the relevant mappings between the WSDL element and the corresponding Java components:

WSDL element	**Java component**
`targetNamespace` attribute of the `<wsdl:definitions>` element	Java package
`<wsdl:portType>`	Java Service Endpoint Interface (SEI)

WSDL element	Java component
`<wsdl:operation>` child element of the `<wsdl:portType>` element	Java methods
`<wsdl:service>`	Service class
`<wsdl:message>`	Service operation parameters

We will use the `wsdl2java` tool to build a service from WSDL. CXF provides many such tools to ease and automate web service development. The `wsdl2java` tool can be used to generate the relevant service components. The tool provides various options or arguments that can be used during the conversion. One can generate the service components with the following command:

```
wsdl2java -ant -impl -server -d <outputdir> mywsdl.wsdl
```

Here is the description of the `wsdl2java` command tool options:

Tool options	Description
`- ant:`	This option will generate the ANT build file `build.xml` that can be used to build the generated code
`- impl:`	This option will generate a service implementation class
`- server:`	This option will generate a `server` component that can be used to publish the service and start the server
`-d <outputdir>:`	This option can be used to direct the generated code to a specific output folder

Let's actually perform the code generation using the `wsdl2java` tool. We will use the existing `OrderProcess.wsdl`, as discussed in an earlier section, to convert it into a JAX-WS service class. Navigate to the `Chapter3/contractfirst` folder of the downloaded source folder, and type in the following command:

```
wsdl2java.bat -d src -ant -impl -server OrderProcess.wsdl
```

This command will generate the following set of files:

- JAXB Input and Output message classes – this tool generates respective Java input and output message components based on the input and output message schema defined in a WSDL format. For `OrderProcess.wsdl`, it will generate `ProcessOrder` as an input class and `ProcessOrderResponse` as an output class which maps to the `processOrder` and `processOrderResponse` XML element. It also generates the `Order` class which maps to the `<xs:complexType name="order">` definition in the WSDL file.
- Service Interface—this service interface contains web service methods. The service interface generated for Order Process WSDL is `OrderProcess.java`.
- Service Implementation class—this class provides a sample implementation which extends the `Service` interface. We would modify this class to add our implementation code. The service implementation generated for Order Process WSDL is `OrderProcessImpl.java`.
- Standalone Server class—this class provides a standalone utility to publish and test the JAX-WS web service using an embedded server. The code generated for the `OrderProcess.wsdl` file is `OrderProcess_OrderProcessPort_Server.java`.
- Build file—the build file can be used to build the generated source code and publish the web service using the standalone server class.

All these components reside under the `demo.order` package. The `wsdl2java` tool devises the package name by mapping it with the `targetNamespace` attribute of the `<wsdl:definitions>` element. If you look at the WSDL contract, the `targetNamespace` has the value `http://order.demo`. The `wsdl2java` tool will derive the package name by reversing the URL and stripping off the leading `http://`. The package name therefore becomes `demo.order`.

Let's look at these artifacts in detail.

JAXB input and output message classes

The `ProcessOrder`, `ProcessOrderResponse`, and `Order` class are generated for OrderProcess WSDL. These classes represent the input and output classes for web service operation. If you open up these files in the editor, then you see various JAXB annotations on classes and methods which are used to map a Java class to XML. The `ProcessOrder` and `ProcessOrderResponse` classes are termed as `Request` and `Response` Wrapper classes. The `Request` Wrapper class holds the input parameter and the `Response` Wrapper class holds the output parameter. As with the JAX-WS specification, the `Request` and `Response` Wrapper classes are generated by default for document literal style web services. As discussed earlier in the SOAP Binding section, in the case of document wrapped style, the web service request consists of a root element which represents the name of the operation, and a child element following the root element represents the payload. The name of the operation is used by the web service framework to determine which method to invoke the implementation class.

To understand the Request and Response Wrapper concepts, let's look at an example of a sample SOAP request message sent by the web service client when it invokes the `processOrder` operation.

```
<soap:Envelope xmlns:soap="http://schemas.xmlsoap.org/soap/envelope/">
<soap:Body>
      <ns2:processOrder xmlns:ns2="http://order.demo/">
         <arg0>
            <customerID>C001</customerID>
            <itemID>I001</itemID>
            <price>200.0</price>
            <qty>100</qty>
         </arg0>
      </ns2:processOrder>
</soap:Body>
</soap:Envelope>
```

As you see in this code, the `soap` body contains the `wrapper root` element "`processOrder`" which maps to the method name "`processOrder`" in the Order Process web service. This is how a web service container like CXF identifies which method to invoke in the case of a document-literal wrapped style. The child element (`arg0`) following the root element represents the SOAP payload which maps to the input parameter (`Order`) of `processOrder` method in the `OrderProcess` class. The CXF framework behind the scenes converts the SOAP payload to the `Order` class by referring to JAX annotations and invokes the method `processOrder`. Once the method is invoked, the response object from the method is converted to the required XML response transparently by the CXF framework before transmitting the response back to the web service client.

The following code snippet shows the generated `ProcessOrder` class:

```
package demo.order;

import javax.xml.bind.annotation.XmlAccessType;
import javax.xml.bind.annotation.XmlAccessorType;
import javax.xml.bind.annotation.XmlType;

/**
 * <p>Java class for processOrder complex type.
 *
 * <p>The following schema fragment specifies the expected content
contained within this class.
 *
 * <pre>
 * &lt;complexType name="processOrder">
 *   &lt;complexContent>
 *     &lt;restriction base="{http://www.w3.org/2001/
XMLSchema}anyType">
 *       &lt;sequence>
 *         &lt;element name="arg0" type="{http://order.demo/}order"
minOccurs="0"/>
 *       &lt;/sequence>
 *     &lt;/restriction>
 *   &lt;/complexContent>
 * &lt;/complexType>
 * </pre>
 *
 *
 */
@XmlAccessorType(XmlAccessType.FIELD)
@XmlType(name = "processOrder", propOrder = {
    "arg0"
})
public class ProcessOrder {

    protected Order arg0;

    /**
     * Gets the value of the arg0 property.
     *
     * @return
     *     possible object is
     *     {@link Order }
     *
     */
    public Order getArg0() {
```

```
        return arg0;
    }

    /**
     * Sets the value of the arg0 property.
     *
     * @param value
     *     allowed object is
     *     {@link Order }
     *
     */
    public void setArg0(Order value) {
        this.arg0 = value;
    }
}
```

As you can see in the previous code listing, the generated `ProcessOrder` class has the JAXB binding defined, which maps the `ProcessOrder` class to the `processOrder` XML element. The `ProcessOrder` contains the `Order` class which maps to the `arg0` element, as shown in the SOAP request example. The `Request` Wrapper class is denoted by the `@RequestWrapper` annotation on the Service Interface, as discussed in the next section.

Service Interface

The `OrderProcess` class is an SEI that defines the abstract `processOrder` method. The following code shows the generated class:

```
@WebService(targetNamespace = "http://order.demo/",
name = "OrderProcess")
@XmlSeeAlso({ObjectFactory.class})
public interface OrderProcess {

    @ResponseWrapper(localName = "processOrderResponse",
targetNamespace = "http://order.demo/", className =
"demo.order.ProcessOrderResponse")
    @RequestWrapper(localName = "processOrder", targetNamespace =
    "http://order.demo/", className = "demo.order.ProcessOrder")
    @WebResult(name = "return", targetNamespace = "")
    @WebMethod
    public java.lang.String processOrder(
        @WebParam(name = "arg0", targetNamespace = "")
        demo.order.Order arg0
    );
}
```

As you can see, the generated code uses lot of annotations to define the SEI. Firstly, it uses the @WebService annotation that defines the class as a web service. The @Xml SeeAlso annotation instructs JAXB to include the ObjectFactory class when performing the data binding. The service method processOrder is defined with relevant method-level annotations. The @RequestWrapper annotations wrap the input message and the @ResponseWrapper annotation wraps the output message and its parameter to a Java class, as defined by its className attribute respectively. Note that if you are using the OrderProcess interface for creating a web service client, as illustrated in the Code-first development approach, you don't need to use the Wrapper objects as input, as this would be created at runtime by the CXF JAX-WS framework, based on the classname defined in @RequestWrapper annotation. Instead, you would work with the Order class itself. CXF JAX-WS runtime hides the complexity of the RequestWrapper and ResponseWrapper classes from developers. The @WebResult provides the logical name for the return type, which is named return. The @WebMethod annotation signifies that the processOrder method is a service method. Finally, the processOrder service method parameter is annotated with @WebParam annotation. The @WebParam annotation is used to customize the mapping of the method parameter to the WSDL message part name. For instance, the Order method parameter would be mapped to the arg0 element name in request XML.

Service implementation class

The generated OrderProcessImpl represents the service implementation class that provides an empty shell for the processOrder method. The following code shows the service implementation class:

```
@javax.jws.WebService(
                      serviceName = "OrderProcessService",
                      portName = "OrderProcessPort",
                      targetNamespace = "http://order.demo/",
                      wsdlLocation = "file:OrderProcess.wsdl",
                      endpointInterface = "demo.order.OrderProcess")
public class OrderProcessImpl implements OrderProcess {

    private static final Logger LOG =
    Logger.getLogger(OrderProcessImpl.class.getName());

    /* (non-Javadoc)
     * @see demo.order.OrderProcess#processOrder(demo.order.Order
arg0 )*
     */
```

```
    public java.lang.String processOrder(demo.order.Order arg0) {
        LOG.info("Executing operation processOrder");
        System.out.println(arg0);
        try {
            java.lang.String _return = "";
            return _return;
        } catch (Exception ex) {
            ex.printStackTrace();
            throw new RuntimeException(ex);
        }
    }
}
```

The class is generated with the `@WebService` annotation having all the relevant attributes. It implements the generated `OrderProcess` SEI and defines an empty implementation of the `processOrder` service method. The developer needs to implement this empty method to complete the implementation.

Standalone server class

The generated `OrderProcess_OrderProcessPort_Server` class represents the standalone server class. The standalone server class gets its name from the `<wsdl:portType>` element and the `<wsdl:port>` element. It is used to publish the service on a given endpoint address and start the server.

```
public class OrderProcess_OrderProcessPort_Server{

    protected OrderProcess_OrderProcessPort_Server() throws Exception
{
        System.out.println("Starting Server");
        Object implementor = new OrderProcessImpl();
        String address = "http://localhost:8080/OrderProcess";
        Endpoint.publish(address, implementor);
    }

    public static void main(String args[]) throws Exception {
        new OrderProcess_OrderProcessPort_Server();
        System.out.println("Server ready...");
}
```

Build file

The ANT `build` file can be used to build the generated Java file. The build process will create the respective classes in the `build` folder. The following code shows this portion of the generated `build.xml` file:

```
<project name="cxf wsdltojava" default="build" basedir=".">
    <property environment="env"/>
    <property name="home.dir" location="${basedir}"/>
    <property name="build.dir" location ="${basedir}/build"/>
    <property name="build.classes.dir" location ="${build.dir}/
classes"/>
    <property name="build.src.dir" location ="${basedir}"/>
...
    <target name="OrderProcessClient" description=
    "Run demo.order.OrderProcess_OrderProcessPort_Client"
    depends="compile">
        <property name="param" value=""/>
        <cxfrun classname="demo.order.OrderProcess_OrderProcessPort_
        Client"
                    param1="file:OrderProcess.xml"
                    param2="${op}"
                    param3="${param}"/>
    </target>

    <target name="OrderProcessServer" description="Run demo.order.
    OrderProcess_OrderProcessPort_Server" depends="compile">
        <cxfrun classname="demo.order.OrderProcess_OrderProcessPort_
        Server"
                    param1="file:OrderProcess.xml"/>
    </target>
...
</project>
```

The ANT `build` file above defines the target both for server and client application. Execute the `ant` command from the path where this file is generated. The `ant` command will build or compile the generated code and put it in the `build` folder. You can then use the following commands to run the server and client programs respectively:

```
ant OrderProcessServer
ant OrderProcessClient
```

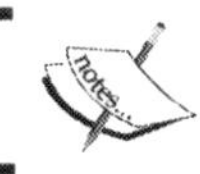

In Chapter 8 we will look at how to use the `WSDL2Java` tool to create a service implementation from a `.NET WSDL` file.

Implementing the service method

Modify the `OrderProcessImpl` class to provide your implementation for `processOrder` method. The following code illustrates this portion of the generated `OrderProcessImpl` implementation class:

```
public class OrderProcessImpl implements OrderProcess {

    private static final Logger LOG =
    Logger.getLogger(OrderProcessImpl.class.getName());

    /* (non-Javadoc)
     * @see demo.order.OrderProcess#processOrder(demo.order.Order
argO )*
     */
    public java.lang.String processOrder(demo.order.Order argO) {
        LOG.info("Executing operation processOrder");
        System.out.println(arg0);
        try {
            java.lang.String _return = "ORD1234";
            return _return;
        } catch (Exception ex) {
            ex.printStackTrace();
            throw new RuntimeException(ex);
        }
    }
}
```

You can provide the required business logic to this `processOrder` method and complete the implementation. We provide a dummy implementation and return a static Order ID "`ORD1234`", as shown above.

Publishing the web service

To publish the generated Order Process service, navigate to the `Chapter3/contractfirst` folder, and type in the following command:

```
ant server
```

This will publish the Order Process web service at `http://localhost:8080/OrderProcess`

Invoking the web service

You can use the web service client from the Code-first development section to invoke the web service. Navigate to the `Chapter3/codefirst` folder of the downloaded source code and type in the following command:

```
ant client
```

In Chapter 8 we will look at how to use the client code generated from WSDL2 Java tool to invoke a service

You will see the order ID being printed in the console.

Using dynamic client

A web service client typically uses service interface to invoke service methods. Till now we developed client applications that used Service Endpoint Interface (SEI) or a proxy to the interface to call the service method. There may be a situation where you need to provide a client that is generated dynamically at the runtime. Dynamic client is typically helpful where you don't want to have an extra overhead for generating and maintaining stub classes for creating clients. As dynamic client inspects the WSDL and creates input and output objects dynamically, based on WSDL definition, it also serves as a component for validating WSDL file and input and output message formats, without actually invoking the web service as part of your unit test environment.

CXF provides an alternate way to build a web service client dynamically. It delivers the concept of dynamic client through the use of the `JaxWsDynamicClientFactory` factory class. CXF also provides a non JAX-WS class named `DynamicClientFactory`. This is useful if your service component is developed using any non JAX-WS API. This chapter will focus on the JAX-WS version of dynamic client factory class.

Creating a simple dynamic client

Let's look at how to create a dynamic client. You need an existing WSDL document to generate a dynamic client. The `JaxWsDynamicClientFactory` factory class will make use of this WSDL and generate the SEI and data classes, at the runtime, in the memory. As part of this exercise, we would reuse the Order Process WSDL that we had generated in the Code-first development section.

We will name the dynamic client class `OrderProcessJaxWsDynamicClient`. The following block of code shows the code listing for `OrderProcessJaxWsDynamicClient.java`:

```
package demo.order.client;

import org.apache.cxf.jaxws.endpoint.dynamic.
JaxWsDynamicClientFactory;

import org.apache.cxf.endpoint.Client;

import java.lang.reflect.Method;

public class OrderProcessJaxWsDynamicClient {
   public OrderProcessJaxWsDynamicClient() {
   }

   public static void main(String str[]) throws Exception {

      JaxWsDynamicClientFactory dcf = JaxWsDynamicClientFactory.
      newInstance();
      Client client = dcf.createClient("http://localhost:8080/
      OrderProcess?wsdl");
      Object order = Thread.currentThread().getContextClassLoader().
loadClass("demo.order.Order").newInstance();
      Method m1 = order.getClass().getMethod("setCustomerID",
      String.class);
      Method m2 = order.getClass().getMethod("setItemID",
      String.class);
      Method m3 = order.getClass().getMethod("setQty",
      Integer.class);
      Method m4 = order.getClass().getMethod("setPrice",
      Double.class);
      m1.invoke(order, "C001");
      m2.invoke(order, "I001");
      m3.invoke(order, 100);
      m4.invoke(order, 200.00);
      Object[] response = client.invoke("processOrder", order);
      System.out.println("Response is " + response[0]);
   }
}
```

The `OrderProcessJaxWsDynamicClient` carries out the following steps:

1. Create an instance of a `JaxWsDynamicClientFactory` factory class. This is done by calling the static `newInstance` method.
2. After getting the instance, you invoke the `createClient` method on this instance to create the client component dynamically. This method retrieves the WDSL document from the URL `http://localhost:8080/OrderProcess?wsdl`. Note that we published the OrderProcess service at `http://localhost:8080/OrderProcess`. This method returns an object of `org.apache.cxf.endpoint.ClientImpl` class.
3. We then dynamically build an instance of an `Order` class using context classloader. We need to pass the `Order` object to the `processOrder` method.
4. The next set of code populates the `Order` bean using Java reflection. Since we are generating a dynamic client, and there is no SEI directly available to the client, we have to use Java reflection API to invoke the service and data methods. The `invoke` method on the `Client` object will make a call to the `processOrder` service method that takes the `Order` bean as a parameter.
5. We then retrieve the output and print it on the console. Our object is represented as a simple string, which contains the `Order Id`.

Now, let's see the dynamic client in action.

Running the dynamic client

We will use the ANT tool to build and execute the code. The source code and build file for the chapter is available in the `Chapter3/dynamiclient` folder of the downloaded source code. Navigate to the `Chapter3/dynamiclient` folder, and run the following command on the command prompt:

1. `ant build`

   This will build the source code.
2. `ant server`

   This will run the server and publish the Order Process web service to the location `http://localhost:8080/OrderProcess`.

   This is the same web service that was developed as part of the Code-first development approach.
3. Open a new command prompt and run the client, which will invoke the service.

   ```
   ant client
   ```

On running the client, you will see the following output:

Oct 13, 2009 6:50:40 PM org.springframework.context.support.AbstractApplicationContext prepareRefresh

INFO: Refreshing org.apache.cxf.bus.spring.BusApplicationContext@32563256: display name [org.apache.cxf.bus.spring.BusApplicationContext@32563256]; startup date [Tue Oct 13 18:50:40 IST 2009]; root of context hierarchy

......

```
INFO: Created classes: demo.order.ObjectFactory, demo.order.Order,
demo.order.ProcessOrder, demo.order.ProcessOrderResponse
Response is ORD1234
```

The output shows the generated order ID. As you see in the above output message highlighted in bold, the `JaxWsDynamicClientFactory` dynamically creates the `demo.order.Order`, `demo.order.ProcessOrder`, and `demo.order.ProcessOrderResponse` classes at runtime.

Using the CXF service model for building dynamic client

The previous code uses Java reflection API. Alternatively, you can use the CXF service model framework to dynamically build the service information and finally invoke the service method through bean introspection. By using service model framework can dynamically obtain the web service information. This approach is better when compared to the earlier approach, particularly when you don't know which class to load for the web service input and output message. This approach doesn't require an extra overhead for obtaining the correct class loader reference to load the required input and output objects, which based on container class loading policy can be problematic. The following image shows the service model framework components that can be used to get or populate the service information:

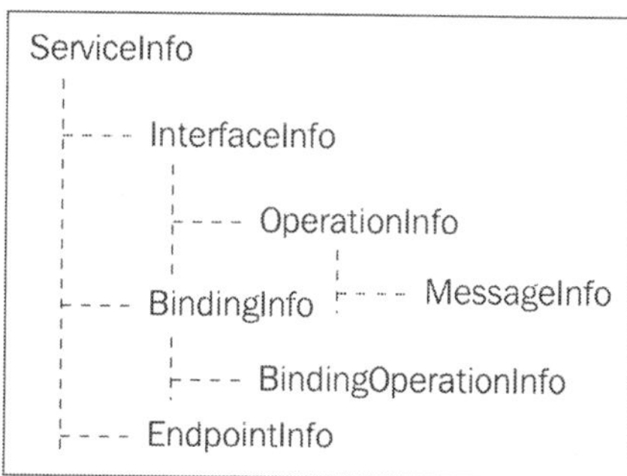

We will change the above Java reflection based code to reflect the service model API. Since the example code is large, we will dissect the code and explain each chunk of it.

```
import java.beans.PropertyDescriptor;
import java.util.List;

import javax.xml.namespace.QName;

import org.apache.cxf.endpoint.Client;
import org.apache.cxf.endpoint.Endpoint;
import org.apache.cxf.jaxws.endpoint.dynamic.
JaxWsDynamicClientFactory;
import org.apache.cxf.service.model.BindingInfo;
import org.apache.cxf.service.model.BindingMessageInfo;
import org.apache.cxf.service.model.BindingOperationInfo;
import org.apache.cxf.service.model.MessagePartInfo;
import org.apache.cxf.service.model.ServiceInfo;
public class OrderProcessJaxWsDynClient {
   public OrderProcessJaxWsDynClient() {
   }

   public static void main(String str[]) throws Exception {
      JaxWsDynamicClientFactory dcf = JaxWsDynamicClientFactory.
      newInstance();
      Client client = dcf.createClient("http://localhost:8080/
      OrderProcess?wsdl");
       Endpoint endpoint = client.getEndpoint();. . .
```

We start off by creating an instance of the `JaxWsDynamicClientFactory` factory class and then invoke the `createClient` method on this instance to create the client component dynamically. The `createClient` method retrieves the WDSL document from the URL `http://localhost:8080/OrderProcess?wsdl`. We then get the service endpoint object from the `Client` object. This is where we will start using the dynamics service model framework.

```
// Make use of CXF service model to introspect the existing WSDL
        ServiceInfo serviceInfo = endpoint.getService().
getServiceInfos().get(0);
        QName bindingName = new QName("http://order.demo/", "
OrderProcessServiceSoapBinding");
        BindingInfo binding = serviceInfo.getBinding(bindingName);
        QName opName = new QName("http://order.demo/", "processOrder");
        BindingOperationInfo boi = binding.getOperation(opName);
// Operation name is processOrder
        BindingMessageInfo inputMessageInfo = null;
        if(!boi.isUnwrapped()){
           //OrderProcess uses document literal wrapped style.
           inputMessageInfo = boi.getWrappedOperation().getInput();
```

```
        }else {
            inputMessageInfo = boi.getUnwrappedOperation().getInput();
        }
        List<MessagePartInfo> parts = inputMessageInfo.
getMessageParts();
        MessagePartInfo partInfo = parts.get(0); gb// Input class is
Order
```

Using the service endpoint object, we will obtain the `ServiceInfo` object. The `ServiceInfo` object is the base object of the service model framework. We can start by obtaining the relevant service information using the `ServiceInfo` object. We will obtain the following details—binding info, the service operation name, and the input parameter name. The `BindingInfo` class represents the service binding information. We will pass the operation qualified name to the `getOperation()` method to retrieve the binding operation information associated with that binding. For `OrderProcess` service, there is only one operation `processOrder`. By using the `BindingOperationInfo` object, we will then get the operation input parameter details. The `BindingMessageInfo` object consists of a list of message parts of type `MessagePartInfo`, which represents an input parameter. For the `OrderProcess` service, there is only one input associated with `processOrder` operation. Therefore, we retrieve the first `MessagePartInfo` object. Once we have obtained the operation and message information, we can use bean introspection to invoke the service method. The following code illustrates the use of bean introspection:

```
List<MessagePartInfo> parts = inputMessageInfo.getMessageParts();
MessagePartInfo partInfo = parts.get(0); // Input class is Order

        // Get the input class Order
        Class<?> orderClass = partInfo.getTypeClass();
        Object orderObject = orderClass.newInstance();
        // Populate the Order bean
        // Set customer ID, item ID, price and quantity
        PropertyDescriptor custProperty =
        new PropertyDescriptor("customerID", orderClass);
          custProperty.getWriteMethod().invoke(orderObject, "C001");
          PropertyDescriptor itemProperty =
          new PropertyDescriptor("itemID", orderClass);
          itemProperty.getWriteMethod().invoke(orderObject, "I001");
          PropertyDescriptor priceProperty =
          new PropertyDescriptor("price", orderClass);
          priceProperty.getWriteMethod().invoke(orderObject,
          Double.valueOf(100.00));
          PropertyDescriptor qtyProperty =
          new PropertyDescriptor("qty", orderClass);
```

```
        qtyProperty.getWriteMethod().invoke(orderObject,
        Integer.valueOf(20));

       // Invoke the processOrder() method and print the result
      // The response class is String
      Object[] result = client.invoke(opName, orderObject);
        System.out.println("The order ID is " + result[0]);
```

As you can see, we are invoking the `processOrder` method that takes the `Order` bean as the input parameter. The `PropertyDescriptor` is used to set and get the properties of the `Order` class. The important thing to observe is that everything is performed dynamically and there is no existing information about the input parameter class. The dynamic client can be used with service model if your web service has many complex dependencies. Now, let's run the dynamic client.

Running the dynamic client which uses Service Model API

We will use the ANT tool to build and execute the code. The source code and `build` file for the chapter is available in the `Chapter3/dynamiclient` folder of the downloaded source code. Navigate to the `Chapter3/dynamiclient` folder, and run the following command on the command prompt:

- `ant build`

  This will build the source code.

- `ant server`

  This will run the server and publish the Order Process web service to the location `http://localhost:8080`. Don't close this window.

- Open a new command prompt, and run the client which will invoke the service.

  `ant modelclient`

  On running the client you will see the following output.

  Oct 13, 2009 6:50:40 PM org.springframework.context.support.AbstractApplicationContext prepareRefresh

  INFO: Refreshing org.apache.cxf.bus.spring.BusApplicationContext@32563256: display name [org.apache.cxf.bus.spring.BusApplicationContext@32563256]; startup date [Tue Oct 13 18:50:40 IST 2009]; root of context hierarchy

```
......
INFO: Created classes: demo.order.ObjectFactory, demo.order.Order,
demo.order.ProcessOrder, demo.order.ProcessOrderResponse
The order ID is ORD1234
```

The output shows the generated order ID. As you can see in the above output message highlighted in bold, the `JaxWsDynamicClientFactory` dynamically creates the `demo.order.Order`, `demo.order.ProcessOrder`, and `demo.order.ProcessOrderResponse` classes at runtime.

Provider and Dispatch services

You can build a JAX-WS service by writing an SEI and annotating it as a web service or generating an SEI from a given WSDL. With SEI-based implementation, you simply write the service method, and the client program makes use of SEI to invoke this service method. Behind the scenes, the operation parameters or messages are converted into XML and vice versa by the JAXB.

`Provider` and `Dispatch` interfaces, part of JAX-WS API, are used to develop a web service that processes or handles messages as raw XML, and not through method invocation. Unlike SEI-based implementation, the messages are not converted into XML using data binding techniques like JAXB. Instead, the messages themselves are in a raw XML format.

The `Provider` and `Dispatch` methods are useful where the XML messages transferred between web service client and web service provider are pretty large and you don't want the extra overhead of converting the XML messages in Java objects. As part of your web service implementation, you would want to deal with XML directly and probably use an effective way to parse XML, rather than relying on the web service framework.

JAX-WS provides the `javax.xml.ws.Provider` interface that offers functionality to create and implement a service provider that will process XML messages. It will take a request in the form of XML messages from the dispatcher client, process the same, and accordingly generate the response. The provider implementation class will be published as a service endpoint on the server. On the other hand, the JAX-WS `javax.xml.ws.Dispatch` interface is used to process the XML message and send the response in XML format to the service provider.

Since both Provider and Dispatcher services deal with the raw XML as a message, we will first look at the different types or modes of messages that can be processed. It is very important to gain a good understanding of the nature of messages that can be exchanged. We will also look at different message types that can be handled by the Provider and Dispatch implementation. Later, we will develop Provider and Dispatch implementations. The section will focus on the topics below in the following order:

- Understanding messaging modes
- Understanding types of message objects
- Implementing Provider service
- Implementing Dispatch service
- Publishing the Provider service
- Running the example

Understanding messaging modes

The `Provider` and `Dispatcher` interfaces allow two types of messages—Message and Payload. They are often considered as two different messaging modes. The difference lies in the message content. The Message mode consists of the actual data along with the control information such as the header, whereas the Payload mode works only with actual data. The Message mode is used when you want to access the SOAP header information associated with the web service request. Most web service specifications such as WS-Security, WS-Policy, and WS-authorization use the SOAP header to propagate context information for web services.

Message mode

In this mode the message is processed in its entirety. An implementation class will process the complete message, the message composed of control or binding information such as the header and the actual message data.

```
@WebServiceProvider()
@ServiceMode(value = Service.Mode.MESSAGE)
public class OrderProcessDOMProvider implements Provider<DOMSource> {
. . .
```

The above code snippet illustrates the processing of a SOAP message with the `Message` mode by a `Provider` implementation. The implementation uses SOAP binding and accepts a complete SOAP message. The complete SOAP message is nothing but the SOAP envelope, which is composed of the header and the actual data. Both the incoming and outgoing messages are complete SOAP messages. One can also specify the mode of messaging using the `@ServiceMode` annotation. This annotation expects a value that will determine the message mode. The value above is defined as `Service.Mode.MESSAGE`, which indicates that the `Provider` implementation will handle the message with the mode as `MESSAGE`.

Payload mode

Payload means the actual data that is sent or received. An implementation class will process only the actual data or payload and not the complete message. The payload of a message is the actual business data that is passed between endpoints. In the case of SOAP binding, the SOAP body is the payload of the message.

```
@WebServiceProvider()
@ServiceMode(value = Service.Mode.PAYLOAD)
public class OrderProcessDOMProvider implements Provider<DOMSource> {
. . .
```

The above code snippet illustrates the processing of SOAP messages with the `Payload` mode by a `Provider` implementation. The implementation accepts a SOAP message, which is part of a SOAP body element. The annotation `@ServiceMode` is used with the value of `Service.Mode.PAYLOAD` to specify the `Payload` mode for the message. The `Payload` mode is the default mode used by the `Provider` implementation, that is, if you do not specify the `@ServiceMode` annotation, it takes `Payload` as the default messaging mode.

Understanding types of message objects

Both the `Provider` and `Dispatch` implementation work with input and output messages that represent one of the following three objects—`javax.xml.transform.Source`, `javax.xml.soap.SOAPMessage`, and `javax.activation.DataSource`.

javax.xml.transform.Source

With a `Provider` implementation, you can provide an input and output message object of the type `java.xml.transform.Source`. Source objects are a direct representation of XML documents. They allow APIs to access and manipulate XML document contents. The `Provider` implementation works with three types of source implementation, `DOMSource`, `SAXSource`, and `StreamSource`.

DOMSource

`DOMSource` object, as the name suggests, represents XML elements or messages in a **Document Object Model** (**DOM**) tree. The DOM tree is a tree of nodes. Each node represents an XML element. `DOMSource` implementation provides methods to access and create a node in the DOM tree.

SAXSource

`SAXSource` object represents an XML elements or messages based on **Simple API for XML** (**SAX**) model. The SAX model is event based. It makes use of `InputSource` and `XMLReader` objects to access and manipulate XML elements.

StreamSource

`StreamSource` object represents XML elements or messages as a stream of bytes.

javax.xml.soap.SOAPMessage

The `SOAPMessage` object is a natural choice for an input or output message for the `Provider` implementation, if you are using the SOAP binding for transmitting messages. It works only in the `Message` mode, which means one has to provide the complete SOAP envelope as messages. A `SOAPMessage` object represents the SOAP envelope which is composed of a `SOAPPart` object and an `AttachmentPart` object. The `SOAPPart` resembles the SOAP envelope, and it contains SOAP headers and the SOAP message body. The `AttachmentPart` object resembles binary data attached to the SOAP message. The `SOAPMessage` object can have zero or several `AttachmentPart` objects.

javax.activation.DataSource

You can also pass messages as a form of `DataSource` object. The `DataSource` object represents an arbitrary collection of data that supports MIME type. It provides access to the data type and the data itself in the form of `InputStream` and `OutputStream`. The `DataSource` object is useful when you want to send messages that are http-bound with the mode as `Message`. An example of using a `DataSource` object would be to transfer image contents such as like fingerprint images for authentication.

In next section, we will implement `Dispatch` and `Provider` components that will process the XML messages. First we will look at implementing the `Dispatch` service implementation that will make a request to the `Provider` implementation in the form of an XML message. Then, we will work on building the `Provider` implementation that will process the request and send the appropriate response. We will revisit the example of the Order Processing Application and show how this can be implemented using the Provider and Dispatcher implementation.

[The source code for provider service implementation is available in the `Chapter3/providerdispatch` folder of the downloaded source code.]

Implementing Provider service

In this section we will look at how to implement a `Provider` web service that directly processes Order XML messages. We will break down the code into sections in order to understand it in detail. The following code snippet shows the code listing of the `OrderProcessDOMProvider` class:

```
@WebServiceProvider()
@ServiceMode(value = Service.Mode.MESSAGE)
public class OrderProcessDOMProvider implements Provider<DOMSource> {

    public OrderProcessDOMProvider() {
    }
. . .
```

The `OrderProcessDOMProvider` provider implementation class implements a `Provider` interface with a type as `DOMSource`. The type has to be specific and cannot be generic. This means that you cannot implement the `Provider<T>` interface. `<T>` must be replaced with one of the `Source` objects discussed in the previous section. The interface defines one abstract method `invoke`. The `invoke` method takes one of the three object types as a parameter, `Source`, `MessageObject`, or `DataSource`. We will look at implementing our `Provider` class with a `Source` type message.

The class declaration is supported with the `@WebServiceProvider` annotation. The `@WebServiceProvider` signifies that the `Provider` class is a JAX-WS-based service provider implementation. The `@WebServiceProvider` is supported with the following attributes:

Attribute	Description
`portName`	It indicates the name of the endpoint where the service is published. It directly maps to a name attribute of the `<wsdl:port>` element in the WSDL document.
`serviceName`	The name of the published service object. It directly maps to a name attribute of the `<wsdl:service>` element in the WSDL document.
`targetNamespace`	It holds the namespace where the service is defined.
`wsdlLocation`	It indicates the location of the WSDL document in the form of a URL.

All the above attributes are optional. If you choose not to provide the attributes, then in such case, the values of these attributes are implicitly provided.

Next, we look at the implementation method. The `invoke()` method performs the following steps:

1. Create the `SOAPMessage` object to hold the incoming XML request. It then prints the message to the system console. You can validate the message to make sure it is the same request we sent from the dispatcher client.

```
public DOMSource invoke(DOMSource request) {
        DOMSource response = new DOMSource();
        try {
            MessageFactory factory = MessageFactory.newInstance();
            SOAPMessage soapReq = factory.createMessage();
            soapReq.getSOAPPart().setContent(request);
MessageFactory factory = MessageFactory.newInstance();
            SOAPMessage soapReq = factory.createMessage();
            soapReq.getSOAPPart().setContent(request);

            System.out.println("Incoming Client Request as a
DOMSource data in MESSAGE Mode");
            soapReq.writeTo(System.out);
            System.out.println("\n");
```

2. Next, we print the order information associated with the node by iterating through child nodes. The following snippet of code shows the code listing:

```
Node processOrderNode = soapReq.getSOAPBody().getFirstChild();
        //Get arg0 - order element
        Node order = processOrderNode.getChildNodes().item(0);
       //Get list of child nodes associated with order and print it
              NodeList list = order.getChildNodes();
              for(int i = 0 ; i<list.getLength() ; i++){
               //Get the child nodes and value as per the order xml
request.
                 System.out.println(list.item(i).getNodeName() + "=" +
                     list.item(i).getFirstChild().getNodeValue());
              }
```

3. We then create a SOAP message from the `MessageFactory` instance. Since we are using SOAP binding, the response XML message here will be a SOAP message. We create the order response in the required XML format and set it in the SOAP body. For simplicity, we set the `Order Id` to a static value "`ORD1234`", as shown in the following block of code:

```
SOAPMessage orderResponse =  factory.createMessage();
              QName processOrderQName =
              new QName("http://order.demo/", "processOrder");
              QName responseQName =
              new QName("http://order.demo/", "return");
         //create the element -
        //<http://order.demo/:processOrder></http://order.demo/:
           processOrder>
              SOAPElement processOrderResponse =
orderResponse.getSOAPBody().addChildElement(processOrderQName);
//create the element inside processOrder - //<http://order.demo/:
return>ORD1234</http://order.demo/:return>
processOrderResponse.addChildElement(responseQName).
addTextNode("ORD1234");
```

4. We then construct a `DOMSource` object and set the soap response as a XML node and return the same:

```
response.setNode(orderResponse.getSOAPPart());
```

As you can see in the above `invoke()` method, unlike SEI-based implementation, the `Provider` implementation works directly with XML messages. The input and output message both have the same type. The developer has to build a message in the form of raw XML. The XML message can resemble a SOAP format or a standard one, as defined by the `wsdl:operation` element in the WSDL file. The XML message should follow the basic norms of SOAP style, RPC, and Document.

The following code illustrates the SOAP response that would be generated by the `OrderProcessDOMProvider` implementation:

```
<soap:Envelope xmlns:soap="http://schemas.xmlsoap.org/soap/envelope/">
<soap:Body xmlns:soap="http://schemas.xmlsoap.org/soap/envelope/">
<ns2:processOrder xmlns:ns2="http://order.demo/
"><arg0><customerID>C001</customerID><itemID>I001</
itemID><price>200.0</price><qty>100</qty></arg0></ns2:processOrder>
</soap:Body>
</soap:Envelope>
```

Publishing the Provider service

We will publish the `OrderProcessDOMProvider` provider service on the endpoint URL `http://localhost:8080/OrderProcessDOMProvider`. The following code shows the `Server` that publishes the `OrderProcessDOMProvider` service provider object:

```
public class Server {

    protected Server() throws Exception {
        System.out.println("Starting Server");

        Object implementor = new OrderProcessDOMProvider();
        String address = "http://localhost:8080/
        OrderProcessDOMProvider";
        Endpoint.publish(address, implementor);


    }

    public static void main(String args[]) throws Exception {
        new Server();
        System.out.println("Server ready...");

        Thread.sleep(5 * 60 * 1000);
        System.out.println("Server exiting");
        System.exit(0);
    }
```

The previous code is similar to the one used for publishing the web service for the Code-first development approach with the exception of publishing the `OrderProcessDOMProvider` class instead of the `OrderProcessImpl` class.

Next, we look at the Dispatcher client implementation that would invoke the web service.

Implementing the Dispatch service

The `Dispatch` component is responsible for making a request in the form of an XML message. We will name the `Dispatch` component as `DispatcherClient`. The `Dispatcher` client performs the following steps:

1. The code first creates the `Service` object. The `Dispatch` object is created from the `Service` object. The service object is constructed using the target namespace and the service `QName`:

```
public final class DispatcherClient {

    public static final String WSDLFile =
    "http://localhost:8080/OrderProcessDOMProvider?wsdl";

    public DispatcherClient() {
    }
    public static void main(String args[]) throws Exception {
   URL wsdlURL = new URL(WSDLFile);
        MessageFactory factory = MessageFactory.newInstance();
        QName domProvider = new QName("http://provider.order.
        demo/", "OrderProcessDOMProviderService");
        QName portName = new QName("http://provider.order.demo/",
        "OrderProcessDOMProviderPort");
        Service service = Service.create(wsdlURL, domProvider);
```

2. Next, the `SOAPMessge` object is created from the `MessageFactory` instance. Since we are using SOAP binding, we create an instance of a `SOAPMessage` object:

```
SOAPMessage soapRequest = factory.createMessage();
```

3. Next, the XML request is created for the `Order`, and set it in the SOAP body. As you can see in the code listing below, the SOAP body is retrieved using the `soapRequest.getSOAPBody()` method and request XML order is set as the child element of the SOAP body.

```
QName processOrderQName = new QName("http://order.demo/",
"processOrder");
```

```
        //create the element - <http://order.demo/:processOrder>
        </http://order.demo/:processOrder>
         SOAPElement processOrderResponse =
         soapRequest.getSOAPBody().addChildElement(processOrderQNa
         me);
         SOAPElement order = processOrderResponse.
addChildElement("arg0");
         order.addChildElement("customerID").addTextNode("Naveen");
         order.addChildElement("itemID").addTextNode("I001");
         order.addChildElement("price").addTextNode("200.00");
         order.addChildElement("qty").addTextNode("200");
```

4. Next, the `DOMSource` object is constructed by passing the SOAP request:

```
DOMSource domRequestMsg = new
DOMSource(soapRequest.getSOAPPart());
```

5. Once the `DOMSource` object is in place, we go about creating the `Dispatch` implementation. The `Dispatch` implementation object is created using the service created above. The method `createDispatch` is used to create the `Dispatch` implementation object. The method takes port name, the `DOMSource` class, and the message mode as parameters. The message mode will be `Mode.MESSAGE` and the port name will be `OrderProcessDOMProviderPort`.

```
Dispatch<DOMSource> domMsg = service.createDispatch(portName,
DOMSource.class, Mode.MESSAGE);
```

6. You then call the `invoke` method on the dispatch implementation that sends the request to the service provider and gets back the response as `DOMSource`. Since the response will be in the form of an XML message, you have to use the `getNode` method of the `DOMSource` object to parse the XML response message. After running the client, the Order ID is printed at the console.

```
 DOMSource domResponseMsg = domMsg.invoke(domRequestMsg);

System.out.println("Client Request as a DOMSource data in
MESSAGE Mode");
        soapReq.writeTo(System.out);
        System.out.println("\n");


        System.out.println("Response from server: " +
domResponseMsg.getNode().getLastChild().getTextContent());
```

The following code shows the SOAP request created by the `DispatcherClient` class:

```
<SOAP-ENV:Envelope xmlns:SOAP-ENV="http://schemas.xmlsoap.org/soap/
envelope/" xmlns:soap="http://schemas.xmlsoap.org/soap/envelope/
"><SOAP-ENV:Header xmlns:SOAP-ENV="http://schemas.xmlsoap.org/soap/
envelope/"/>
<SOAP-ENV:Body xmlns:SOAP-ENV="http://schemas.xmlsoap.org/soap/
envelope/">
<processOrder xmlns="http://order.demo/">
<arg0 xmlns="http://order.demo/"><customerID xmlns="http://order.
demo/">Naveen</customerID><itemID xmlns="http://order.demo/">I001</
itemID><price xmlns="http://order.demo/">200.00</price><qty
xmlns="http://order.demo/">200</qty>
/arg0>
</processOrder>
</SOAP-ENV:Body>
</SOAP-ENV:Envelope>
```

Running the provider dispatch example

We will use the ANT tool to build and execute the code. The source code and the build file for the chapter is available in the `Chapter3/providerdispatch` folder of the downloaded source code. Navigate to the `Chapter3/providerdispatch` folder and run the following command on the command prompt:

- `ant build`

  This will build the source code.

- `ant server`

  This will run the server and publish the Order Process web service to the location `http://localhost:8080/OrderProcessDOMProvider`. Do not close this window.

- Open a new command prompt, and run the client which will invoke the service.

  `ant client`

  On running the client, you will see the following output:

```
INFO: ...
Incoming Client Request as a DOMSource data in MESSAGE Mode
<SOAP-ENV:Envelope xmlns:SOAP-ENV="http://schemas.xml-soap.org/soap/envelope/"><SOAP-ENV:Header xmlns:SOAP-ENV="http://schemas.xmlsoap.org/soap/envelope/"/><SOAP-ENV:Body xmlns:SOAP-ENV="http://schemas.xmlsoap.org/soap/envelope/"><processOrder xmlns="http://order.demo/"><arg0 xmlns="http://order.demo/"><customerID xmlns="http://order.demo/">Naveen</customerID><itemID xmlns="http://order.demo/">I001</itemID><price xmlns="http://order.demo/">200.00</price><qty xmlns="http://order.demo/">200</qty></arg0></processOrder></SOAP-ENV:Body></SOAP-ENV:Envelope>
Response from server: ORD1234
```

The output in the client shows the Response order ID `ORD1234` from the server.

On the server console, you will see the following output:

```
Incoming Client Request as a DOMSource data in MESSAGE Mode
<SOAP-ENV:Envelope xmlns:SOAP-ENV="http://schemas.xmlsoap.org/
soap/envelope/" xmlns:soap="http://schemas.xmlsoap.org/soap/
envelope/"><SOAP-ENV:Header xmlns:SOAP-ENV="http://schemas.xmlsoap.
org/soap/envelope/"/><SOAP-ENV:Body xmlns:SOAP-ENV="http://schemas.
xmlsoap.org/soap/envelope/"><processOrder xmlns="http://order.
demo/"><arg0 xmlns="http://order.demo/"><customerID xmlns="http://
order.demo/">Naveen</customerID><itemID xmlns="http://order.
demo/">I001</itemID><price xmlns="http://order.demo/">200.00</
price><qty xmlns="http://order.demo/">200</qty></arg0></
processOrder></SOAP-ENV:Body></SOAP-ENV:Envelope>

customerID=Naveen
itemID=I001
price=200.00
qty=200
```

As you can see above, the server prints the incoming SOAP request and prints out the `customerId`, `itemId`, `price`, and `qty` details associated with order.

Web service context

Every message that is exchanged between the client and service provider has some contextual information attached to it. The context here is the web service that gives information about the service message being passed between the endpoints. The context information is often called metadata, that is, the data about the message. The context information is stored in the form of key-value pairs. Context information is simply the properties that provide information on the incoming and outgoing message. The properties are stored as a Java Map object. These properties hold two types of information, data about the message and the underlying transport protocol that is used to route the message.

CXF provides access to these context properties in the form of a JAX-WS based `MessageContext` object. The `javax.xml.ws.handler.MessageContext` interface extends `java.util.Map<String key, Object obj>`. The Message context object is associated with a scope and can be in any one of the following scopes:

- Application

  The message context properties defined in an application scope can be shared by a service provider, service consumer, and the JAX-WS handler implementations. Any message context property set in service consumer code or service provider code is defaulted to Application scope.

- Handler

  Handler scoped properties are only available to the JAX-WS handler implementations. A message context property set in Handlers is not available to the service implementation code or a service client. Any message context property defined by the handler implementation is, by default, handler scoped.

> Handlers are used to perform additional processing of inbound and outbound messages. In Chapter 5 we will look at how to use handlers to intercept SOAP messages.

You can change the scope with the help of the `setScope` method of the `MessageContext` object. The `setScope` method takes two parameters, namely,the key and the scope. The key is the message context property key that you want to change to reflect the new scope. The scope value can be `MessageContext.Scope.APPLICATION` or `MessageContext.Scope.HANDLER`.

This chapter will focus on working with message property context in JAX-WS service implementation.

Implementing Context in service

Service implementation class developed using JAX-WS can access the message context properties through the use of the `WebServiceContext` interface. The `WebServiceContext` interface defines the `getMessageContext` method that can be used to obtain the `MessageContext` object. The `MessageContext` object can then be used to get or set the message context property.

Let's revisit the JAX-WS `OrderProcess` service code that we developed as part of the Code-first development approach. We will modify it to incorporate the `MessageContext` implementation.

```
@WebService(endpointInterface="demo.order.OrderProcess",
portName="OrderProcessPort")
public class OrderProcessImpl implements OrderProcess {

   @Resource
   WebServiceContext wsc;

   public String processOrder(Order order) {
      System.out.println("Getting the operation info from the message
      context ");
      MessageContext ctx = wsc.getMessageContext();
      QName operation = (QName) ctx.get(Message.WSDL_OPERATION);

      System.out.println("The operation name is " + operation);
. . .
```

As you can see in the above code snippet, we have modified the `processOrder` method to include the following steps:

1. The `WebServiceContext` property has been added to `OrderProcessImpl` class and annotated with an `@Resource` annotation. The `@Resource` annotation is used to inject resource objects. The CXF container at runtime will inject an instance of `WebServiceContext` when the `processOrder` method is being invoked.
2. We then invoke the `getMessageContext` method on the injected `WebServiceContext` object. The method returns the `MessageContext` object.
3. The message context object can then be used to access the message context properties. These properties are stored by the object as key-value pair. The above code uses the `WSDL_OPERATION` key to get the information on the wsdl operation being invoked. Inside the `processOrder` method, you are calling `ctx,get(Message.WSDL_OPERATION)` which will return the name of the operation in question as `QName`.

Running the web service context example

We will use the ANT tool to build and execute the code. The source code and build file for the chapter is available in the `Chapter3/context` folder of the downloaded source code. Navigate to the `Chapter3/context` folder, and run the following command on the command prompt:

- `ant build`

  This will build the source code.

- `ant server`

  This will run the publish the Order Process web service to the location `http://localhost:8080/OrderProcess`.

- Open a new command prompt, and run the client which will invoke the service `ant client`.

  On running the client, you will see the following output.

  ```
  INFO: Creating Service {http://order.demo/}OrderProcessImplService
  from WSDL: http://localhost:8080/OrderProcess?wsdl
  The order ID is ORD1234
  ```

  The output shows the generated order ID.

  On the console where the server is running, you will see the following output:

  ```
  Processing order...
  Getting the operation info from the message context
  The operation name is {http://order.demo/}processOrder.
  ```

As you can see, it is very simple to get the contextual information of the message. The following table shows some of the relevant properties that can be accessed in a JAX-WS-based service implementation:

Property	Description
`ENDPOINT_ADDRESS`	The endpoint address of the published service
`HTTP_REQUEST_METHOD`	The name of the request method used to send the message
`QUERY_STRING`	The query string attached to URL while making the request
`MTOM_ENABLED`	It determines whether or not the service provider can use MTOM attachments
`CONTENT_TYPE`	The MIME type of the message
`WSDL_SERVICE`	The service name as a `QName`

Property	Description
`WSDL_PORT`	The port name as a `QName`
`WSDL_INTERFACE`	The SEI name as a `QName`
`WSDL_OPERATION`	The service operation name as a `QName`

Simple frontend

Unlike JAX-WS, simple frontend does not provide any formal specification or standard to develop and deploy a web service. Instead it makes use of simple factory components to build a service. The factory components use Java-based reflection API internally to create service and client components. It's simpler to use and does not require any tool to build the service. JAX-WS, on the other hand, is a formal specification that addresses the development and deployment of web service.

The following table explains the difference between JAX-WS and Simple frontend:

JAX-WS	Simple frontend
JAX-WS is a Sun Java specification that specifies APIs to develop and deploy web services	A reflection based API to develop and deploy web service
Supports Java 5 annotation-based development	Annotations are not supported

In this section we will use simple frontend API to develop a service and client component.

Developing a simple frontend

Let's start with the building of web service using simple frontend. We will look at the following steps:

1. Creating service implementation class and interface
2. Creating server implementation
3. Creating client proxy component to invoke our web service

Creating service implementation class and interface

We will revisit the example of an Order Processing application. We will create an interface for the Order Processing application named `OrderProcess` and an implementation class named `OrderProcesImpl`. The `OrderProcessImpl` class will have a service method `processOrder` that will process the given order and generate the unique ID. The following block of code shows the code listing of the `OrderProcess` interface and the `OrderProcessImpl` class:

```
public interface OrderProcess {
    String processOrder(Order order);
}

public class OrderProcessImpl implements OrderProcess {

    public String processOrder(Order order) {
      System.out.println("Processing order...");
      String orderID = validate(order);
        return orderID;
    }
. . . // Refer to chapter3/simplefrontend source code for complete
listing
```

The previous code is similar to one developed for Code-first development approach, without the use of web service annotation. We do not need to annotate our class here as we are using the simple frontend to build our web service.

> We do not need an interface here, but it is good practice to separate the service contract and the implementation. Moreover, it helps in modeling the client as a proxy component.

Next, we will create a server component that will publish our web service.

Creating server implementation

We will create a server component that will publish our `OrderProcess` web service. The server component is created by using a simple frontend class called `ServerFactoryBean`. The `ServerFactoryBean` class publishes the service as an endpoint that can be referenced through the endpoint URL. Let's create the server component to publish the `OrderProcess` service.

```
public class SimpleServer {
   public static void main(String[] arg) {
      // Create service implementation
```

```
        OrderProcessImpl orderProcessImpl = new OrderProcessImpl();

        // Create Server
        ServerFactoryBean svrFactory = new ServerFactoryBean();
        svrFactory.setServiceClass(OrderProcess.class);
        svrFactory.setAddress("http://localhost:8080/
        SimpleOrderProcess");
        svrFactory.setServiceBean(orderProcessImpl );
        svrFactory.create();
    }
}
```

The previous code instantiates the `ServerFactoryBean` class which in turn uses Java reflection to build the service. We provide the service interface and the class name to the factory bean class. In this case, it will be the `OrderProcess` interface and the `OrderProcessImpl` class respectively. We also need to set the endpoint URL `http://localhost:8080/SimpleOrderProcess` to the factory. The service will be published at the said URL.

Finally, the `create` method of the factory publishes the service as an endpoint. The `OrderProcess` service will be published on this URL. You can test the validity of the service by invoking the following URL:

```
http://localhost:8080/SimpleOrderProcess?wsdl
```

This should show the order process WSDL. If you are able to see the WSDL, then it effectively means that the service is published successfully on the server.

Next, we will develop the client component that will invoke the `OrderProcess` service.

Creating client

The client proxy component is used to invoke the `processOrder` method of the `OrderProcess` service.

```
package demo.order.client;

import org.apache.cxf.frontend.ClientProxyFactoryBean;

import demo.order.Order;
import demo.order.OrderProcess;

    public class SimpleClient {
        public static void main(String[] args) {
```

```
        ClientProxyFactoryBean factory =
        new ClientProxyFactoryBean();
        factory.setServiceClass(OrderProcess.class);
        factory.setAddress("http://localhost:8080/
        SimpleOrderProcess");
        OrderProcess client = (OrderProcess) factory.create();
        Order order = new Order();
        order.setCustomerID("C001");
        order.setItemID("I001");
        order.setPrice(100.00);
        order.setQty(20);

          String result = client.processOrder(order);
          System.out.println("The order ID is " + result);
    }


}
```

As you can see from the previous code, the proxy will be created using the simple frontend factory class called `ClientProxyFactoryBean`. You need to provide the service class and the endpoint address to the factory component. The `create` method returns the implementation object of the type `OrderProcess`. It is typecast to the `OrderProcess` service interface, which can then be used to invoke the `processOrder` method.

Running the simple frontend example

We will use the ANT tool to build and execute the code. The source code and `build` file for the chapter is available in the `Chapter3/simplefrontend` folder of the downloaded source code. Navigate to the `Chapter3/simplefrontend` folder, and run the following command on the command prompt:

- `ant build`

  This will build the source code.
- `ant server`

  This will run the server and publish the Order Process web service to the location `http://localhost:8080/SimpleOrderProcess`.

- Open a new command prompt, and run the client which will invoke the service.

  ```
  ant client
  ```

  On running the client, you will see the following output.

  The order ID is ORD1234

  The output shows the generated order ID.

Summary

The CXF JAX-WS-based framework provides a complete web service stack which eases web service development and deployment. In this chapter we learnt the concepts and core technology associated with web services using CXF JAX-WS API. We looked at how to create web services using the Code-first and Contract-first approach. We looked at how to create dynamic web service clients and work directly with XML messages using the Provider and Dispatch implementation. The chapter also demonstrated the use of web service context where the user can access the context information of the service message. Lastly, we looked at the CXF-based Simple frontend API to develop web services.

4
Learning about Service Transports

Web service transport uses higher level protocols to route or transfer messages between service endpoints. The higher level protocols include: **HTTP**, **FTP**, **JMS**, **SMTP**, and so on. These protocols are also known as **application protocols**. The application protocols are part of the **TCP/IP** suite that operates at the application layer. The application protocols directly communicate with a low-level protocol such as **TCP** to perform data routing. The following figure illustrates the semantics of application and transport protocol:

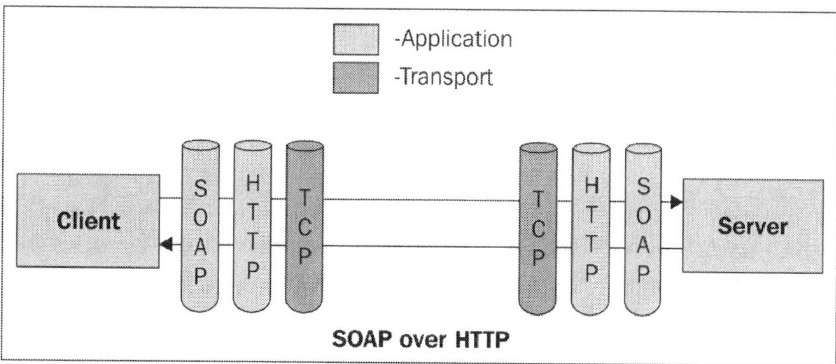

This figure depicts the data flow from the client to the server and vice versa using the application protocol.

Transport protocols in CXF

CXF provides support for the following transport protocols:

- HTTP
- HTTPs
- JMS
- Local

While HTTP, **HTTPs,** and JMS run over TCP routing protocol for remote routing, the **local** transport is used to transmit service messages locally within a single JVM. The transports are **message routers**. In the context of CXF, web service messages that are part of service operations are routed between service endpoints using a specific transport.

The transport details are provided when defining an endpoint. An **endpoint** is a physical manifestation of the service. Simply put, it is an instantiated service. The endpoint definition is composed of binding details and transport details. The transport details are often called **networking** details. The endpoint is defined as part of a `<wsdl:service>` element in the WSDL contract. The following code fragment illustrates the endpoint:

```
<wsdl:service name="OrderProcessImplService">
  <wsdl:port binding="tns:OrderProcessImplServiceSoapBinding"
            name="OrderProcessImplPort">
  <soap:address location="http://localhost:8080/orderapp/
                  OrderProcess" />
  </wsdl:port>
</wsdl:service>
```

The `OrderProcessImplService` is the actual service name which is bound to a SOAP binding name and port name. The binding details specify the operations and the input/output messages while the port name specifies the transport URL. The following section briefly discusses the `<wsdl:port>` element.

HTTP transport

HTTP is a standard web transport protocol. HTTP transport is widely used with web service as most services are published over the web. HTTP transport has become the most commonly used and standard communication channel for service endpoints. CXF provides support for HTTP transport in the following two ways:

- SOAP over HTTP
- HTTP only

SOAP over HTTP

Simple Object Access Protocol (**SOAP**) is the language format of web service messages that are transmitted or exchanged between consumer and service provider. These messages are often exchanged over the Web and therefore, the SOAP messages are routed over HTTP protocol. This ensures interoperability as the client and the service providers can be running on different platforms. SOAP payloads can also use other transports such as SMTP, FTP, JMS. But the most common and prevalent transport is HTTP and therefore all SOAP implementations automatically and very naturally support HTTP as their routing application protocol.

There are two types of SOAP messages that can be transported over HTTP, SOAP 1.1 and SOAP 1.2.

SOAP 1.1 over HTTP

You can define the SOAP 1.1 binding with the use of the `<soap:binding>` element. This element is the direct child of the `<wsdl:binding>` element. It signifies that this service is bound to the SOAP version 1.1 protocol format, that is, the message will follow the SOAP 1.1 format. The `<soap:binding>` element comes with a `transport` attribute in which you can specify which transport protocol to use. In this case it will be HTTP. It takes the value in the form of the following URI:

`http://schemas.xmlsoap.org/soap/http`

The following WSDL code fragment shows the SOAP 1.1 binding with HTTP transport:

```
<wsdl:binding name="OrderProcessServiceSoapBinding"
              type="tns:OrderProcess">
   <soap:binding style="document" transport=
                        "http://schemas.xmlsoap.org/soap/http" />
 . . .
</wsdl:binding>
```

The previous code fragment tells us that you are sending SOAP 1.1 messages over HTTP. You also need to specify the service endpoint address that will use SOAP 1.1 HTTP binding.

The following WSDL code fragment illustrates the use of the SOAP 1.1 endpoint address:

```
<wsdl:service name="OrderProcessService
   <wsdl:port binding="tns:OrderProcessServiceSoapBinding"
              name="OrderProcessPort">
      <soap:address location="http://localhost:8080/OrderProcess">
   </wsdl:port>
</wsdl:service>
```

You need to specify the <soap:address> element for sending SOAP 1.1 messages. The element is the direct child element of the <wsdl:port> element, which is part of the <wsdl:service> element. The <soap:address> element takes one attribute named location, which specifies the endpoint address.

SOAP 1.2 over HTTP

You can define SOAP 1.2 binding with the use of the <soap12:binding> element. This element is the direct child of <wsdl:binding> element. It signifies that this service is bound to the SOAP version 1.2 protocol format, that is, the message will follow the SOAP 1.2 format. The <soap12:binding> element comes with a transport attribute in which you can specify which transport protocol to use. The value is the same for both SOAP 1.1 and 1.2. The value is a URI which indicates SOAP 1.2 binding with HTTP.

```
http://schemas.xmlsoap.org/soap/http
```

The following WSDL code fragment shows the SOAP 1.2 binding with HTTP transport:

```
    <wsdl:binding name="OrderProcessServiceSoapBinding"
                  type="tns:OrderProcess">
    <soap12:binding style="document" transport=
                         "http://schemas.xmlsoap.org/soap/http" />
 . . .
    </wsdl:binding>
```

The previous code fragment signifies that you are sending SOAP 1.2 messages over HTTP. You then specify the service endpoint address that will use SOAP 1.2 HTTP binding.

The following WSDL fragment illustrates the use of the SOAP 1.2 endpoint address:

```
<wsdl:service name="OrderProcessService">
<wsdl:port binding="tns:OrderProcessServiceSoapBinding"
              name="OrderProcessImplPort">
      <soap12:address location="http://localhost:8080/
                                  OrderProcess">
</wsdl:port>
</wsdl:service>
```

You need to specify the <soap12:address> element for sending SOAP 1.2 messages. The element is the direct child element of the <wsdl:port> element which is part of the <wsdl:service> element. The <soap12:address> element takes one attribute named location. The location attribute specifies the endpoint address.

SOAP 1.2 is the latest release from the W3C Group. There are a lot of improvements compared to SOAP 1.1. A discussion on the features of each version is beyond the scope of this book. More information can be found at `http://www.w3.org/TR/soap12-part0/`

HTTP only

Web service messages typically follow SOAP protocol format. But you may choose to send messages using the HTTP protocol format depending on the application requirement. The **HTTP only** transport sends web service messages in HTTP protocol format. It uses the HTTP `GET` and `POST` methods to perform request and response between consumer and service endpoints.

The following WSDL fragment shows the HTTP only binding:

```
<binding name="OrderProcessServiceHttpBinding"
         type="OrderProcess">
    <http:binding verb="GET"/>
    <operation name="processOrder">
       <http:operation location="processOrder"/>
       <input>
           <http:urlEncoded/>
       </input>
       <output>
           <mime:content type="text/html"/>
       </output>
    </operation>
</binding>
```

The previous code fragment describes HTTP binding, which means the input and output message will be in HTTP protocol format. It sends the message as a `GET` request. The input message has the value `http:urlEncoded`, which means the message parameter will take the form of a `name=value` pair. The output message or the return type will be string formatted as HTML.

You also need to specify the service endpoint address that will use HTTP only binding.

The following WSDL fragment illustrates the use of the HTTP endpoint address:

```
<wsdl:service name="OrderProcessService">
   <wsdl:port binding="tns:OrderProcessServiceHttpBinding"
              name="OrderProcessPort">
      <http:address location="http://localhost:8080/OrderProcess">
```

```
        </wsdl:port>
    </wsdl:service>
```

You need to specify the `<http:address>` element for sending messages in HTTP format. The element is the direct child element of the `<wsdl:port>` element, which is part of the `<wsdl:service>` element. The `<http:address>` element has one attribute `location`. The `location` attribute specifies the endpoint address.

The `<http:address>` endpoint address is also used for messages that are not in a SOAP or HTTP format. This element is specified when the message format is other than SOAP.

In the following sections we will explore concepts called **HTTP Conduit** and **HTTP Destination** that can be used to change the HTTP transport behavior.

HTTP conduit

Conduit simply means channel or pipe. HTTP conduits are channels allow us to apply certain HTTP related properties or attributes which can affect the way messages are exchanged between endpoints. You typically specify HTTP connection attributes such as whether to allow chunking, connection timeout, and so on. The conduit is always defined by the client or consumer of the service. The following code fragment illustrates the use of a sample HTTP conduit:

```
<beans ...
  xmlns:http-conf="http://cxf.apache.org/transports/http/configuration"
...
   <http-conf:conduit name="{http://order.demo} OrderProcessImplPort.
                            http-conduit">
<http-conf:client Connection="Keep-Alive" AllowChunking="false" />
      <http-conf:tlsClientParameters secureSocketProtocol="SSL">
      </http-conf:tlsClientParameters>
</http-conf:conduit>
...
</beans>
```

Firstly, you need to define the HTTP configuration namespace to use the conduit. The following XML fragment shows the *http-conf* namespace along with schema location:

```
xmlns:http-conf="http://cxf.apache.org/transports/http/
                                    configuration"
xsi:schemaLocation="
         http://cxf.apache.org/transports/http/configuration
         http://cxf.apache.org/schemas/configuration/http-conf.xsd
```

The `<http-conf:conduit>` element represents the HTTP conduit. It is used to specify certain attributes while invoking the service endpoint. The `<http-conf:conduit>` element has one `name` attribute that indicates the name of the conduit. The name has a standard convention, and it takes the form of `{WSDL_endpoint_target_namespace}PortName.http-conduit`. You can also specify a wildcard such as `*.http-conduit` as the conduit name. The child element `<http-conf:tlsClientParameters>` indicates that this conduit will use secure transport. There are many other child elements that can be used with the conduit. One of the significant child elements is `<http-conf:client>`. It is used to specify different HTTP connection attributes from the client perspective. The attributes are more like client-side HTTP headers. The following table shows some of the attributes that can be used with the `<http-conf:client>` element.

Attribute	Description
`ConnectionTimeout`	It indicates time in milliseconds. The client attempts to send the request before the connection times out. The default value is `30,000`. The value of `0` means request will never timeout.
`AllowChunking`	It indicates whether the request can be sent in chunks to the server. The default is `true`.
`CacheControl`	It communicates directives on the behavior of the cache when the message request is communicated to the server.
`ContentType`	It indicates the MIME data that is sent to the server.

HTTP destination

The server-side endpoints use destinations to specify HTTP attributes while serving the connection to its client. The following code illustrates the use of a sample HTTP destination:

```
<beans ...
...
<http-conf:destination name="{http://order.demo}OrderProcessImplPort.
http-destination">
   <http-conf:server HonorKeepAlive="true" />
</http-conf:destination>
</beans>
```

Like the conduit, the HTTP destination also uses *http-conf* namespace. The `<http-conf:destination>` element represents the HTTP destination to which certain HTTP attributes can be set. The said element takes a `name` attribute that holds a value expressed as `{WSDL_endpoint_target_namespace}PortName.http-destination`.

The most significant child element is `<http-conf:server>`. It is used to specify different HTTP connection attributes from the server perspective. The following table shows some of the attributes that can be used with the `<http-conf:server>` element:

Attribute	Description
`ReceiveTimeout`	It indicates the time in milliseconds, the server attempts to receive the request before the connection times out. The default value is `30,000`. `0` means the server will never timeout.
`HonorKeepAlive`	It indicates whether to accept a client request for keeping the connection alive after the response is sent. The default value is `false`.
`CacheControl`	It communicates directives on the behavior of the cache when the message response is sent back to the client.
`ContentType`	It indicates the MIME data that is sent to the client.

HTTPs transport

HTTPs stands for HTTP secure. It is a combination of HTTP and secured protocol. The protocol is used to access sensitive information such as payments and financial data on secured websites. HTTPs creates a secure transport layer over a normal insecure one. The client browser connects to secure websites using the `https://` URL. The client can make a secure connection to a secure website only if the site has its certificate registered in the client browser or if the site certificate is registered with certain **Certificate Authorities** (**CA**) and at least one of the CA is supported by the client browser. The certificate is typically created using the pair of private/public keys known to the client and the server. The public/private keys are generated using a cryptography algorithm such as RSA.

The following table shows the difference between the two protocols:

Http	Https
URL begins with `http://`	URL begins with `https://`
It operates on default port `80`	It uses default port `443`
It is a text-based insecure protocol	It is a secured protocol

CXF supports HTTPs protocol through which service messages can be exchanged securely. In this section we will develop an order process web service and a consumer that will exchange messages securely through HTTPs transport. You will need to perform the following steps:

1. Developing service SEI and the implementation class
2. Generating crypto key
3. Creating a server and client bean configuration
4. Creating a client component to use the service
5. Configuring the server to support SSL
6. Developing a client
7. Building and deploying

The source code and build file is available in the `Chapter4/HTTPs` folder of the downloaded source code.

Developing the service and implementation class

We will use the same `OrderProcess` SEI and `OrderProcessImpl` class which were demonstrated in earlier sections.

```
import javax.jws.WebService;

@WebService
public interface OrderProcess {
    String processOrder(Order order);
}
```

Generating crypto key

We will use the Java-based `keytool` application to generate the crypto key. The server and client program will use this key to communicate in a secure fashion. You need to have the Java 5 SDK kit installed on your machine. The JDK installation `bin` folder has the `keytool` application. Run the `keytool` application by entering the following command in the command prompt window:

```
keytool -genkey -alias Tomcat -keyalg RSA -storepass changeit -keypass
changeit -keystore orderprocess.jks -dname "cn=localhost"
```

The above command will generate the key in the location where it is executed.

Let's take a look at the options and understand what they mean:

- `-genkey`—option generates a public/private key
- `-alias`—option is used to provide a unique name to the generated key
- `-keyalg`—option is used to specify the algorithm to be used to generate a key
- `-storepass`—option is to provide a password for a key store
- `-keypass`—option is to provide a password for a key itself
- `-keystore`—is used to specify a `keystore` filename
- `-dname`—is used to specify a domain name or the website name

The command along with the above options generates a public/private key which is encrypted using RSA crypto algorithm. The generated key is given an alias name *Tomcat*. The key is stored in a file named `orderprocess.jks`. The file is known as a **key store** file. A key store accommodates all the public/private keys. The file extension `jks` means Java Key Store. The file extension is not mandatory, and you may specify the file without the `jks` extension. The key and the key store is given the password `changeit`. The password is used to access the `keystore` and retrieve the keys. The `-dname` option here is significant. It indicates your website name. For testing web applications running on a local host, the `-dname` must be assigned a value `localhost`.

The command also generates a `.keystore` file under the `C:\Documents and Settings\<your_login_name>` folder in the `Windows` environment, or user home directory if not on Windows. This file is also a key store. If you do not want to explicitly specify the key store filename using the `–keystore` option, then you can also use this alternate `.keystore` file.

Usually, every secured site is digitally signed in the form of certificate. For our example we will not use a certificate.

Creating client and server bean configuration

We will be using Spring-based configuration files to develop consumer and service endpoints. Both consumer and service endpoints will exchange messages through HTTPs protocol. The following code illustrates the server configuration:

```
<?xml version="1.0" encoding="UTF-8"?>
<beans xmlns="http://www.springframework.org/schema/beans"
  xmlns:xsi="http://www.w3.org/2001/XMLSchema-instance"
  xmlns:http-conf="http://cxf.apache.org/transports/http/
configuration"
  xmlns:jaxws="http://cxf.apache.org/jaxws"
```

```
    xsi:schemaLocation="
                http://cxf.apache.org/transports/http/configuration
                http://cxf.apache.org/schemas/configuration/http-conf.xsd
                http://www.springframework.org/schema/beans
                http://www.springframework.org/schema/beans/spring-beans.
                xsd
            http://cxf.apache.org/jaxws
            http://cxf.apache.org/schemas/jaxws.xsd">

    <import resource="classpath:META-INF/cxf/cxf.xml" />
    <import resource="classpath:META-INF/cxf/cxf-extension-soap.xml" />
    <import resource="classpath:META-INF/cxf/cxf-servlet.xml" />
    <jaxws:endpoint id="orderProcess" implementor="demo.order.
  OrderProcessImpl" address="/OrderProcess" />
  </beans>
```

The server configuration file contains only one `<jaxws:endpoint>` element which is used to define the service endpoint for the `OrderProcess` service. The `OrderProcess` endpoint address will be relative URI `/OrderProcess`.

The client configuration uses SSL properties to enable secure connectivity with the service endpoint. The following code illustrates the client configuration file:

```
<?xml version="1.0" encoding="UTF-8"?>
<beans xmlns="http://www.springframework.org/schema/beans"
  xmlns:xsi="http://www.w3.org/2001/XMLSchema-instance"
  xmlns:sec="http://cxf.apache.org/configuration/security"
  xmlns:http-conf="http://cxf.apache.org/transports/http/
  configuration"
  xmlns:jaxws="http://cxf.apache.org/jaxws"
  xsi:schemaLocation="
            http://cxf.apache.org/configuration/security
            http://cxf.apache.org/schemas/configuration/security.xsd
            http://cxf.apache.org/transports/http/configuration
            http://cxf.apache.org/schemas/configuration/http-conf.xsd
            http://cxf.apache.org/jaxws
            http://cxf.apache.org/schemas/jaxws.xsd
            http://www.springframework.org/schema/beans
            http://www.springframework.org/schema/beans/spring-beans.
            xsd">

   <jaxws:client id="orderClient" serviceClass="demo.order.
OrderProcess" address="https://localhost:8443/orderappssl/
OrderProcess" />
   <http-conf:conduit name="*.http-conduit">
      <http-conf:tlsClientParameters secureSocketProtocol="SSL">
```

```
            <sec:keyManagers keyPassword="changeit">
                <sec:keyStore type="JKS" password="changeit" file="C:\tmp\
                 orderprocess.jks" />
            </sec:keyManagers>
        </http-conf:tlsClientParameters>
    </http-conf:conduit>
</beans>
```

Firstly, the client configuration uses `<jaxws:client>` to register the `OrderProcess` service bean. It then defines the HTTP conduit, which allows us to set SSL-related properties. The following code fragment shows the SSL configuration:

```
...
        <http-conf:tlsClientParameters secureSocketProtocol="SSL">
          <sec:keyManagers keyPassword="changeit">
              <sec:keyStore type="JKS" password="changeit" file=
               "C:\tmp\orderprocess.jks" />
          </sec:keyManagers>
        </http-conf:tlsClientParameters>
...
```

The `<http-conf:tlsClientParameters>` element defines the secure channel. It specifies the `secureSocketProtocol` attribute with the value of `SSL`. The child element `<sec:keyManagers>` is configured with the password and key store location.

> If we remember the key generated in the above section using the `keytool` command-line tool, the same parameters are provided here by the client to unlock the key.

The above elements are supported by the namespace `sec`:

```
...
   xmlns:sec="http://cxf.apache.org/configuration/security"
...
   xsi:schemaLocation="
            http://cxf.apache.org/configuration/security
            http://cxf.apache.org/schemas/configuration/security.xsd
...
```

You must specify the above namespace and the schema location entries.

Configuring the server to support SSL

You might be wondering why we haven't added the SSL properties in the service endpoint bean configuration file. The reason is we are using the Tomcat server for our deployment. The Tomcat server comes with its own SSL configuration. You will need to enable the server to communicate over a secure channel. The SSL configuration can be found in the `server.xml` file, which is located under the `%CATALINA_HOME%\conf` folder. You need to uncomment the following commented entry in this file:

```
<Connector port="8443" maxHttpHeaderSize="8192"
           maxThreads="150" minSpareThreads="25"
           maxSpareThreads="75"
           enableLookups="false" disableUploadTimeout="true"
           acceptCount="100" scheme="https" secure="true"
           clientAuth="false" sslProtocol="TLS" />
```

After uncommenting it, you need to add two more attributes, `keystoreFile` and `keystorePass` to the `<Connector>` element. The modified entry will look as follows:

```
<Connector port="8443" maxHttpHeaderSize="8192"
           maxThreads="150" minSpareThreads="25"
           maxSpareThreads="75"
           enableLookups="false" disableUploadTimeout="true"
           acceptCount="100" scheme="https" secure="true"
           clientAuth="false" sslProtocol="TLS"
       keystoreFile="C:\tmp\orderprocess.jks"
       keystorePass="changeit"
       />
```

The above updated entry ensures that the server will accept HTTPs connections. You can now safely invoke the order process service using HTTPs.

Developing the client component

The `Client` class will obtain the `OrderProcess` bean and invoke its `processOrder` method. The following code illustrates the consumer code:

```
...
    public static void main(String args[]) throws Exception {
        ClassPathXmlApplicationContext context =
        new ClassPathXmlApplicationContext(new String[]
        {"demo/order/client/client-bean.xml"});
        OrderProcess client = (OrderProcess) context.
        getBean("orderClient");
```

```
...
        String orderID = client.processOrder(order);
        String message = (orderID == null) ? "Order not approved" :
        "Order approved; order ID is " + orderID;
        System.out.println(message);
        System.exit(0);
...
```

Building and deploying

The next step is to build and deploy our code. We will use ANT to build the code. The code will be deployed on the Tomcat web server.

Your ANT build file will look as follows:

```
<?xml version="1.0"?>
<project name="Order Process HTTPS " default="build" basedir=".">
<import file="common_build.xml"/>

    <target name="client" description="run demo client"
     depends="build">
        <cxfrun classname="demo.order.client.Client" />
    </target>

    <property name="cxf.war.file.name" value="orderappssl"/>
    <target name="war" depends="build">
     <cxfwar filename="${cxf.war.file.name}.war" webxml=
     "webapp/WEB-INF/web.xml" />
    </target>
</project>
```

You generate the server side `WAR` file and run the client. The ANT build file is used to build and compile the code. The `build` folder will be created under the project root folder.

You then start the Tomcat web server. It is started by entering the following command at your project root:

```
catalina start
```

The server will publish the `OrderProcess` service and listen on the SSL port `8443`.

Once the server is started you invoke the client by entering the following command:

```
ant client
```

The previous command will run the `Client` class, which will invoke the `processOrder` method of the `OrderProcess` bean. The method invocation will initiate message exchange on the secure layer.

For more information on building the source code using the ANT tool, see the Appendix A *Getting Ready with Code Examples*. The appendix covers step-by-step information on organizing and building the source code.

The source code and build file is available in the `Chapter4/HTTPs_Jetty` folder of the downloaded source code.

Configuring SSL for Jetty runtime

In the previous section we looked at configuring SSL using the Tomcat web container. In this section we will configure SSL using a standalone web server. We will configure Jetty, a standalone web server, to accept SSL connections. Jetty is an open source miniature web server licensed under Apache License 2.0. CXF provides support for the Jetty runtime engine. You can configure the Jetty runtime by defining the `<httpj:engine-factory>` element in the server side configuration file. The following code illustrates the Jetty runtime configuration:

```
<beans ...
...
xmlns:httpj="http://cxf.apache.org/transports/http-jetty/
configuration"
xsi:schemaLocation="http://cxf.apache.org/schemas/configuration/http-
jetty.xsd"
...
   <httpj:engine-factory bus="cxf">
      <httpj:engine port="9001">
      ...
      </httpj:engine>
   </httpj:engine-factory>
</beans>
```

You first need to define a namespace URI for a Jetty engine, which is `http://cxf.apache.org/transports/http-jetty/configuration`, and the prefix is `httpj`. The namespace should also be supported with the schema location. You then define the `<httpj:engine-factory>` element that represents the jetty runtime engine factory. The element has one attribute bus that specifies the application bus. The default bus is `cxf`, and you can choose to provide the default value. The bus is the core engine of a CXF framework and manages the jetty infrastructure components in this context. You then define the `<httpj:engine>` child element. This element takes port number as an attribute. The `<httpj:engine>` element represents one instance of the jetty server. The server listens for an incoming request on the specified port.

The engine element has many child elements. The section will focus on one such child element `httpj:tlsServerParameters`. This element is used to configure SSL-related properties to enable secure access to a server.

We will revisit our previous example and replace the Tomcat server with CXF-provided Jetty runtime. We will now create one server configuration file that will look as follows:

```
<?xml version="1.0" encoding="UTF-8"?>
<beans xmlns="http://www.springframework.org/schema/beans"
  xmlns:xsi="http://www.w3.org/2001/XMLSchema-instance"
  xmlns:sec="http://cxf.apache.org/configuration/security"
  xmlns:http="http://cxf.apache.org/transports/http/configuration"
  xmlns:httpj="http://cxf.apache.org/transports/http-jetty/
  configuration"
  xmlns:jaxws="http://cxf.apache.org/jaxws"
  xsi:schemaLocation="
            http://cxf.apache.org/jaxws
            http://cxf.apache.org/schemas/jaxws.xsd
            http://cxf.apache.org/configuration/security
            http://cxf.apache.org/schemas/configuration/security.xsd
            http://cxf.apache.org/transports/http/configuration
            http://cxf.apache.org/schemas/configuration/http-conf.xsd
            http://cxf.apache.org/transports/http-jetty/configuration
            http://cxf.apache.org/schemas/configuration/http-jetty.xsd
            http://www.springframework.org/schema/beans
            http://www.springframework.org/schema/beans/spring-beans.
xsd">

   <httpj:engine-factory bus="cxf">
    <httpj:engine port="9001">
     <httpj:tlsServerParameters>
       <sec:keyManagers keyPassword="changeit">
            <sec:keyStore type="JKS" password="changeit" file=
            "c:\tmp\orderprocess.jks"/>
       </sec:keyManagers>
     </httpj:tlsServerParameters>
    </httpj:engine>
   </httpj:engine-factory>
 </beans>
```

As you can see from the above code, SSL configuration parameters are defined as part of the `<sec:keyManagers>` child element of the `<httpj:tlsServerParameters>` element. All you do is provide the location of your key store file along with the password as part of the `<sec:keyStore>` element.

Since we are not using Tomcat server, we have to write the server code that will publish the `OrderProcess` service on the Jetty runtime. The following code illustrates the `Server` class that creates the service endpoint and publishes it:

```
import org.apache.cxf.Bus;
import org.apache.cxf.bus.spring.SpringBusFactory;
import javax.xml.ws.Endpoint;

import demo.order.OrderProcessImpl;

public class Server {
   public Server() {
      SpringBusFactory factory = new SpringBusFactory();
      Bus bus = factory.createBus("demo/order/server/server-bean.
      xml");
      factory.setDefaultBus(bus);
      OrderProcessImpl orderProcessImpl = new OrderProcessImpl();
      Endpoint.publish("https://localhost:9001/OrderProcessSSL",
      orderProcessImpl);
   }

public static void main(String[] args)    {
   new Server();
      System.out.println("Server ready ...");
   }
}
```

The code first instantiates the `SpringFactoryBus` class to create the `bus` from this server configuration file. The `createBus` method takes the server configuration XML file as a parameter and creates the bus. This bus is set as a default bus. Remember that the jetty runtime uses the *cxf* bus by default, so indirectly you are using the same default CXF bus. The `Endpoint` class then publishes the `OrderProcessImpl` service implementation class on the secured URL. The endpoint URL is `https://localhost:9001/OrderProcessSSL`.

Once the server is created, follow the same sequence of steps to run the client program, which were discussed in the previous section. The `Client` class will consume the `OrderProcess` service and invoke its `processOrder` method.

JMS transport

Web services play an important role when it comes to asynchronous communication. This nature of communication is very common in enterprise platform integration connecting disparate systems. JMS is a Java standard that provides a platform to develop applications that can communicate asynchronously with external systems. CXF provides support for JMS transport for its services, and enables them to exchange messages asynchronously.

In JMS, the messages are exchanged using two popular communication models, **Point-to-Point (P2P)** and **Publisher-Subscriber (Pub-Sub)**.

In the P2P model the messages are exchanged through the concept of queues. Each message has only one consumer. P2P is used to process messages synchronously and asynchronously. In the Pub-Sub model, the messages are exchanged through the concept of topics. A consumer subscribes to a topic in order to receive the message. A message in this model can only be exchanged asynchronously. Queue and Topic are called as **destinations**.

The following figure shows the P2P JMS communication model:

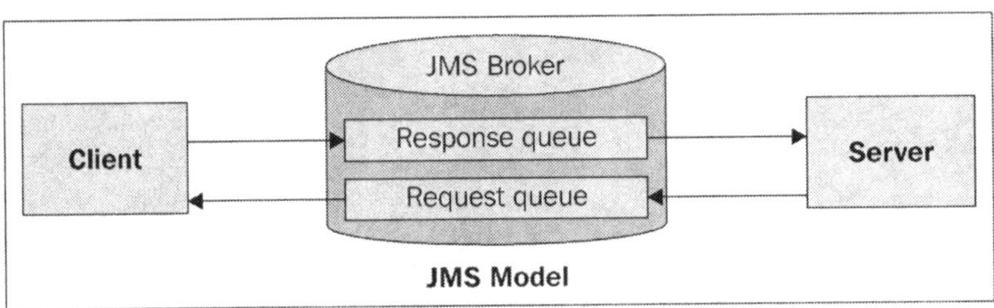

The client makes a request by sending the message to a destination queue and waits for the response from the server. The server receives the message, processes it, and returns the response back to the queue. The resulting message is then consumed by the client.

JMS can be considered as a glue technology that connects disparate or distinct systems. When using JMS, you typically perform the following steps:

1. Set up the JNDI context
2. Lookup for the queue connection factory
3. Fetch the queue from the connection factory
4. Make a connection in the form of a `Session` object
5. Create a `provider` and `consumer` object
6. Perform the message exchange using the above objects
7. Close the connection

Imagine as a developer you have to write the code for the above tasks. It can be tedious and time consuming. CXF provides a convenient approach to connect your services through JMS using a Spring-based configuration. It completely abstracts the process of creating and looking up destination objects.

In this section, you will develop an order process web service that will exchange messages with the consumer using JMS transport. You will need to perform the following steps:

1. Developing service SEI and the implementation class
2. Developing an embedded broker
3. Creating a server and a client bean configuration
4. Creating a client component to consume the service
5. Performing build and deployment

You will use **Apache ActiveMQ provider** as a message broker. For the purpose of deployment, you will use Tomcat as a web server.

The source code and build file is available in the `Chapter4/JMS` folder of the downloaded source code.

Developing the service and implementation class

You will use the same `OrderProcess` SEI and `OrderProcessImpl` class that was demonstrated in earlier sections.

```
import javax.jws.WebService;

@WebService
public interface OrderProcess {
    String processOrder(Order order);
}
```

Developing an embedded broker

An embedded broker is a miniature broker application which will act as a JMS provider to accept messages from the consumer and the server. You will use ActiveMQ as a messaging provider. Apache ActiveMQ is an open source enterprise messaging provider. It provides support for a wide variety of protocols and cross-language client applications. It also provides a platform to implement messaging using enterprise integration patterns. ActiveMQ supports JMS standard v1.1.

The following code illustrates the `MessageBroker` class that uses ActiveMQ as a JMS provider:

```
import org.apache.activemq.broker.BrokerService;
import org.apache.activemq.store.memory.MemoryPersistenceAdapter;

public final class MessageBroker {
    private MessageBroker() {
    }

    public static void main(String[] args) throws Exception {
        BrokerService broker = new BrokerService();
        broker.setPersistenceAdapter(new MemoryPersistenceAdapter());
        broker.addConnector("tcp://localhost:61616");
        broker.start();
        System.out.println("JMS broker ready ...");
    }
}
```

You will first instantiate the `BrokerService` class. The `BrokerService` class represents the JMS broker that is used to set up the messaging infrastructure. The `setPersistenceAdapter` method sets the persistence layer for the messages. The persistence adapter is the object of the `MemoryPersistenceAdapter` class. It means that the messages will be persisted in-memory. Then you define the connectivity using the `addConnector` method. The method takes the URI in the form of `<protocol>://<hostname>:<port>`. The broker will listen on this URI. You will provide `localhost` as your hostname and `61616` as a port number on which the broker will accept the messages. The communication protocol will be `tcp`. The `start()` method will start the broker.

Creating a server and client bean configuration

You will use Spring-based configuration files to develop consumer and service endpoints. Both consumer and service endpoints will open a link with the message broker for message exchange through message queues. The following code illustrates the server configuration:

```
<?xml version="1.0" encoding="UTF-8"?>
<beans xmlns="http://www.springframework.org/schema/beans"
   xmlns:xsi="http://www.w3.org/2001/XMLSchema-instance"
   xmlns:jaxws="http://cxf.apache.org/jaxws"
   xmlns:jms="http://cxf.apache.org/transports/jms"
   xmlns:p="http://www.springframework.org/schema/p"
   xsi:schemaLocation=" http://www.springframework.org/schema/beans
```

```
                http://www.springframework.org/schema/beans/spring-
                beans.xsd
                http://cxf.apache.org/jaxws
                http://cxf.apache.org/schemas/jaxws.xsd ">

<import resource="classpath:META-INF/cxf/cxf.xml" />
<import resource="classpath:META-INF/cxf/cxf-extension-soap.xml" />
<import resource="classpath:META-INF/cxf/cxf-servlet.xml" />
<import resource="classpath:META-INF/cxf/cxf-extension-jms.xml" />

<jaxws:endpoint id="orderProcess" implementor="demo.order.
OrderProcessImpl" address="jms://" >
   <jaxws:features>
   <bean class="org.apache.cxf.transport.jms.JMSConfigFeature"
   p:jmsConfig-ref="jmsConfig" />
    </jaxws:features>
</jaxws:endpoint>

<bean id="jmsConfig" class="org.apache.cxf.transport.jms.
JMSConfiguration"
   p:connectionFactory-ref="jmsConnectionFactory"
   p:targetDestination="test.cxf.jmstransport.queue" />

<bean id="jmsConnectionFactory" class=
"org.apache.activemq.ActiveMQConnectionFactory">
   <property name="brokerURL" value="tcp://localhost:61616" />
</bean>
</beans>
```

The `<jaxws-endpoint>` element is used to define the service endpoint for the `OrderProcess` service. The `<jaxws-features>` is used to apply features to the service endpoint. In this case, we use the `JMSConfigFeature` bean, to which we set the JMS configuration. The configuration defines the **JMS connection factory** and **destination queue**. The connection factory `ActiveMQConnectionFactory` is used to obtain the connection to the broker. The destination name provided is `test.cxf.jmstransport.queue`. The complete JMS configuration is represented by `JMSConfiguration` object.

The client configuration is similar to service configuration. The following code illustrates the client configuration file:

```
<beans xmlns="http://www.springframework.org/schema/beans"
xmlns:xsi="http://www.w3.org/2001/XMLSchema-instance"
xmlns:jaxws="http://cxf.apache.org/jaxws"
xmlns:p="http://www.springframework.org/schema/p"
```

```
xsi:schemaLocation="http://www.springframework.org/schema/beans
                    http://www.springframework.org/schema/beans/
                    spring-beans.xsd
                    http://cxf.apache.org/jaxws
                    http://cxf.apache.org/schemas/jaxws.xsd">
  <jaxws:client id="orderClient" serviceClass="demo.order.
  OrderProcess" address="jms://" >
    <jaxws:features>
      <bean class="org.apache.cxf.transport.jms.JMSConfigFeature"
      p:jmsConfig-ref="jmsConfig"/>
    </jaxws:features>
  </jaxws:client>
  <bean id="jmsConfig" class="org.apache.cxf.transport.jms.
  JMSConfiguration"
    p:connectionFactory-ref="jmsConnectionFactory"
    p:targetDestination="test.cxf.jmstransport.queue" />
  <bean id="jmsConnectionFactory" class="org.apache.activemq.
  ActiveMQConnectionFactory">
    <property name="brokerURL" value="tcp://localhost:61616" />
  </bean>
</beans>
```

The client configuration uses `<jaxws:client>` to register the `OrderProcess` service. It uses the same sequence to specify the JMS configuration, as defined by the server configuration. The message broker is a central point message provider that sits between client and server. Both client and server exchange messages via the broker.

The bean element for JMS configuration uses `p: namespace` to define its attribute value. The `p: namespace` gives you an alternate way of specifying your bean properties.

Developing a client component

The `Client` class will obtain the `OrderProcess` bean and invoke its `processOrder()` method. The following code illustrates the consumer code:

```
public final class Client {

    public Client() {
    }

    public static void main(String args[]) throws Exception {
        ClassPathXmlApplicationContext context =
        new ClassPathXmlApplicationContext(new String[] {"demo/order/
        client/client-bean.xml"});
```

```
        OrderProcess client = (OrderProcess) context.
        getBean("orderClient");
        Order order = new Order();
        order.setCustomerID("C001");
        order.setItemID("I001");
        order.setQty(100);
        order.setPrice(200.00);

        String orderID = client.processOrder(order);
        String message = (orderID == null) ? "Order not approved" :
       "Order approved; order ID is " + orderID;
        System.out.println(message);
        System.exit(0);
    }
}
```

Performing build and deployment

The next step is to build and deploy our code. You will use ANT to build the code and it will be deployed on the Tomcat web server. The code needs to be organized into folders, as shown below:

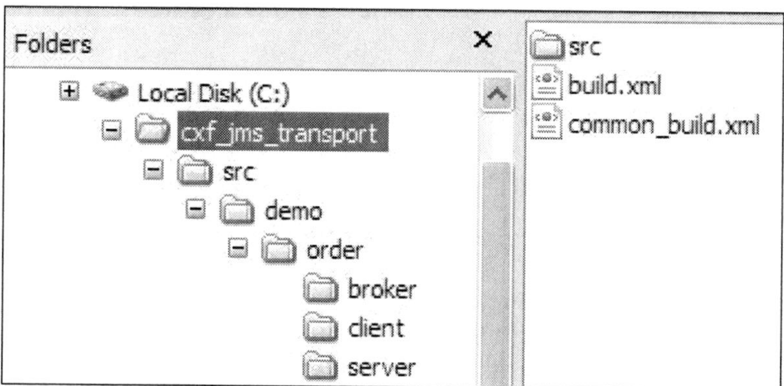

The following code illustrates the ANT build file:

```
<?xml version="1.0"?>
<project name="Order Process JMS Queue" default="build" basedir=".">
    <property environment="env"/>
    <condition property="activemq.home" value="${env.ACTIVEMQ_HOME}">
        <isset property="env.ACTIVEMQ_HOME"/>
    </condition>
```

```
    <fail message="this sample need to use activemq, please setup
     ACTIVEMQ_HOME in your environment"
        unless="activemq.home"/>
    <condition property="activemq.version" value="${env.ACTIVEMQ_
     VERSION}">
  <isset property="env.ACTIVEMQ_VERSION"/>
    </condition>
    <fail message="this sample need to use activemq, please setup
     ACTIVEMQ_VERSION in your envrionment"
        unless="activemq.version"/>

    <property name="thirdparty.classpath" location=
    "${activemq.home}/activemq-all-${activemq.version}.jar"/>

    <import file="common_build.xml"/>

    <target name="start.jmsbroker" description="run jms broker"
     depends="build">
       <cxfrun classname="demo.order.broker.MessageBroker" />
    </target>

    <target name="client" description="run demo client"
     depends="build">
        <cxfrun classname="demo.order.client.Client" />
    </target>

    <target name="server" description="run demo server"
     depends="build">
        <cxfrun classname="demo.order.server.Server" />
    </target>
...
```

The first part checks for the environment variable `ACTIVEMQ_HOME` and `ACTIVEMQ_VERSION`. You need to set this environment variable before proceeding with the build. Depending on your ActiveMQ installation, this environment variable should hold the following values:

```
set ACTIVEMQ_HOME = C:\apache-activemq-5.2.0
set ACTIVEMQ_VERSION = 5.2.0
```

You have to define the path for the third party JAR file. As we are using ActiveMQ as an external message provider, you will specify `activemq-all-5.2.0.jar` as a third-party JAR file. You then define three targets each for broker, client, and server respectively. To build and execute the code, perform the following steps:

1. The following command on your project root will compile the code and place it under the `build` folder:

   ```
   ant
   ```

2. Once the code is built successfully, you need to start the message broker. The `ant start.jmsbroker` command is used to start the message broker. The following figure shows the message broker startup output:

   ```
   C:\cxf_tutorial\book\chap_4\jms>ant start.jmsbroker
   Buildfile: build.xml

   maybe.generate.code:

   compile:

   build:

   start.jmsbroker:
        [java] JMS broker ready ...
   ```

3. You will then start the Tomcat web server. It is started by giving the following command at your project root:

   ```
   catalina start
   ```

4. The server will register the `OrderProcess` service and connect to the message broker on port `61616`

   Once the server is started, you invoke the client by giving the following command:

   ```
   ant client
   ```

5. The above command will run the `Client` class, which will invoke the `processOrder()` method of the `OrderProcess` bean. The method invocation will initiate message exchange via the broker.

Local transport

CXF provides support for local transport. **Local transport** means routing of service messages within a single JVM. Both the server and the client must be launched inside a JVM. The messages are serialized and piped between the endpoints. The following figure shows the working of local transport:

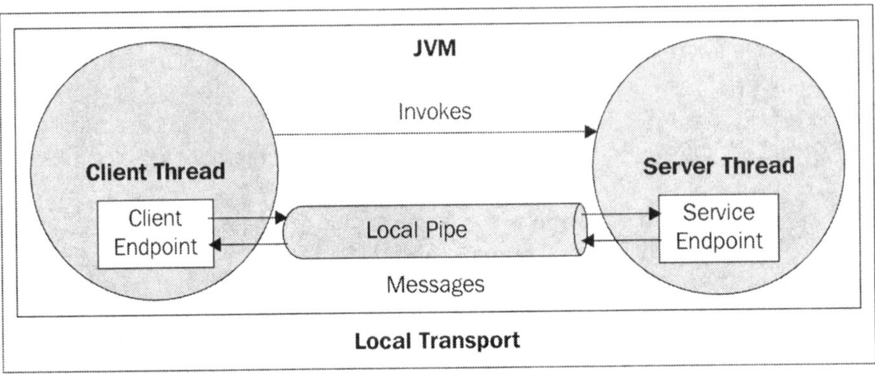

This works more like local EJBs. You may have local endpoints that communicate with each other to address a small workflow before routing it to the external endpoint.

To signify a local transport, you simply need to specify the `local://` URI convention while defining the endpoint. In this section, you will develop the order process web service and a consumer that will exchange messages using local transport.

You need to perform the following steps:

1. Developing SEI and an implementation class
2. Developing a server
3. Creating client bean configuration
4. Developing a client

The source code and build file is available in the `Chapter4/Local` folder of the downloaded source code.

Developing SEI and an implementation class

You will use the same `OrderProcess` SEI and the `OrderProcessImpl` class, demonstrated in earlier chapters.

```
import javax.jws.WebService;

@WebService
public interface OrderProcess {
    String processOrder(Order order);
}
```

Developing a server

The server component is very simple. The following code illustrates the `Server` class:

```
package demo.order.server;

import javax.xml.ws.Endpoint;
import demo.order.OrderProcessImpl;

public class Server {

    public Server() throws Exception {
        OrderProcessImpl orderProcessImpl = new OrderProcessImpl();
      Endpoint.publish("local://OrderProcess", orderProcessImpl);
    }

    public static void main(String args[]) throws Exception {
        new Server();
        System.out.println("Server ready...");
    }
}
```

As you can see, all you need to do is define your endpoint with the URI prefixed as `local://` and you are all set. The URI `local://OrderProcess` signifies that the `OrderProcess` service will be published for local use by the client inside the JVM.

Creating client bean configuration

The following code shows the Spring-based client bean configuration:

```
<beans xmlns="http://www.springframework.org/schema/beans"
xmlns:xsi="http://www.w3.org/2001/XMLSchema-instance"
xmlns:jaxws="http://cxf.apache.org/jaxws"
xsi:schemaLocation="http://www.springframework.org/schema/beans
                http://www.springframework.org/schema/beans/spring-
                beans.xsd
                http://cxf.apache.org/jaxws
```

```
                http://cxf.apache.org/schemas/jaxws.xsd">
    <jaxws:client id="orderClient" serviceClass="demo.order.
OrderProcess" address="local://OrderProcess" />
</beans>
```

The above client bean configuration is a simple JAX-WS client that registers the `OrderProcess` service class to use local endpoint `local://OrderProcess`.

Developing a Client

The `Client` class obtains the `OrderProcess` bean and invokes its `processOrder()` method. The following code illustrates the consumer code:

```
public final class Client {

    public Client() {
    }

    public static void main(String args[]) throws Exception {
        Server.main(new String[]{""});
        ClassPathXmlApplicationContext context =
        new ClassPathXmlApplicationContext(new String[]
        {"demo/order/client/client-bean.xml"});

        OrderProcess client = (OrderProcess) context.
        getBean("orderClient");
      Order order = new Order();
      order.setCustomerID("C001");
      order.setItemID("I001");
      order.setQty(100);
      order.setPrice(200.00);

        String orderID = client.processOrder(order);
        String message = (orderID == null) ? "Order not approved" :
"Order approved; order ID is " + orderID;
      System.out.println(message);
        System.exit(0);
    }
}
```

One important thing to notice is that you invoke your `Server` class from the client code itself. The following code snippet will first start the `Server` class:

```
Server.main(new String[]{""});
```

Remember, both client and server should be a part of the same JVM for the local transport to work.

Building and executing

The ANT build file will look like as follows:

```
<?xml version="1.0"?>
<project name="Order Process Local transport" default="build"
basedir=".">
    <import file="common_build.xml"/>

    <target name="client" description="run demo client"
    depends="build">
        <cxfrun classname="demo.order.client.Client" />
    </target>
</project>
```

As you can see, there is no server target. There is only one client target defined, which means you use one single `main()` method to run both the client and the server.

> Running one single JVM means you have only one `main()` method running.

You can run the code by giving the `ant client` command. Upon executing the command, it will show the following output:

```
C:\cxf_tutorial\book\chap_4\local>ant client
Buildfile: build.xml

maybe.generate.code:

compile:

build:

client:
     [java] Server ready...
     [java] Processing order...
     [java] Order approved; order ID is ORD1234

BUILD SUCCESSFUL
Total time: 5 seconds
```

Summary

In this chapter, you learned how to configure the following CXF supported transports:

- HTTP
- HTTPs
- JMS
- Local

The chapter introduced you to the concept of HTTP conduit, which enables the client program to apply policies/properties to HTTP and HTTPs protocols. You learned how to generate a crypto key and a keystore for HTTPs-based service communication. You also learned how to invoke a service using the JMS configuration features. The chapter also provided a working example of a standalone Jetty runtime. Finally, you learned the concept of local transport that allows the client and service program to exchange messages within a single JVM.

5

Implementing Advanced Features

In the previous chapter we learned about various types of CXF transports such as HTTP, HTTPs, JMS, and so on, which can be used to invoke a service. In this chapter we will learn advanced concepts like features, interceptors, and invokers. The chapter will explain how to create a custom component for each of these advanced features and apply it to your service.

The chapter will cover the following topics:

- Understanding CXF interceptors
- Developing custom interceptors
- Understanding CXF features
- Understanding CXF invokers
- Developing custom invokers

Understanding CXF interceptors

In the web service scenario, the consumer and service provider communicate with each other through the exchange of messages. The messages are marshalled at the client end and unmarshalled at the server end. In web service terminology, **marshalling** is the process of converting Java objects to XML files, which are to be sent over a network. **Unmarshalling** refers to converting an XML file back to a Java object.

When the consumer makes a request on the remote service, the data is first marshalled and placed over the network to be sent to the server. The server receives this marshalled data, unmarshalls it, and invokes the service method. The process is repeated in the same manner when the server sends back the response to the client. Marshalling and unmarshalling are the core services that are provided by client and service runtime. In CXF these special kinds of services are offered through the concept of interceptors.

Interceptors are POJOs that intercept your message to provide or apply certain core services to it. CXF supports many such interceptors that provide core services to the message that is being exchanged between consumer and service endpoint. These interceptors do the work of marshalling and unmarshalling, manipulating message headers, performing authorization checks, validating the message data, and so on. CXF provides built-in core interceptors that act upon messages. You can also develop your own custom interceptor, which can change to process the message before it is passed to the server. Interceptors are invoked in chain and organized in phases. In this section we will cover the following topics:

- Understanding interceptor phase and chain
- Overview of interceptor API

Understanding interceptor phase and chain

Interceptors are ordered or structured in phases. A **phase** can be thought of as a category that holds interceptors having similar or common functionality. A phase indicates or signifies an action that is performed by its interceptors on the messages. Some of the actions are marshalling, unmarshalling, user authorization, data compression, and so on. Interceptors within a phase are organized sequentially in the order of execution.

A **phase** tells the **interceptor** of its location in the **chain**. A chain is a collection of phases. Phases are connected together in an ordered list to form an interceptor chain. There are two types of interceptor chains, an inbound chain and an outbound chain. Both these chains have their set of phases. For example, interceptors in an UNMARSHAL phase, for an inbound chain, unmarshalls the message data into objects to be used by the application server.

The following figure shows the interceptor chain and phases:

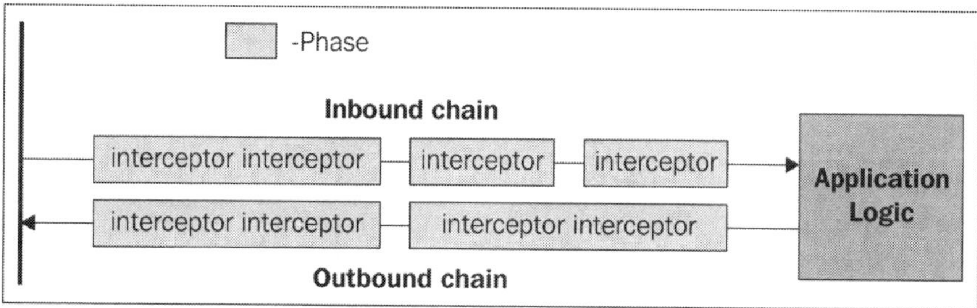

There are typically three types of chains associated with an endpoint:

- Inbound chain—it processes incoming messages
- Outbound chain—it processes outgoing messages
- Fault chain—it processes error messages

The previous figure shows message processing in the chain. It shows the service-side interceptors.

- For every request to a service, an inbound interceptor is created at the server end, and for every response, an outbound interceptor is created.
- The message goes through a chain and is processed by interceptors in phases in a particular order or sequence.
- The inbound interceptors manipulate the message before it reaches the application logic on the server side.
- The outbound interceptors manipulate the message before it is sent to the client.
- If an error condition occurs, then the interceptor chain unwinds itself to the calling program. It effectively means the control will go back to previous interceptors in a reverse chain and terminate at the application logic.

Overview of the interceptor API

Let's examine interceptor API and what classes can be used by the developers to write the custom interceptor.

The interceptor API is specified in two CXF packages: `org.apache.cxf.interceptor` and `org.apache.cxf.phase`. The interfaces in the `org.apache.cxf.interceptor` package allow you to develop the custom interceptors. The classes in this package resemble some of the core interceptors offered by CXF. The components in the `org.apache.cxf.phase` package allow you to develop interceptors and aggregate them in phases.

The core interceptors indirectly implement the `PhaseInterceptor` interface by extending the `AbstractPhaseInterceptor` abstract class. The `PhaseInterceptor` extends the `Interceptor` interface. Let's start by looking at these interfaces and the abstract class for developing custom interceptors.

Interceptor interface

When you write a custom interceptor, you need to directly or indirectly implement the `Interceptor` interface. The `Interceptor` interface defines two methods, `handleMessage` and `handleFault`.

The following code illustrates the CXF Interceptor interface:

```
package org.apache.cxf.interceptor;
public interface Interceptor<T extends Message> {
   void handleMessage(T message) throws Fault;
   void handleFault(T message);
}
```

You need to implement the above `Interceptor` interface and its methods to develop the custom interceptor. Let's look at the methods:

- `handleMessage` – the method expects an object of a type derived from `org.apache.cxf.message.Message`. It is the core method that processes the message. The method is called on all the interceptors sequentially in a chain. To write a custom interceptor one has to implement this method and provide message processing logic.
- `handleFault:` – the method expects an object of a type derived from `org.apache.cxf.message.Message`. It is called when there arises an error condition while processing the message. In this case, the method is called on the interceptor which processed the message, which in turn invokes this method on the previous interceptor in the chain recursively in reverse order. The method is used to handle exceptions.

The PhaseInterceptor interface

Most of the core interceptors implement the `Interceptor` interface indirectly through the `PhaseInterceptor` interface. The following code illustrates this interface:

```
package org.apache.cxf.phase;
...
public interface PhaseInterceptor<T extends Message> extends
Interceptor<T> {
   Set<String> getAfter();
   Set<String> getBefore();
```

```
        String getId();
        String getPhase();
    }
```

The `PhaseInterceptor` interface defines methods that allow the interceptors to work in chain. It defines the following four methods:

- `getAfter`—this method returns a `Set` containing IDs of the interceptors that should be executed before this interceptor. It effectively means that this interceptor will be placed in chain after the interceptors in the set.
- `getBefore`—this method returns a `Set` containing IDs of the interceptors that should be executed after this interceptor. It effectively means that this interceptor will be placed in chain before the interceptors in the set.
- `getId`—this method returns the ID of the interceptor. Every interceptor in the chain has a unique ID associated with it.
- `getPhase`—this method returns the phase in which this interceptor is executed.

A developer must extend the `AbstractPhaseInterceptor` class, which in turn implements the `PhaseInterceptor` interface to create a custom interceptor that participates in a phase. The next section talks about the `AbstractPhaseInterceptor` class.

> The `getAfter` and `getBefore` return the set of IDs of interceptors participating in the same phase as that of the interceptor on which these methods are invoked.
>
> If you do not wish to have your interceptor participate in the phase, then your interceptor can directly implement the `Interceptor` interface and should not use the `PhaseInterceptor` interface.

The AbstractPhaseInterceptor class

The interceptor API provides a convenient class named `AbstractPhaseInterceptor`, which provides a blank implementation of the `PhaseInterceptor` interface methods. More importantly, it defines the constructor with which, you can specify the phase name for your interceptor. When you specify the phase, your interceptor is ordered according to the phase in the chain. It also provides a blank implementation of the `handleFault` method of the `Interceptor` interface. Developer needs to override this method. The developers though still have to implement the `handleMessage` method of the `Interceptor` interface. The following code illustrates the use of the `AbstractPhaseInterceptor` abstract class:

```
public class MyPhaseedInterceptor extends AbstractPhaseInterceptor {
  public MyPhasedInterceptor() {
     super(Phase.INVOKE); // Put this interceptor in this phase
  }
  public void handleMessage(Message msg) throws Fault {
     // process the message
  }
}
```

As you can see from the previous code, a developer only needs to implement the `handleMessage` method. The methods of the `PhaseInterceptor` interface are already implemented by the `AbstractPhaseInterceptor` abstract class. The developer can override the `handleFault` method, the blank implementation of which has been already provided in the abstract class. The significant thing to observe is the constructor. It tells us that this interceptor is part of the `INVOKE` phase. The phases are ordered in a chain and are determined by a class named `PhaseInterceptorChain`. Most of the core interceptors offered by CXF use the `AbstractPhaseInterceptor` class. The following table shows the phases for an inbound chain:

Phase	Description
RECEIVE	Transport level processing
(PRE/USER/POST)_STREAM	Stream level processing/transformations
READ	Suitable for reading headers
(PRE/USER/POST)_PROTOCOL	Protocol processing
UNMARSHAL	Unmarshalling of the request
(PRE/USER/POST)_LOGICAL	Processing of the unmarshalled request
PRE_INVOKE	Pre invocation actions
INVOKE	Invocation of the service
POST_INVOKE	Invocation of the outgoing chain if there is one

The following table shows the phases for an outbound chain:

Phase	Description
SETUP	Setup for the following phases
(PRE/USER/POST)_LOGICAL	Processing of objects about to be marshalled
PREPARE_SEND	Opening of the connection
PRE_STREAM	Stream level processing
PRE_PROTOCOL	Misc protocol actions

Phase	Description
WRITE	Writing of the protocol message
MARSHAL	Marshalling of the objects
(USER/POST)_PROTOCOL	Processing of the protocol message
(USER/POST)_STREAM	Processing of the byte level message
SEND	Final sending of the message and closing of the transport stream

The following UML diagram summarizes the use of interceptors in phase:

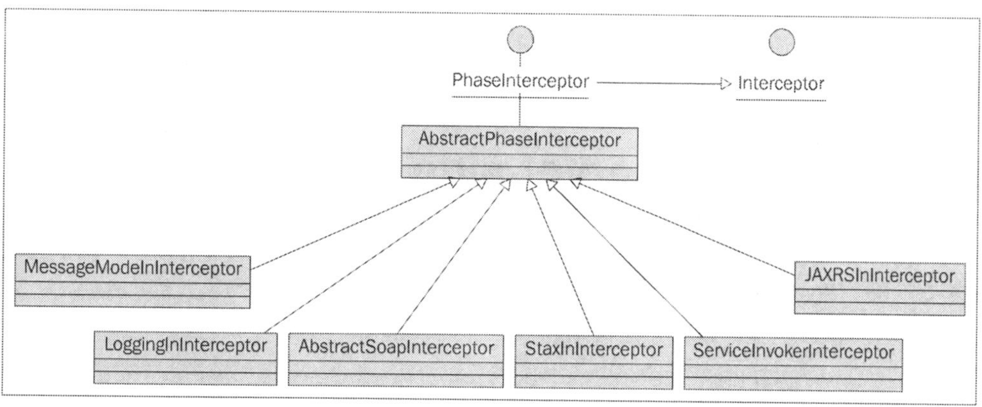

The above diagram shows some of the core interceptors offered by CXF. In the next section, we will use one of the previous interceptors named `AbstractSoapInterceptor` and illustrate this as part of developing the custom interceptor.

Developing the custom interceptor

In order to demonstrate the capabilities of interceptors, we assume a use case where only valid authenticated users can access the order processing web service. We expect that the user credentials required to access the web service are available in the SOAP header along with the payload.

To demonstrate these requirements, we create two interceptors, one on the client side, and the other on the server side. The client interceptor is responsible for intercepting the outgoing SOAP message and adding user credentials in the SOAP header. The server side interceptor intercepts an incoming SOAP message, extracts the user credentials from the SOAP message, and validates it. If the user credential fails, then it throws an exception back, in which case the web service operation doesn't execute.

We will develop our custom interceptor using the following steps:

- Developing the server side interceptor
- Adding the server side interceptor to the order process service
- Developing the client side interceptor
- Adding a client side interceptor to the client code
- Developing the standalone server for publishing the order process web service
- Building and running the order process web service and interceptor
- Testing the custom interceptor for a negative condition

The source code and build file is available in the `Chapter5/Interceptor` folder of the downloaded source code.

Developing the server side interceptor

We will first develop the server side interceptor. We will name this implementation class as `OrderProcessUserCredentialInterceptor`. The following is the code listing of the `OrderProcessUserCredentialInterceptor` class:

```
import javax.xml.namespace.QName;

import org.apache.cxf.binding.soap.SoapMessage;
import org.apache.cxf.binding.soap.interceptor.
AbstractSoapInterceptor;
import org.apache.cxf.headers.Header;
import org.apache.cxf.interceptor.Fault;
import org.apache.cxf.phase.Phase;
import org.w3c.dom.Element;
import org.w3c.dom.Node;

public class OrderProcessUserCredentialInterceptor extends
AbstractSoapInterceptor {

   private String userName;
   private String password;

   public OrderProcessUserCredentialInterceptor() {
      super(Phase.PRE_INVOKE);
   }

   public void handleMessage(SoapMessage message) throws Fault {

      System.out.println("OrderProcessUserCredentialInterceptor
      handleMessage invoked");
      QName qnameCredentials = new QName("OrderCredentials");
      // Get header based on QNAME
      if (message.hasHeader(qnameCredentials)) {
         Header header = message.getHeader(qnameCredentials);
```

```
            Element elementOrderCredential= (Element) header.getObject();
            Node nodeUser = elementOrderCredential.getFirstChild();
            Node nodePassword = elementOrderCredential.getLastChild();
            if (usernamel != null) {
               userName = nodeUser.getTextContent();
            }
            if (passwordel != null) {
               password = nodePassword.getTextContent();
            }
         }
         System.out.println("userName reterived from SOAP Header is "
         + userName);
         System.out.println("password reterived from SOAP Header is "
         + password);
         // Perform dummy validation for John
         if ("John".equalsIgnoreCase(userName) && "password".
         equalsIgnoreCase(password)) {
            System.out.println("Authentication successful for John");
         } else {
            throw new RuntimeException("Invalid user");
         }
      }
      public String getUserName() {
         return userName;
      }
      public void setUserName(String userName) {
         this.userName = userName;
      }
      public String getPassword() {
         return password;
      }
      public void setPassword(String password) {
         this.password = password;
      }
   }
```

Let's analyze some of the important lines of the code. The `OrderProcessUserCredentialInterceptor` extends the `AbstractSoapInterceptor` class. The `AbstractSoapInterceptor` class provides methods to access the SOAP header and version information.

Next, we define the default constructor for `OrderProcessUserCredentialInterceptor`, which calls the `super (Phase.PRE_INVOKE)` method to register the invocation phase, at which the `OrderProcessUserCredentialInterceptor` invoker needs to be executed. The `OrderProcessUserCredentialInterceptor` is executed by the CXF framework during the `PRE_INVOKE` phase, before invoking the order process web service operations.

```
public SOAPUserCredentialInterceptor() {
        super(Phase.PRE_INVOKE);
}
```

The `handleMessage` method gets invoked by the CXF interceptor framework during the phase registered by the `OrderProcessUserCredentialInterceptor` class. The `SoapMessage` class provides a method to get the list of SOAP headers or get the SOAP header based on the namespace. We then retrieve the `<OrderCredentials>` element from the SOAP header based on the namespace by calling the method `message.getHeader(qnameCredentials)`.The web service client sets the username and password in an `<OrderCredentials>` element, which is added to the SOAP header element when creating the web service request.

The following is the sample SOAP header request which contains the `<OrderCredentials>` element. The code listed above carries out the function of retrieving the username and password from the `<OrderCredentials>` element.

```
<soap:Header>
       <OrderCredentials>
          <username>John</username>
          <password>password</password>
       </OrderCredentials>
</soap:Header>
```

We will look at how to set this object when we create the client side interceptor. We then retrieve the username and password node from the `<OrderCredentials>` element and get the value associated with the username and password node. As part of our implementation, we provide a dummy authentication implementation for a user `John`, where the password for user `John` will be the value `password`. If the password doesn't match, then an exception occurs. You can provide your own implementation based on your requirements, for instance, to look up the database to retrieve user authentication information and perform a validation.

Adding a server side interceptor to the Order Process service

Next we add the `OrderProcessUserCredentialInterceptor` class to the Order Process web service. You can add interceptors with a configuration file or define annotations on the service interface or service class. We would use annotations on the `OrderProcessImpl` service implementation class.

The following code shows the revised `OrderProcessImpl.java` with relevant interceptor annotation:

```
import javax.jws.WebService;

@org.apache.cxf.interceptor.InInterceptors (interceptors = {"demo.
order. OrderProcessUserCredentialInterceptor" })
@WebService
public class OrderProcessImpl implements OrderProcess {

    public String processOrder(Order order) {
      System.out.println("Processing order...");
      String orderID = validate(order);
        return orderID;
    }
}
```

As you can see in the previous code listing, we have added an `InInterceptors` annotation that defines an inbound interceptor, which would be invoked before the web service is executed.

```
@org.apache.cxf.interceptor.InInterceptors (interceptors = {"demo.
order.server.OrderProcessUserCredentialInterceptor" })
```

With this, we have added the interceptor to our Order Process web service. Next, we would create the client interceptor, which would intercept the outgoing SOAP message, and set the user credentials in the SOAP header.

Developing the client side interceptor

We will now develop the client side interceptor. We will name this implementation class as `OrderProcessClientHandler`. The following is the code listing of the `OrderProcessClientHandler` class:

```
import javax.xml.namespace.QName;
import javax.xml.parsers.DocumentBuilder;
import javax.xml.parsers.DocumentBuilderFactory;
import javax.xml.parsers.ParserConfigurationException;
import org.apache.cxf.binding.soap.SoapMessage;
```

```
import org.apache.cxf.binding.soap.interceptor.
AbstractSoapInterceptor;
import org.apache.cxf.binding.soap.interceptor.
SoapPreProtocolOutInterceptor;
import org.apache.cxf.headers.Header;
import org.apache.cxf.interceptor.Fault;
import org.apache.cxf.phase.Phase;
import org.w3c.dom.Document;
import org.w3c.dom.Element;
public class OrderProcessClientHandler extends AbstractSoapInterceptor
{
    public String userName;
    public String password;
    public OrderProcessClientHandler() {
        super(Phase.WRITE);
        addAfter(SoapPreProtocolOutInterceptor.class.getName());
    }
    public void handleMessage(SoapMessage message) throws Fault {
            System.out.println("OrderProcessClientHandler handleMessage
            invoked");
            DocumentBuilder builder = null;
            try {
                builder = DocumentBuilderFactory.newInstance().
                newDocumentBuilder();
            } catch (ParserConfigurationException e) {
                e.printStackTrace();
            }
            Document doc = builder.newDocument();
            Element elementCredentials =
            doc.createElement("OrderCredentials");
            Element elementUser = doc.createElement("username");
            elementUser.setTextContent(getUserName());
            Element elementPassword = doc.createElement("password");
            elementPassword.setTextContent(getPassword());
            elementCredentials.appendChild(elementUser);
            elementCredentials.appendChild(elementPassword);
            // Create Header object
            QName qnameCredentials =  new QName("OrderCredentials");
            Header header = new Header(qnameCredentials,
            elementCredentials);
            message.getHeaders().add(header);
    }
    public String getPassword() {
        return password;
    }
    public void setPassword(String password) {
        this.password = password;
    }
```

```
        public String getUserName() {
            return userName;
        }
        public void setUserName(String userName) {
            this.userName = userName;
        }
    }
```

Let's analyze some of the important lines of the code.
The `OrderProcessClientHandler` extends the `AbstractSoapInterceptor` class. The `AbstractSoapInterceptor` class provides methods to access the SOAP header and version information.

Next, we define the default constructor for `OrderProcessClientHandler`, which calls the `super(Phase.WRITE)` constructor method and `addAfter(SoapPreProtocolOutInterceptor.class.getName())` to register the invocation phase at which the `OrderProcessClientHandler` interceptor needs to be executed. The `addAfter` method specifies that the `OrderProcessClientHandler` interceptor needs to be added to the interceptor chain after the CXF in-built `SoapPreProtocolOutInterceptor` interceptor class. The method is part of the base class `AbstractPhaseInterceptor`. The `OrderProcessClientHandler` is executed by the CXF framework during the `WRITE` phase and after the `SoapPreProtocolOutInterceptor` interceptor class. The `SoapPreProtocolOutInterceptor` interceptor is responsible for setting up the SOAP version and header, and hence any additions to the SOAP header element need to be done after the `SoapPreProtocolOutInterceptor`.

```
    public OrderProcessClientHandler() {
            super(Phase.WRITE);
            addAfter(SoapPreProtocolOutInterceptor.class.getName());
    }
```

The `OrderProcessClientHandler` class `handleMessage` method receives the `SoapMessage` as the input, which provides access to the SOAP header information associated with the SOAP payload.

We next create the `<OrderCredentials>` root XML element and add the `username` and `password` element to it. We then create a `Header` object and set the `OrderCredentials` elements in the `header` object, along with the namespace by calling the constructor `new Header(qnameCredentials, elementCredentials)`. We then finally add the `Header` element to the SOAP Header using the `message.getHeaders().add(header)` method.

Next, we need to add the `OrderProcessClientHandlerinterceptor` to the web service client.

Adding a client side interceptor to the client code

You can add interceptors with a configuration file or programmatically using the CXF `org.apache.cxf.endpoint.Client` interface. We will use this to add outbound interceptors.

The following code shows the `Client` class:

```
import demo.order.OrderProcess;
import demo.order.Order;

import org.apache.cxf.frontend.ClientProxy;
import org.springframework.context.support.
ClassPathXmlApplicationContext;

public final class Client {

    public Client() {
    }

    public static void main(String args[]) throws Exception {
        ClassPathXmlApplicationContext context =
        new ClassPathXmlApplicationContext(new String[]
        {"demo/order/client/client-beans.xml"});

        OrderProcess client = (OrderProcess) context.
        getBean("orderClient");
        OrderProcessClientHandler clientInterceptor =
        new OrderProcessClientHandler();
        clientInterceptor.setUserName("John");
        clientInterceptor.setPassword("password");
        org.apache.cxf.endpoint.Client cxfClient = ClientProxy.
        getClient(client);
        cxfClient.getOutInterceptors().add(clientInterceptor);

      Order order = new Order();
      order.setCustomerID("C001");
      order.setItemID("I001");
      order.setQty(100);
      order.setPrice(200.00);

        String orderID = client.processOrder(order);
        String message = (orderID == null) ? "Order not approved" :
        "Order approved; order ID is " + orderID;
      System.out.println(message);
    }
}
```

As you can see in the given code, we create an instance of the `OrderProcessClientHandler` class and set the username and password. We then retrieve the `org.apache.cxf.endpoint.Client` object using the `ClientProxy.getClient(client)` method and add the `OrderProcessClientHandler` instance as an outbound interceptor to the `org.apache.cxf.endpoint.Client` instance using the `cxfClient.getOutInterceptors().add()` method. Thus, we have completed our client and server interceptors' functionality.

The following is the `client-beans.xml` configuration file used to configure the web service client:

```
<?xml version="1.0" encoding="UTF-8"?>
<beans xmlns="http://www.springframework.org/schema/beans"
   xmlns:xsi="http://www.w3.org/2001/XMLSchema-instance"
   xmlns:jaxws="http://cxf.apache.org/jaxws"
   xsi:schemaLocation="http://www.springframework.org/schema/beans
                       http://www.springframework.org/schema/beans/
                       spring-beans.xsd
                       http://cxf.apache.org/jaxws
                       http://cxf.apache.org/schemas/jaxws.xsd">

   <jaxws:client id="orderClient" serviceClass="demo.order.
OrderProcess" address="http://localhost:8080/OrderProcess" />

</beans>
```

Next, we write a standalone server utility to publish the Order Process web service to the endpoint address `http://localhost:8080/OrderProcess`. The standalone server utility provides a quick way to test your web service as well as the interceptors, which are invoked during execution prior to deployment in the application server.

Developing the standalone server for publishing the Order Process web service

We will now develop the standalone server utility which will publish the Order Process web service. We will name this implementation class as `OrderProcessServerStart`. The following provides the code listing of the `OrderProcessServerStart` class:

```
import org.apache.cxf.jaxws.JaxWsServerFactoryBean;

public class OrderProcessServerStart {

   public static void main(String[] args) {

      OrderProcess orderProcess = new OrderProcessImpl();
```

```
        JaxWsServerFactoryBean server = new JaxWsServerFactoryBean();
        server.setServiceBean(orderProcess);
        server.setAddress("http://localhost:8080/OrderProcess");
        server.create();
        System.out.println("Server ready....");
        Thread.sleep(5 * 60 * 1000);
    System.out.println("Server exiting");
          System.exit(0);    }
}
```

We start off by creating the `JaxWsServerFactoryBean` instance. We then set the implementation class instance `OrderProcessImpl` and set the address where the `OrderProcess` web service needs to be deployed which is `http://localhost:8080/OrderProcess` and invoke the create method on the `JaxWsServerFactoryBean` instance. The `create` method creates an embedded jetty service instance and deploys the Order Process web service.

Building and running the Order Process web service and interceptor

Before running the program, we organize the code in the appropriate folder structure. We organize the code in the folder structure which is shown below:

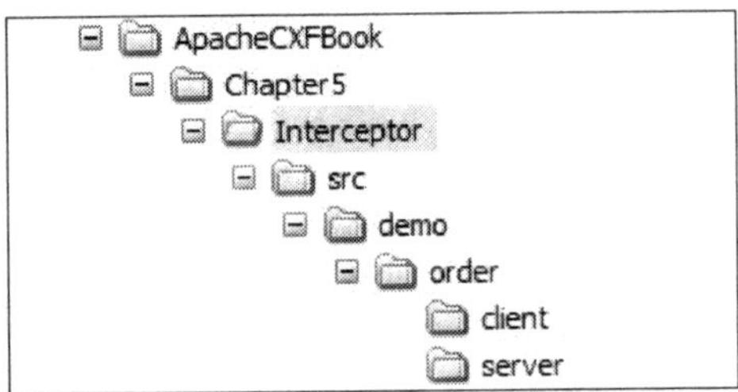

Once the code is organized, we build and deploy it in the Jetty embedded server. It will typically involve three steps:

- Building the code
- Deploying the code
- Executing the code

Building the code

We create the `build.xml` file to add a target for running the standalone server utility. The following code illustrates the `build.xml` build script:

```
<?xml version="1.0" encoding="UTF-8"?>
<project name="CXF Book examples" default="build" basedir=".">
...
    <target name="client" description=
    "run demo client" depends="build">
        <property name="param" value=""/>
        <cxfrun classname="demo.order.client.Client" />
    </target>
    <target name="server" description=
    "run demo server" depends="build">
        <cxfrun classname="demo.order.OrderProcessServerStart"/>
    </target>
</project>
```

As you can see, we have added a target server which runs the server standalone class `demo.order.OrderProcessServerStart` and a target client that runs the client class `demo.order.client.Client`.

For more information on building the source code using the ANT tool, see the Appendix *Getting Ready with Code Examples*. The Appendix covers step-by-step information on organizing and building the source code.

```
Command Prompt

C:\ApacheCXFBook\Interceptor>ant
Buildfile: build.xml
    [mkdir] Created dir: C:\ApacheCXFBook\Interceptor\build
 [loadfile] Do not set property srcbuild.classpath as its length is 0.

maybe.generate.code:

compile:
    [mkdir] Created dir: C:\ApacheCXFBook\Interceptor\build\classes
    [mkdir] Created dir: C:\ApacheCXFBook\Interceptor\build\src
    [javac] Compiling 7 source files to C:\ApacheCXFBook\Interceptor\build\class
es
     [copy] Copying 1 file to C:\ApacheCXFBook\Interceptor\build\classes

build:

BUILD SUCCESSFUL
Total time: 3 seconds
C:\ApacheCXFBook\Interceptor>
```

Deploying the code

After the code build is performed, we deploy it in the embedded jetty container for testing. To deploy the built code, navigate to your project root folder, and give the following command:

```
ant server
```

This executes the Java program `demo.order.OrderProcessServerStart` that starts the embedded jetty server, which deploys and publishes the Order Process web service and makes it available at the URL `http://localhost:8080/OrderProcess`

After running the above command, you will see the following output. Do not close the window while the server is running.

```
C:\ApacheCXFBook\Chapter5\Interceptor>ant server
Buildfile: build.xml

maybe.generate.code:

compile:
    [javac] Compiling 1 source file to C:\ApacheCXFBook\Chapter5\Interceptor\bui
ld\classes

build:

server:
     [java] Server ready....
```

Executing the code

After the code deployment is over, we are all set to run the web service client. You will execute the Java client program `Client.java` to invoke the Order Process web service. Run the client program by giving the following command in the command prompt window:

```
ant client
```

As you can see from the previous screenshot, we are using ant to run the client program. Upon executing this command, it will generate the following output:

```
C:\ApacheCXFBook\Chapter5\Interceptor>ant client
Buildfile: build.xml

maybe.generate.code:

compile:
    [javac] Compiling 1 source file to C:\ApacheCXFBook\Chapter5\Interceptor\bui
ld\classes

build:

client:
     [java] OrderProcessClientHandler handleMessage invoked
     [java] Order approved; order ID is ORD1234

BUILD SUCCESSFUL
Total time: 19 seconds
```

As you can see in the previous output, the `OrderProcessClientHandler` interceptor is invoked, which sets the username and password in the SOAP header.

On the console where you executed the ant server, you see the user credentials being printed by the `OrderProcessUserCredentialInterceptor` interceptor.

```
C:\ApacheCXFBook\Chapter5\Interceptor>ant server
Buildfile: build.xml

maybe.generate.code:

compile:
    [javac] Compiling 1 source file to C:\ApacheCXFBook\Chapter5\Interceptor\bui
ld\classes

build:

server:
     [java] Server ready....
     [java] OrderProcessUserCredentialInterceptor handleMessage invoked
     [java] userName reterived from SOAP Header is John
     [java] password reterived from SOAP Header is password
     [java] Authentication successful for John
     [java] Processing order...
```

As we have supplied valid credentials the `OrderProcessUserCredentialInterceptor` interceptor is successfully executed and we see the Order Process web service being executed as denoted by the **Processing Order...** system output message shown in the previous screenshot.

Testing the custom interceptor for negative condition

Next, we try out a negative scenario by setting the username as `Jack` in the SOAP header. Open up the `Client.java` in an editor, and make the following modifications, as highlighted in bold below to provide the username as `Jack`.

```
import demo.order.OrderProcess;
import demo.order.Order;
```

```
import org.apache.cxf.frontend.ClientProxy;
import org.springframework.context.support.
ClassPathXmlApplicationContext;
public final class Client {
        public Client() {
        }
    //Code not shown , same as earlier Client code
OrderProcess client = (OrderProcess) context.getBean("orderClient");
         OrderProcessClientHandler clientInterceptor =
         new OrderProcessClientHandler();
         clientInterceptor.setUserName("John");
         clientInterceptor.setPassword("nopassword");
         org.apache.cxf.endpoint.Client cxfClient =
         ClientProxy.getClient(client);
         cxfClient.getOutInterceptors().add(clientInterceptor);
         System.exit(0);
         // END SNIPPET: client
    }
}
```

As with our server side interceptor implementation, the `OrderProcessUserCredentialInterceptor` throws an exception if the password for `John` is not equal to value `password`. Thus, the above request would result in an error being thrown, and the web service operation would not be executed.

Next we build the modified `Client.java`. Navigate to the project `root` folder, and run the following command in sequence the `ant build`, followed by `ant client`.

If you look at the server output, you notice that the web service operation is not executed, you would not see the **Processing Order system out** message being printed at the console as an exception is thrown by `OrderProcessUserCredentialInterceptor`.

```
[java] OrderProcessUserCredentialInterceptor handleMessage invoked
[java] userName reterived from SOAP Header is John
[java] password reterived from SOAP Header is nopassword
```

On the client side, you would see an SOAP fault exception with the message **Invalid user or password** being printed at the console, as shown in the following screenshot:

```
C:\ApacheCXFBook\Chapter5\Interceptor>ant client
Buildfile: build.xml

maybe.generate.code:

compile:
    [javac] Compiling 1 source file to C:\ApacheCXFBook\Chapter5\Interceptor\bui
ld\classes

build:

client:
     [java] OrderProcessClientHandler handleMessage invoked
     [java] Exception in thread "main" javax.xml.ws.soap.SOAPFaultException: Inv
alid user or password
     [java]     at org.apache.cxf.jaxws.JaxWsClientProxy.invoke(JaxWsClientProxy
.java:146)
     [java]     at $Proxy44.processOrder(Unknown Source)
     [java]     at demo.order.client.Client.main(Client.java:31)
     [java] Caused by: org.apache.cxf.binding.soap.SoapFault: Invalid user or pa
ssword
     [java]     at org.apache.cxf.binding.soap.interceptor.Soap11FaultInIntercep
tor.unmarshalFault(Soap11FaultInInterceptor.java:75)
     [java]     at org.apache.cxf.binding.soap.interceptor.Soap11FaultInIntercep
```

Thus, we have successfully tested the interceptors for the Order Process web service.

Understanding CXF features

A `Feature` is a component that provides extra capability to the server, client, and bus, over and above their existing functionality. The CXF bundle provides feature components that allow the developer to add extra features to the endpoints and bus.

The following table lists the feature components supported by CXF:

Feature	Description
`ColocFeature`	Enables collocating services with different transport protocols
`FailoverFeature`	Enables clients to failover from the initial target endpoint to another compatible endpoint for the target service
`StaxDataBindingFeature`	Performs data binding using XML streaming
`LoggingFeature`	Enables inbound and outbound logging
`GZIPFeature`	Enables gzip compression to the service messages
`JMSConfigFeature`	Enables JMS transport configuration
`WSAddressingFeature`	Enables and controls the use of WS-Addressing
`RMFeature`	Enables and controls the use of WS-RM (Reliable Messaging)

Features are an indirect form of interceptors. You can use a `Feature` component instead of directly using an interceptor. When you apply a feature to the service endpoint, the server bean factory will invoke the `initialize` method of that particular feature class. This method will invoke the respective interceptor class for that feature. For example, you can use `LoggingFeature` to enable logging of inbound and outbound messages. The `LoggingFeature` class, behind the scenes, will invoke the `initialize` method which will register the `LoggingInInterceptor` and `LoggingOutInterceptor` components so as to perform the logging. With features, you can avoid direct use of interceptors. It is the most convenient way of applying extra functionality to your web service. Every feature class extends the `AbstractFeature` class. This class provides API to add extra capabilities to the server, client, or bus. When the feature is applied to the bus, all the service endpoints automatically inherit that feature.

In the next section, we will use one of the features offered by CXF and apply it to our Order Process web service.

Applying the GZIP feature to the Order Process web service

In this section we will develop the Order Process web service that will use the CXF-offered `GZIPFeature` to compress the service request and response in a `gzip` format. You will need to perform the following steps:

1. Developing service SEI and implementation class
2. Developing a server component
3. Creating a client bean configuration file
4. Creating a client component to consume the service
5. Building and executing the code

The source code and build file is available in the `Chapter5/Feature` folder of the downloaded source code.

Developing service and implementation class

We will use the same `OrderProcess` SEI and `OrderProcessImpl` class that is demonstrated in earlier sections.

```
import javax.jws.WebService;
@WebService
public interface OrderProcess {
    String processOrder(Order order);
}
```

Developing a server component

The following code illustrates the `Server` component:

```
import org.apache.cxf.jaxws.JaxWsServerFactoryBean;
import org.apache.cxf.transport.http.gzip.GZIPFeature;
import demo.order.OrderProcess;
import demo.order.OrderProcessImpl;
public class Server {
    public static void main(String[] args) throws Exception {
        OrderProcess orderProcess = new OrderProcessImpl();
GZIPFeature gzip = new GZIPFeature();
gzip.setThreshold(1);
        JaxWsServerFactoryBean server = new JaxWsServerFactoryBean();
        server.setServiceBean(orderProcess);
        server.setAddress("http://localhost:8080/feature/
OrderProcessGZIP");
        server.getFeatures().add(gzip);
        server.create();
        System.out.println("Server ready....");
        Thread.sleep(5 * 60 * 1000);
            System.out.println("Server exiting");
            System.exit(0);
    }
}
```

You will use `JAXWsServerFactoryBean` class to create the server. One of the things you will set is the `GZIPFeature` feature class. The following code line adds the gzip feature:

```
sf.getFeatures().add(gzip);
```

The `getFeatures` method returns the `List` of existing features for this JAX-WS server factory bean. If there are no existing features then it will return a blank list. You then add the `GZIPFeature` object to the list. It basically signifies that the server will compress the response in a `gzip` format and send it back to the client. We also set a threshold value of `1`. It means skip 1 byte and compress the remaining content. The idea here is to show the significance of threshold. The threshold value of `0` means full content compression. If no threshold value is provided, then by default it performs full content compression. The service endpoint address will be `http://localhost:8080/feature/OrderProcessGZIP`.

Creating the client bean configuration file

The following code shows the client configuration file:

```
<?xml version="1.0" encoding="UTF-8" ?>
<beans xmlns="http://www.springframework.org/schema/beans"
xmlns:xsi="http://www.w3.org/2001/XMLSchema-instance"
xmlns:http-conf="http://cxf.apache.org/transports/http/configuration"
xmlns:jaxws="http://cxf.apache.org/jaxws"
xsi:schemaLocation="http://www.springframework.org/schema/beans
               http://www.springframework.org/schema/beans/spring-
               beans.xsd
               http://cxf.apache.org/transports/http/configuration
               http://cxf.apache.org/schemas/configuration/http-conf.
               xsd
               http://cxf.apache.org/jaxws http://cxf.apache.org/
               schemas/jaxws.xsd">

   <http-conf:conduit name="*.http-conduit">
      <http-conf:client AcceptEncoding="gzip" />
   </http-conf:conduit>
   <jaxws:client id="orderClient" serviceClass="demo.order.
OrderProcess" address="http://localhost:9000/feature/OrderProcessGZIP">
      <jaxws:features>
         <bean class="org.apache.cxf.transport.http.gzip.GZIPFeature"
>
            <property name="threshold" value="1" />
         </bean>
      </jaxws:features>
   </jaxws:client>
</beans>
```

From the code you can see above, you will first define the HTTP conduit to specify the client side HTTP properties. You specify the properties as part of the `<http-conf:client>` element. This element takes the `AcceptEncoding` attribute, which indicates that the client application can accept encoded responses. The encoding type value here is `gzip`. You then define the client endpoint using the `<jaxws:client>` element with the service class as `demo.order.OrderProcess`. The service endpoint address is `http://localhost:8080/feature/OrderProcessGZIP`. Since we want the request also to be `gzip` compressed, we provide the `<jaxws:features>` child element to the `<jaxws:client>` element. In the `<jaxws:features>` element, you define the `GZIPFeature` class as part of the `<bean>` element. The `<property>` tag defines the threshold for `gzip` compression. The value in this case is `1`.

Creating a client component to consume the service

The `Client` class obtains the `OrderProcess` bean and invokes its `processOrder()` method. The following code illustrates the consumer code:

```
public final class Client {

    public Client() {
    }

    public static void main(String args[]) throws Exception {
        ClassPathXmlApplicationContext context =
        new ClassPathXmlApplicationContext(new String[] {"demo/order/
        client/client-beans.xml"});

        OrderProcess client = (OrderProcess) context.
        getBean("orderClient");
      Order order = new Order();
      order.setCustomerID("C001");
      order.setItemID("I001");
      order.setPrice(100.00);
      order.setQty(20);
      String result = client.processOrder(order);

        System.out.println("The Order ID is : " + result);
        System.exit(0);
    }
}
```

In the next section we will build and execute the code.

Building and executing the code

Before running the program we will organize the code in the appropriate folder structure. We organize the code in the folder structure, shown below:

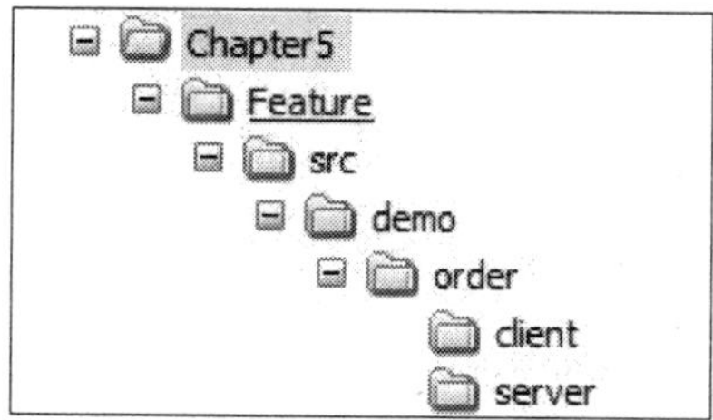

You will build the code using the ANT tool. You can provide the ant command at the project root folder in the command prompt window to build the code.

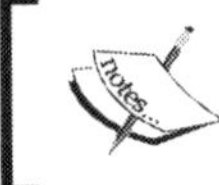

For more information on building the source code using the ANT tool, see the Appendix *Getting Ready with Code Examples*. The Appendix covers step-by-step information on organizing and building the source code.

Executing the code requires you to launch the server and then run the client program. The command `ant server` starts the server. Once the server is started, you can give the `ant client` command to execute the client code. You will not see any compressed data in the server and client console output. The compression will be at the SOAP level, that is, after the message is marshalled and before it is unmarshalled.

You use the Apache-offered `tcpmon` tool to see the outgoing and incoming SOAP requests and response messages. You need to change the `tcpmon tcp` listener port to an arbitrary port number such as `9000` and provide the same port in the client configuration file in the `address` attribute of the `<jaxws:client>` element. Then change the server port in `tcpmon` to `8080`. This makes sure that the client first sends a request to the `tcpmon` server, which in turn will send it to our embedded jetty server.

`tcpmon` is a utility tool that can be used to see data packets in transit sent between the client and the server program using TCP protocol.

The following screenshot shows the output of the `tcpmon` tool:

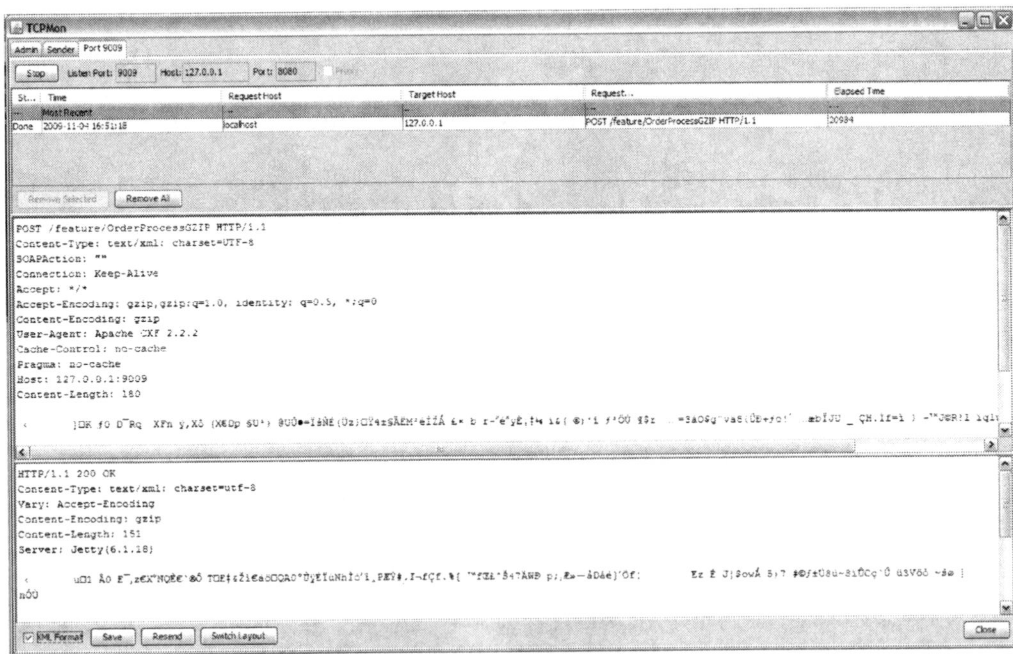

The previous screenshot shows the SOAP request and response message in transit in a `gzip` compressed form.

Understanding CXF Invoker

In an earlier section, we looked at Feature components that can be added to your service endpoint to enable that feature. In this section, we will talk about yet another CXF component named Invoker. Invoker, in web service context, simply means to invoke a method of the service, and the `Invoker` component does exactly the same. So what is special about the `Invoker` component? Well, it provides you with the ability to customize your service method execution. It provides you with the ability to control the service invocation. It effectively means you can prefix or add more functionality to your service business method before the method is actually invoked. Invokers are applied to a service endpoint.

Invoker acts more like simple filter components. It gives you the ability to intercept the message before the service method is called or invoked. Invokers though cannot be called as interceptors. In CXF, interceptors process messages at different phases in an inbound or outbound chain. Invokers do not have phases, they merely invoke a service method with the ability to intercept the message just before the service method is invoked. It means you can write a piece of code that could manipulate the message before the operation is invoked. We will discuss the concept through the following topics:

- Overview of Invoker API
- Developing custom invoker

Overview of Invoker API

Before we demonstrate the practical use of the invoker component, let's look and understand the invoker API and what classes can be used by developers to write the custom invoker. The invoker API is part of a package named `org.apache.cxf.service.invoker`. The interfaces and classes in this package allow you to develop a custom invoker. We will discuss two main components in this package, the `Invoker` interface and the `AbstractInvoker` class.

The Invoker interface

When you write a custom invoker, you need to directly or indirectly implement the `Invoker` interface. The `Invoker` interface defines a method called `invoke` that takes objects of type `org.apache.cxf.message.Exchange` and `java.lang.Object` as parameters. The following code shows the `Invoker` interface:

```
import org.apache.cxf.message.Exchange;
public interface Invoker {
   Object invoke(Exchange exchange, Object o);
}
```

You need to implement the above `Invoker` interface and the `invoke` method to write your own invoker. This will provide functionality to the `invoke` method. Most of the time, you will have to indirectly implement the `Invoker` interface by extending the `AbstractInvoker` class.

The AbstractInvoker class

The invoker API provides a more important and useful abstract class named `AbstractInvoker`. It provides a ready implementation of the `invoke` method. A developer should override this method and provide extension to the existing service functionality. The `invoke` method simply uses Java reflection to invoke the service method. The `AbstractInvoker` class defines one abstract method `getServiceObject`. The developer needs to implement this method by returning the service object. The following code illustrates the use of the `AbstractInvoker` class:

```
import org.apache.cxf.message.Exchange;
public class MyInvoker extends AbstractInvoker {
   // Service bean
   private Object bean;
   public MyInvoker(Object bean) {
      this.bean = bean;
   }
   @Override
   public Object invoke(Exchange exchange, Object o) {
      // Provide your own extension logic here before the
      // service method is invoked
      // Invokes the service method
      return super.invoke(exchange, o);
   }
   public Object getServiceObject(Exchange exchange) {
      return bean;
   }
}
```

The previous code shows a sample `MyInvoker` class that extends `AbstractInvoker`. The constructor takes the service bean as a parameter. This bean is returned from the `getServiceObject` method. The developer must implement the `getServiceObject` method by returning the service bean instance. The developer should override the `invoke` method and provide the functionality on the top of the existing service method functionality. The `super.invoke` method will call the `invoke` method of the `AbstractInvoker` class which in turn will invoke the service method. Remember, invokers are applied to the service endpoint and they invoke its service method.

In the next section we will look at real world examples on how to use invokers.

The source code and build file is available in the `Chapter5/Invoker` folder of the downloaded source code.

Developing custom invoker

We will take the same use case of authentication security check discussed in the earlier *Developing custom interceptor* section. The users of the Order Process web service will be authenticated. Again, as part of assumption, we will have the user credentials already defined in the SOAP header. The components to be developed will remain the same. There will be changes to only two components, `OrderProcessUserCredentialInterceptor.java` and `OrderProcessServerStart.java`. We will call our class file `OrderProcessUserCredentialInterceptor.java` as `AuthenticationInvoker.java`. You will now see how we can use invoker to perform authentication before the `processOrder` method is called on the `OrderProcess` service.

The following code illustrates the `AuthenticationInvoker` class:

```
import java.util.List;
import javax.xml.namespace.QName;
import org.apache.cxf.binding.soap.SoapHeader;
import org.apache.cxf.common.util.ClassHelper;
import org.apache.cxf.headers.Header;
import org.apache.cxf.message.Exchange;
import org.apache.cxf.service.invoker.AbstractInvoker;
import org.apache.cxf.service.model.OperationInfo;
import org.w3c.dom.Element;
import org.w3c.dom.Node;
import demo.order.OrderProcessImpl;
public class AuthenticationInvoker  extends AbstractInvoker {
   private String userName;
   private String password;
   private Object bean;
   public AuthenticationInvoker(Object bean) {
```

```
            this.bean = bean;
    }
    @Override
    public Object invoke(Exchange exchange, Object o) {
        // Get method and class details from the request
        OperationInfo opInfo = exchange.get(OperationInfo.class);
        String methodName = opInfo.getInputName();
        Class<?> realClass = ClassHelper.getRealClass(bean);
        QName qnameOrderCredential = new QName("OrderCredentials");
         // Perform security check only if the service class is
OrderProcessImpl
        // and method name is processOrder
        if (realClass == OrderProcessImpl.class && "processOrder".
        equals(methodName)) {
            List list = (List) exchange.getInMessage().get
           (Header.HEADER_LIST);
            for (int  i = 0 ; i< list.size() ; i++  ) {
                // Get the SOAP header
                SoapHeader header = (SoapHeader) list.get(i);
                if(header.getName().equals(qnameOrderCredential)) {
                    Element orderCredential= (Element) header.getObject();
                    Node usernamel = orderCredential.getFirstChild();
                    Node passwordel = orderCredential.getLastChild();
                    if (usernamel != null) {
                        userName = usernamel.getTextContent();
                    }
                    if (passwordel != null) {
                        password = passwordel.getTextContent();
                    }
                } else {
                     throw new RuntimeException("Request doesn't contain
                     OrderCredentials namespace");
                }
            }
            System.out.println("userName reterived from SOAP Header is "
            + userName);
            System.out.println("password reterived from SOAP Header is "
            + password);
            // Perform dummy validation for John
            if ("John".equalsIgnoreCase(userName) && "password".
            equalsIgnoreCase(password)) {
                System.out.println("Authentication successful for John");
            } else {
                throw new RuntimeException("Invalid user or password");
            }
        }
              // Call super class invoke method
          // This will invoke processOrder method
```

```
        return super.invoke(exchange,o);
    }
    @Override
    public Object getServiceObject(Exchange arg0) {
        return bean;
    }
. . .
// Getter and setter for username and password
}
```

The previous code is pretty similar to that defined in `OrderProcessUserCredentialInterceptor.java` for the interceptor. The primary difference is that here we are using invoker that will check for the name of the service class and method. If the service class is `OrderProcessImpl` and the method to be invoked is `processOrder`, then only the authentication security check will be performed on the user.

Let's scan the `AuthenticationInvoker` class and see what the invoker part actually does.

Firstly the `AuthenticationInvoker` class extends the abstract class `AbstractInvoker`. It means the class must implement the `getServiceObject` method. The method implementation here simply returns the instance of the service bean `OrderProcessImpl`.

The class overrides the invoke method which is part of the `AbstractInvoker` abstract class. We provide the complete authentication security check logic here and then call our `processOrder` method. See the following code snippet:

```
OperationInfo opInfo = exchange.get(OperationInfo.class);
String methodName = opInfo.getInputName();
Class<?> realClass = ClassHelper.getRealClass(bean);
. . .
// Perform security check only if the service class is
OrderProcessImpl
// and method name is processOrder
if (realClass == OrderProcessImpl.class && "processOrder".
equals(methodName)) {
    // perform authentication
```

As you can see from the previous code snippet, we check if the service class is `OrderProcessImpl` and the method to be invoked is `processOrder`, and only then will we perform the authentication. We perform the introspection of the service bean in question, which is `OrderProcessImpl`, and get its metadata (which is the class name and method name). We get the class name using the CXF offered utility class `ClassHelper`. The method name is fetched using the CXF service model API component `OperationInfo`. Using these details, we check if they are the same and accordingly perform authentication.

The `processOrder` method of the `OrderProcessImpl` bean is called by invoking `super.invoke` which will call the `invoke` method of the `AbstractInvoker` abstract class.

You must be wondering from where the `OrderProcessImpl` service bean came from. This is passed through our server class `OrderProcessServerStart`. The following code shows the `OrderProcessServerStart` class:

```
import org.apache.cxf.jaxws.JaxWsServerFactoryBean;
import demo.order.OrderProcessImpl;
import demo.order.OrderProcess;
public class OrderProcessServerStart {
    public static void main(String[] args) {
        // Service instance
        OrderProcess orderProcess = new OrderProcessImpl();
        JaxWsServerFactoryBean jaxServer = new JaxWsServerFactoryBean();
        jaxServer.setServiceBean(orderProcess);
        jaxServer.setAddress("http://localhost:8080/OrderProcess");
        // Set the Invoker
        jaxServer.setInvoker(new AuthenticationInvoker(orderProcess));
        jaxServer.create();
            System.out.println("Server ready...");
        Thread.sleep(5 * 60 * 1000);
            System.out.println("Server exiting");
            System.exit(0);
    }
}
```

As you can see from the previous code snippet, the only change we make is to set the invoker to our `JaxWsServerFactoryBean` class. The `setInvoker` method used takes the `AuthenticationInvoker` invoker as a parameter. The instance of service class `OrderProcessImpl` is passed as an argument to the constructor of the `AuthenticationInvoker` class. This basically tells the server factory bean that we will use an invoker named `AuthenticationInvoker` that will perform the authentication check if the service bean passed is `OrderProcessImpl`.

The rest of the components to be developed are the same as shown in the *Developing custom interceptor section of this chapter*. We build and execute the code as instructed in the *Building and running the Order Process web service and interceptor* section. The folder structure will look like the following:

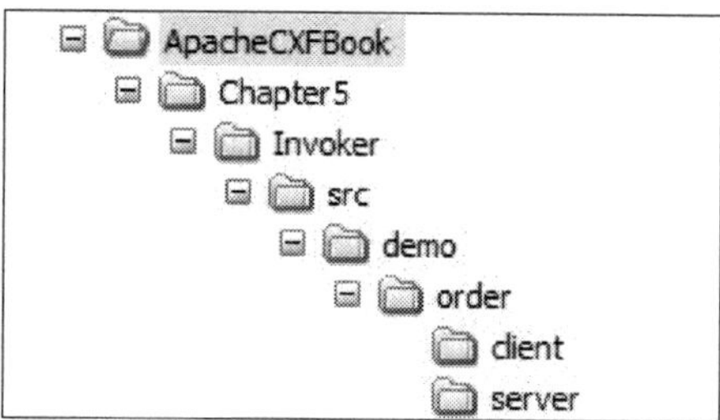

You start the server using the `ant server` command. Once the server is started, run the client by giving the `ant client` command. The client program will show the following output:

```
C:\ApacheCXFBook\Chapter5\Invoker>ant client
Buildfile: build.xml

maybe.generate.code:

compile:

build:

client:
     [java] OrderProcessClientHandler handleMessage invoked
     [java] Order approved; order ID is ORD1234
```

The server program will show the following output:

```
server:
     [java] Server ready...
     [java] userName retrieved from SOAP Header is John
     [java] password retrieved from SOAP Header is password
     [java] Authentication successful for John
     [java] Processed order...
     [java] Server exiting
```

The previous screenshot shows successful authentication.

Summary

The chapter introduced you to the concept of Interceptors that enables you to process the message in transit. One can process the message before the request to the service and after the response from the service. You learned the significance of the interceptor chain and phase. You also learned how to develop a custom SOAP interceptor that intercepts a SOAP message and manipulates the header. The chapter briefed you about the concept of Features, which are components, offered by CXF that can be used directly instead of interceptors. Finally, you learned to develop Invokers that can be used to control the service method execution.

6
Developing RESTful Services with CXF

Web services have become a standard way to achieve interoperability between systems. There are two main approaches for developing web services; one is by using the **Simple Object Access Protocol** (**SOAP**) and the other is by using the **Representational State Transfer** (**REST**) architecture style.

In earlier chapters, we looked at how to develop SOAP-based web services using CXF and JAX-WS support. Developing SOAP-based web services requires various contracts to be defined and negotiated between the provider and consumer, such as using a **Web Service Description Language** (**WSDL**) for describing the message, adhering to various web service specifications (WS Specifications like WS-Security), and choosing a document-literal or RPC style for web service communication.

Services built using the REST architecture style (termed as RESTful services) encapsulate data in a simple XML form and transport it over HTTP just like a web page request to the web server. This simplifies the development of web services without imposing overheads caused by the SOAP-based development approach. RESTFul web services are particularly useful when it is only necessary to transmit and receive simple XML messages.

In this chapter we will introduce the RESTful style of developing web services and look at how to develop RESTful services using the CXF framework. We will cover the following topics in the chapter:

- Overview of REST and RESTful services
- Java API for RESTful services
- CXF JAX-RS implementation
- Developing end-to-end RESTful services using CXF JAX-RS implementation

For a list of web service specifications, refer to the following URL:
`http://www.oasis-open.org/committees/tc_cat.php?cat=ws`

Overview of REST and RESTful services

REST stands for Representational State Transfer. REST is neither a technology nor a standard; it's an architectural style, a set of guidelines for exposing resources over the web. The REST architecture style is related to a resource, which is a representation identified by a **Uniform Resource Indicator** (**URI**) as described at `http://cxf.soaweb.co.in/book`. The resource can be any piece of information such as Book, Order, Customer, Employee, and so on. The client queries or updates the resource through the URI by exchanging representations of the resource. The representations contain actual information in a format such as HTML, XML, or **JavaScript Object Notation** (**JSON**) that is accepted by the resource. The client needs to be aware of the representation returned by the client. Usually the client specifies which representations it wants, like `http://cxf.soaweb.co.in/index.html` and the server returns the required resource, for instance, the required page with HTML content. All resources share a uniform interface for the transfer of state between client and resource. All the information required to process a request on a resource is contained within the request itself, thereby making the interaction stateless.

The World Wide Web is a classic example of REST architecture style. As implemented on the World Wide Web, URIs identify the resources (`http://cxf.soaweb.co.in/book`), and HTTP is the protocol by which resources are accessed. HTTP provides a uniform interface and a set of methods to manipulate the resource. A client program, like a web browser, can access, update, add, or remove a web resource through URI using various HTTP methods. HTTP provides standard methods such as `GET`, `POST`, `PUT`, `DELETE`, `HEAD`, `TRACE`, and `Options`. Each of these methods represents actions that can be performed on the resource. For instance, the `HTTP GET` is used for retrieving the information only and should never change the resource state, while methods like `PUT`, `POST`, `DELETE` influence a state change in its representation.

Web services built using the principles of REST architecture are termed as RESTful web services. Web services developed using the REST approach are viewed as resources and identified by their URI. The web service exposes the set of operations using standard HTTP methods like `GET` or `POST`. The web service clients invoke one of the methods defined on the resources using the URI over the HTTP protocol.

The following is an example of a RESTful service, which provides employee details within a department and how clients can access the service.

URI for the RESTful service—`http://<host>/department/deptname/employee`:

- `GET`—returns a list of employees in a department
- `POST`—creates an employee record in a department
- `DELETE`—deletes an employee record in a department

URI for the RESTful service—`http://<host>/department/deptname/employee/naveen`:

- `GET`—returns information about an employee naveen
- `PUT`—updates information about the employee naveen
- `DELETE`—deletes information about the employee naveen

> The `PUT` method also creates a new resource, if there is none available. If a resource exists, then `PUT` will overwrite it. The Sequence of `PUT` requests will keep updating or overwriting the last resource and therefore it is termed as *idempotent*. `POST` on the other hand will always create a new resource. For instance, if an amount transferred is being initiated via a POST request using a browser and the user inadvertently clicked the initiate transfer button again, you might end up having the amount transferred twice.

In the above example, the resource being exposed is an `employee` object. The `employee` object is represented by the URI `/employee`. Every employee's information is retrieved by appending an identifier to the employee such as `/employee/naveen`. The HTTP methods `GET`, `POST`, `PUT`, and `DELETE` internally map to the operations that need to be carried out on the employee object.

The following is an example of a POST request for `http://<host>/department/deptname/employee`

```
POST /department/deptname/employee HTTP/1.1
Content-Type: */*
Accept: application/xml
User-Agent: Apache CXF 2.2.2
Cache-Control: no-cache
Pragma: no-cache
Host: 127.0.0.1:9001
<employee><firstname>rajeev</firstname><lastname>hathi</lastname>
<dob>10/26/78</dob></employee>
```

As you can see from the above example, the request is a plain XML message over the HTTP protocol. The HTTP header method `POST` specifies that the request is a POST request.

Data supported by the RESTful web service is normally XML, but it can support other widely used formats like JavaScript Object Notation (JSON). The `Content-Type` MIME tag associated with HTTP headers specifies the format of the message, for instance `application/json` specifies the JSON message format, while `application/xml` defines the XML format. The `Accept` tag specifies the format of the message accepted by the client, which in this case is `application/xml`. The format of the message is the representation of the resource that we discussed in the REST overview section. We will look at how to set the `Content-Type` and `Accept` tag when we deal with the HTTP format for executing the sample application.

Java API for RESTful services

In the earlier example, we looked at the employee HTTP POST request. If we need to provide an implementation for realizing the employee HTTP request, we carry out the following steps:

- Identify whether it's an HTTP POST request.
- Convert the XML content associated with HTTP POST request into the required format expected by your implementation, for instance a Java object.
- Perform the required operation, for instance insert the employee object in the database.
- Convert the response back into an HTTP format, for instance set the HTTP Status as 200 denoting a successful response and convert the response into the required format (XML or JSON), and set it in the HTTP body.

Based on your requirements, you need to provide an implementation for all HTTP methods, for instance GET, PUT, and DELETE. Don't you think it would be good to have a standard way for developing RESTful services in Java and simplify the creation of RESTFul services? That's where the **Java API for RESTful Web services (JAX-RS)** specification comes in with the aim of simplifying RESTful services development.

Java API for RESTful Web services (JAX-RS) is a specification that determines the semantics to create web services according to the Representational State Transfer (REST) architectural style. JAX-RS uses annotations for implementing RESTful web services based on HTTP. You use the annotations on Plain Old Java objects (POJO) to expose it as a RESTful resource. The classes are annotated with the request made by the URI, for instance `/employee` and methods on the POJO define what request (or content type) the class or methods accept and what HTTP methods the class or methods support (such as `GET` and `POST`).

At runtime, the framework that implements the JAX-RS specification is responsible for invoking the right Java implementation by mapping the HTTP request to one of the RESTful Java resource methods that satisfies the request. The JAX-RS specification provides an algorithm to match an HTTP request to one of the resource methods that can be implemented by the runtime framework which implements the JAX-RS specification. The basis of the algorithm is to determine the `Java Resource` class and method based on the HTTP URI of the request (for instance `/employee`), the content type (for instance `application/xml`), and HTTP method (for instance `GET`).

The JAX-RS specification provides the following goals:

- POJO-centric

  The JAX-RS API provides a set of annotations and associated classes/interfaces that can be used with POJOs in order to expose them as RESTful resources.
- HTTP-centric

  As RESTful resources are exposed over HTTP, the specification provides clear mapping between HTTP Protocol and the corresponding JAX-RS API classes, methods, and guidelines on how to match the HTTP request to the resource class and method.
- Format independence

  The API provides a pluggable mechanism to allow HTTP content type to be added in a standard manner. For example, application/xml is one of the HTTP content types and, based on the content type, the RESTful resources should have a mechanism to serve the request.
- Container independence

  The application developed using JAX-RS should be able to run in any container. The specification defines a standard mechanism on how to deploy an application using JAX-RS APIs.
- Inclusion in the Java Enterprise Edition container

  The specification defines how RESTful resources can be hosted in a Java EE 6 container and leverage the capabilities offered by the container.

[For more about the JAX-RS specification, refer to the JSR website at `http://jcp.org/en/jsr/detail?id=311`]

CXF JAX-RS implementation

CXF provides an implementation of the JAX-RS 1.0 specification along with various features that assist developers in building enterprise-based RESTful services.

The following are the various features offered by the CXF framework for creating RESTful services:

- Spring Integration

  The Spring framework has become the de facto framework for building Enterprise Java applications. CXF provides integration with the Spring framework, which simplifies configuration and deployment of RESTful applications. Spring provides dependency injection which promotes loose coupling and provides various services to POJO like declarative transaction management. All the capabilities provided by Spring can be leveraged when developing RESTful POJO-based applications using CXF.

The Appendix B *Getting Started with Spring framework* chapter provides an introduction to the Spring framework and the Spring IoC container.

- Pluggable data binding

  Data binding is about mapping the HTTP request, for instance JSON or XML over HTTP, to the required Java objects which your implementation expects. Similarly, the response from the Java implementation needs to be mapped to the required format, for eample XML or JSON format, before sending the response over HTTP. CXF handles this mapping transparently behind the scenes by providing data binding components. CXF supports various data binding mechanisms such as JAXB, JSON, XMLBean, and Aegis. CXF allows you to specify the binding mechanism declaratively.

- Client API

  The JAX RS specification does not provide client side APIs for invoking a JAX-RS enabled REST service. CXF simplifies this by providing Client APIs to invoke RESTful services which can also be configured using the Spring dependency framework.

- Security

  Applications built using CXF JAX-RS implementation can leverage Spring framework features like declarative security to restrict a resource class and methods access based on application requirements, instead of handling the security requirements programmatically.

- Filters

  Filters are used to perform pre processing or post processing of messages. CXF provides an ability to create and configure filters for inspecting the message, logging the message, and modifying the request or response based on the application requirements.

CXF also allows developers to create RESTful services using JAX-WS Provider and Dispatch APIs. We discussed JAX-WS Dispatch and Dispatcher APIs in Chapter 3, where provider and consumer use raw XML for communication. Similarly, you can use JAX-WS Provider and Dispatch APIs to create RESTful services which use XML as the data format. CXF ships an example in the `samples/restful` folder of the distribution of how to create RESTful services using JAX-WS Provider and Dispatch APIs. In this chapter we will focus only on how to build RESTful services using the CXF JAX-RS implementation.

Before we study closely CXF based RESTful services development, we will look at an overview of the example called Book Shop application that we will build in this chapter.

Developing end-to-end RESTful services using CXF JAX-RS implementation

In this section we will develop a RESTful service that will enable us to perform CRUD operations using JAX-RS implementation. We will look at a case study of a Book Shop application.

The Book Shop application is an online application which provides categorization of technology books such as Java or .NET. The Book Shop application lets the administrator create new categories for adding books, modifying an existing category, getting a particularly category, or deleting a category. Once a categorization exists, the application provides the ability to add books and associate it with the respective category.

For simplicity we will look at the following examples:

- Creating a category
- Updating a category
- Deleting a category
- Getting a list of categories
- Getting a specific category
- Adding books to a category
- Getting a list of books associated with a category

The application exposes these functions over the web by using the RESTful style using some URI. The client application interacts with the book shop application by sending an XML request over HTTP. In next chapter we will look at how the Book Shop application provides supports for the JSON format.

Developing the RESTful service

To develop the RESTful service, we typically perform the following steps:

- Create Java data objects for Request and Response.
- Provide Binding for the `Request` and `Response` objects
- Create the `Implementation` class and annotate the `Implementation` class with JAX-RS annotations to create a RESTful implementation
- Unit test the RESTful service
- Create clients to invoke various methods of the RESTful service
- Deploy the RESTful service in a container

The source code of this chapter is available in the `chapter6/restapp` folder of the source code distribution. Refer to Appendix *Getting Ready with the Code Examples* for detailed instructions on how to download the source code from the Packt site.

Creating Java data objects for Request and Response

For the Book Shop application we create two Request data objects called `Category` and `Book`. The `Category` object contains the category information, whereas `Book` contains book information.

We will now develop the `Category` object. We will name this implementation class as `Category`. The following is the code listing of the `Category.java` object.

```
package demo.restful;

import java.util.Collection;

import javax.xml.bind.annotation.XmlRootElement;

@XmlRootElement(name = "Category")
public class Category {

   private String categoryId;

   private String categoryName;
```

```
        private Collection<Book> books;

        public String getCategoryId() {
            return categoryId;
        }

        public void setCategoryId(String categoryId) {
            this.categoryId = categoryId;
        }

        public String getCategoryName() {
            return categoryName;
        }

        public void setCategoryName(String categoryName) {
            this.categoryName = categoryName;
        }

        public Collection<Book> getBooks() {
            return books;
        }

        public void setBooks(Collection<Book> books) {
            this.books = books;
        }
    }
```

As you can see above, we have added an annotation `@XmlRootElement` to the Java class. We will look at this annotation in detail in the next section.

The `Category` object holds books references, which is modeled as a collection in the `Category` object.

We will now develop the `Book` object. We will name this implementation class as `Book`. The following is the code listing of the `Book.java` object:

```
    package demo.restful;

    import javax.xml.bind.annotation.XmlRootElement;

    @XmlRootElement(name = "Book")
    public class Book {

        private String bookId;

        private String bookISBNnumber;

        private String bookName;

        //Let assume one author only
        private String author;

        public String getBookId() {
            return bookId;
        }
```

```
    public void setBookId(String bookId) {
        this.bookId = bookId;
    }
    public String getBookISBNnumber() {
        return bookISBNnumber;
    }
    public void setBookISBNnumber(String bookISBNnumber) {
        this.bookISBNnumber = bookISBNnumber;
    }
    public String getBookName() {
        return bookName;
    }
    public void setBookName(String bookName) {
        this.bookName = bookName;
    }
    public String getAuthor() {
        return author;
    }
    public void setAuthor(String author) {
        this.author = author;
    }
}
```

We will use the same Request data object for Response. For Response, we would send the `response` object back along with the HTTP status. We will look into this when implementing the service.

Providing binding for the Request and Response data objects

The Request and Response data objects need to be serialized in the required format, such as XML or JSON, for communicating between a RESTful service and a client. To serialize the data objects, you need to use one of the data binding components or create your own custom data binding components, which create a mapping between Java objects and XML (or the required format).

CXF uses **JAXB** as the default data binding component. JAXB uses annotations to define the mapping between Java objects and XML.

The `@XmlRootElement` annotations associated with `Category` class map the `Category` class to an XML root element. The attributes contained within the `Category` object by default are mapped to `@XmlElement`. The `@XmlElement` annotations are used to define elements within the XML. The `@XmlRootElement` and `@XmlElement` annotations allow you to customize the namespace and name of the XML element. If no customizations are provided, the JAXB runtime by default would use the same name for the attribute as the XML element. CXF handles this mapping of Java objects to XML transparently behind the scenes.

The following is an XML Request that maps to the `Category` data object:

```
<?xml version="1.0" encoding="UTF-8" standalone="yes"?>
<Category>
<categoryName>Microsoft NET</categoryName>
<categoryId>002</categoryId>
<books><author>NaveenBalani</author>
<bookISBNnumber>ISB003</bookISBNnumber>
<bookId>003</bookId>
<bookName>Spring NET Series</bookName>
</books>
</Category>
```

Developing the implementation class

We will now develop the implementation class to realize our Book shop application. We will name this implementation class `CategoryService`.

The following code illustrates the service implementation class `CategoryService.java`.

```
package demo.restful;

//JAX-RS Imports
import javax.ws.rs.Consumes;
import javax.ws.rs.DELETE;
import javax.ws.rs.GET;
import javax.ws.rs.POST;
import javax.ws.rs.PUT;
import javax.ws.rs.Path;
import javax.ws.rs.PathParam;
import javax.ws.rs.Produces;
import javax.ws.rs.core.Response;
import javax.ws.rs.core.Response.Status;

/*
 * CategoryService class.
```

```
    */
   @Path("/categoryservice")
   @Produces("application/xml")
   public class CategoryService {

      @GET
      @Path("/category/{id}")
      public Category getCategory(@PathParam("id") String id) {

         return null;
      }

      @POST
      @Path("/category")
      @Consumes("application/xml")
      public void addCategory(Category category) {

      }

      @DELETE
      @Path("/category/{id}")
      public void deleteCategory(@PathParam("id") String id) {

      }

      @PUT
       @Path("/category")
      public void updateCategory(Category category) {

      }

      @POST
      @Path("/category/book")
      @Consumes("application/xml")
      public void addBooks(Category category) {

      }

      @GET
      @Path("/category/{id}/books")
      @Consumes("application/xml")
      public void getBooks(@PathParam("id") String id) {

      }
   }
```

As we can see from the above code, our implementation class `CategoryService` is pretty straightforward. It defines methods to add a category, delete a category, get a category, update a category, add books to a category, and get the books associated with a category.

The `CategoryService` also had various annotations defined on the class and methods definition. These annotations are JAX-RS annotations, which are used at runtime to create the RESTful service resource. In JAX-RS terminology, a class which has the JAX-RS annotations defined is termed as a **Resource** class.

The `CategoryService` defines the `@Path` and `@Produces` annotations above the class declaration. The `@Path` annotation defines the URI path that a resource class or class method will serve a request for. For example, for the `CategoryService`, we have defined `@Path("/categoryservice")`, which means the URI request, such as `http://localhost:9080/restapp/categoryservice`, would be served by the `CategoryService`.

The `@Produces` annotation defines the content type that the method or resource class can produce and send back to the client. You can define the `@Produces` annotation on a class as well as methods, in which case, the method level annotations would override class annotations. If `@Produces` annotation is not specified, then the runtime container will assume that any content type can be produced. For the `CategoryService` class, we have defined `@Produces("application/xml")` annotation, which implies that the `CategoryService` produces only `application/xml`.

Each method in `CategoryService` is mapped to the HTTP methods that they support. In JAX-RS terminology, the HTTP methods annotations, that is, `@GET` and `@POST` are called **Request Method Designators**, while the methods of a resource class annotated with a request method designator are termed as **Resource methods**.

The Resource class, such as `CategoryService`, which has a `@Path` annotation defined, is termed as a `Root Resource` class. The `Root Resource` class provides **Request Method Designators to process the request.** The following table summarizes the Request Method Designators for `CategoryService` methods:

Resource Method	Request Method Designators	Description
`getCategory`	`@GET`	The `@GET` annotation indicates that the annotated method responds to HTTP GET requests.
`addCategory`	`@POST`	The `@POST` annotation indicates that the annotated method responds to HTTP POST requests.
`deleteCategory`	`@DELETE`	The `@DELETE` annotation indicates that the annotated method responds to HTTP DELETE requests.

Resource Method	Request Method Designators	Description
`updateCategory`	`@PUT`	The `@PUT` annotation indicates that the annotated method responds to HTTP PUT requests. The PUT request would typically update the resource.
`addBooks`	`@POST`	The `@POST` annotation indicates that the annotated method responds to HTTP POST requests
`getBooks`	`@GET`	The `@GET` annotation indicates that the annotated method responds to HTTP GET requests

Associated with each method are the `@Produce` annotations which determine what content type they produce, and the `@Path` attribute identifies the URI that would be served by the method. The `@Path` may also include variables embedded in the URI, like `/category/{id}`, as in the case of the `getCategory()` method. While resolving the URI served by the method, the `@Path` attribute associated with the class would also be taken into consideration. If the method doesn't specify a `@Path` annotation, it's inherited from a class.

In JAX-RS terminology, URI path templates are URIs with zero or more embedded parameters within the URI syntax. The `/category/{id}` is an example of the URI path template.

For instance, if the HTTP GET request URL is `http://localhost:9080/restapp/categoryservice/category/001`, then the container will map this request to `CategoryService` class as it provides `@Path` annotation with `/categoryservice` value and the method that would be invoked would be `getCategory` as it specifies the `@Path` annotation with value ("`/category/{id}`"), which matches any URI request starting with `/category/{id}` , where `{id}` is some value , like `001`.

The following table summarizes the URI exposed by each method and examples of HTTP URI that would invoke the resource method:

Resource Method	Request Method Designators	@Path	Example of a HTTP URI request that matches the resource method
getCategory	@GET	/category/{id}	http://localhost:9080/restapp/categoryservice/category/001
addCategory	@POST	/category	http://localhost:9080/restapp/categoryservice/category
deleteCategory	@DELETE	/category/{id}	http://localhost:9080/restapp/categoryservice/category/001
updateCategory	@PUT	/category	http://localhost:9080/restapp/categoryservice/category
addBooks	@POST	/category/book	http://localhost:9080/restapp/categoryservice/category/book
getBooks	@GET	/category/{id"}/books	http://localhost:9080/restapp/categoryservice/category/001/books

The path used for addBooks is `/category/book`. We could have also used `/category/{id}/book` to add books associated with Category. We choose `/category/book` as we might want to add a category along with books in one request instead of firing two requests `addCategory()` followed by `addBooks()`.

We will next look at the `@PathParam` annotation. The `@PathParam` annotation is used to map a given URI Path template variable to the method parameter. For instance, if you look at the `getCategory()` method, as shown below, its defines the `@PathParam("id")` for `@Path ("/category/{id}")`

```
@Path("/category/{id}")
public Category getCategory(@PathParam("id") String id)
```

Any URI request such as `/category/nnn`, for instance, `/category/001`, would map the value `001` to `String id`, which essentially means the String ID now has the value `001`.

Adding Data Access logic to the implementation class

The implementation class `CategoryService` needs to talk to a data store, like the database or flat files for accessing the Category and Books information. To do this we create a Data Access object and provide a dummy implementation. Creating a Data Access object is a common way to access the application's data store.

We will now develop the Data Access object. We will name this implementation class as `CategoryDAO`.

Refer to `http://java.sun.com/blueprints/corej2eepatterns/Patterns/DataAccessObject.html` for more information on the Data Access object pattern.

The following code illustrates the `CategoryDAO.java`:

```
package demo.restful;

import java.util.ArrayList;
import java.util.Collection;
import java.util.HashMap;
import java.util.Map;

/*
 * DataAcess object for performing CRUD operations.
 * Dummy implementation.
 */
public class CategoryDAO {
   private static Map<String, Category> categoryMap =
   new HashMap<String, Category>();
   private static Map<String, Collection<Book>> bookMap =
   new HashMap<String, Collection<Book>>();

   static {
         //Populate some static data
      Category category1 = new Category();
      category1.setCategoryId("001");
      category1.setCategoryName("Java");
      categoryMap.put(category1.getCategoryId(), category1);

      Book book1 = new Book();
      book1.setAuthor("Naveen Balani");
      book1.setBookName("Spring Series");
      book1.setBookId("001");
      book1.setBookISBNnumber("ISB001");

      Book book2 = new Book();
      book2.setAuthor("Rajeev Hathi");
      book2.setBookName("CXF Series");
```

```
        book2.setBookId("002");
        book2.setBookISBNnumber("ISB002");

        Collection<Book> booksList = new ArrayList<Book>();
        booksList.add(book1);
        booksList.add(book2);

        bookMap.put(category1.getCategoryId(), booksList);
    }

    public void addCategory(Category category) {
        categoryMap.put(category.getCategoryId(), category);
    }

    //Add Books associated with the Category
    public void addBook(Category category) {
        bookMap.put(category.getCategoryId(), category.getBooks());
    }

    public Collection<Book> getBooks(String categoryId) {
        return bookMap.get(categoryId);
    }

    public Category getCategory(String id) {
        Category cat = null;
        //Dummy implementation to return a new copy of category to
        //avoid getting overridden by service
        if(categoryMap.get(id) != null) {
        cat = new Category();
        cat.setCategoryId(categoryMap.get(id).getCategoryId());
        cat.setCategoryName(categoryMap.get(id).getCategoryName());
        }
        return cat;
     }


    public void deleteCategory(String id) {
        categoryMap.remove(id);
        // Remove association of books
        bookMap.remove(id);
    }

    public void updateCategory(Category category) {
        categoryMap.put(category.getCategoryId(), category);
    }
}
```

As you can see in the above code listing, we have created CRUD operations (Create, Read, Update, Delete) for the `Category` object. For simplicity, we have created two Static maps, `categoryMap` and `booksMap`, which hold dummy `Category` and `Book` objects. In a real implementation scenario, you would typically access the database to get this information.

Next, we integrate the `CategoryDAO` implementation class with the `CategoryService`. The code listing below provides the revised `CatalogService` implementation:

```
package demo.restful;

//JAX-RS Imports
import javax.ws.rs.Consumes;
import javax.ws.rs.DELETE;
import javax.ws.rs.GET;
import javax.ws.rs.POST;
import javax.ws.rs.PUT;
import javax.ws.rs.Path;
import javax.ws.rs.PathParam;
import javax.ws.rs.Produces;

/*
 * CategoryService class - Add/Removes category for books
 */

@Path("/categoryservice")
@Produces("application/xml")
public class CategoryService {

   public CategoryDAO getCategoryDAO() {
      return categoryDAO;
   }

   //Wired using Spring
public void setCategoryDAO(CategoryDAO categoryDAO) {
      this.categoryDAO = categoryDAO;
   }

   @GET
   @Path("/category/{id}")
   public Category getCategory(@PathParam("id") String id) {

   System.out.println("getCategory called with category id: "
   + id);

   Category cat = (Category) getCategoryDAO().getCategory(id);

   return cat;
   }

   @POST
```

```
@Path("/category")
@Consumes("application/xml")
public void addCategory(Category category) {
System.out.println("addCategory called");
Category cat = (Category) getCategoryDAO().getCategory(
        category.getCategoryId());
}
@DELETE
@Path("/category/{id}")
public void deleteCategory(@PathParam("id") String id) {
System.out.println("deleteCategory with category id : " +
id);
getCategoryDAO().deleteCategory(id);
}
@PUT
@Path("/category")
public void updateCategory(Category category) {
System.out.println("updateCategory with category id : "
        + category.getCategoryId());
getCategoryDAO().updateCategory(category);
}
@POST
@Path("/category/book")
@Consumes("application/xml")
public void addBooks(Category category) {
System.out.println("addBooks with category id : "
        + category.getCategoryId());
Category cat = (Category) getCategoryDAO().getCategory(
        category.getCategoryId());
getCategoryDAO().addBook(category);
}
@GET
@Path("/category/{id}/books")
@Consumes("application/xml")
public Category getBooks(@PathParam("id") String id) {
System.out.println("getBooks called with category id : "+
id);
Category cat = (Category) getCategoryDAO().getCategory(id);
```

```
        cat.setBooks(getCategoryDAO().getBooks(id));

        return cat;
        }
    }
```

The code highlighted above shows the changes made to the `CategoryService`. As you can see, each method implementation uses the `CategoryDAO` object to carry out the corresponding operation. We don't create an instance of the `CategoryDAO` object. Instead, the reference for the `CategoryDAO` object is injected through the Spring configuration file. Since CXF provides integration with the Spring framework, you can leverage the dependency injection capability of Spring in your applications.

The following is the code snippet for the Spring configuration file, named `restapp.xml` and used by the application:

```
<?xml version="1.0" encoding="UTF-8"?>
<beans xmlns="http://www.springframework.org/schema/beans"
      xmlns:xsi="http://www.w3.org/2001/XMLSchema-instance"
      xsi:schemaLocation="http://www.springframework.org/schema/beans
      http://www.springframework.org/schema/beans/
      spring-beans-2.0.xsd">

   <bean id="categoryService" class="demo.restful.CategoryService">
      <property name="categoryDAO">
         <ref bean="categoryDAO" />
      </property>
   </bean>


   <bean id="categoryDAO" class="demo.restful.CategoryDAO">
       <!--  wire dependency-->
    </bean>
```

As you can see above, we have defined the `categoryDAO` bean and wired the reference to the `categoryService` bean. Our client will load this file at the first step. The instantiation of the bean and wiring of the bean is handled by the Spring framework.

> If you are not familiar with Spring framework, then refer to the Appendix B *Getting Started with Spring framework* chapter on how to create a sample application using the Spring framework and Spring IoC container.

Creating the client

JAX-RS doesn't provide a standard approach for creating RESTful clients. The CXF framework provides two approaches for creating clients. Each of these approaches lets you configure clients using Spring.

- Proxy-based API

  Proxy-based API allows you to use the resource classes and interfaces that you have created for RESTful service implementation. Proxy shields the client from creating the HTTP request manually and inspects the RESTful service implementation to create the HTTP request. To use the proxy-based API approach, you need to use the `org.apache.cxf.jaxrs.client.JAXRSClientFactory` class and pass the RESTful service implementation class as the input to create a proxy. Once the proxy is created, any method that you invoke on proxy would invoke the required RESTFul service implementation. The next code snippet explains how to use the `JAXRSClientFactory` to create a proxy to `CategoryService`. Once we get a handle to the proxy, we can than call the corresponding methods on it, for instance `getBooks()` method as shown below:

  ```
  CategoryService store = JAXRSClientFactory.create("http://
  localhost:9000", CategoryService.class);
  //Makes remote call to Category RESTFul service
  store.getBooks("001");
  ```

- HTTP centric clients

  HTTP centric clients use the `org.apache.cxf.jaxrs.client.WebClient` instances to invoke the RESTful service. We will use the HTTP-centric approach to communicate with the `CategoryService` RESFTful service and look into the APIs in detail when creating the client.

We will now develop the client which will invoke the `CategoryService` RESTful service. We will name this implementation class as `CategoryServiceClient`.

The following code illustrates the class `CategoryServiceClient.java`:

```
package demo.restful.client;

import java.util.Iterator;

import org.apache.cxf.jaxrs.client.WebClient;

import demo.restful.Book;
import demo.restful.Category;

public class CategoryServiceClient {

   public static void main(String[] args) {

      // Service instance
```

```
        WebClient client = WebClient.create("http://localhost:9000/");
        Category category = client.path("categoryservice/category/001").
        accept(
              "application/xml").get(Category.class);
        System.out.println("Category details from REST service.");
        System.out.println("Category Name " +
        category.getCategoryName());
        System.out.println("Category Id " + category.getCategoryId());
        System.out.println("Book details for Category "+
        category.getCategoryId() + " from REST service");

        String bookString = "categoryservice/category/"+
        category.getCategoryId() + "/books";
        WebClient clientBook = WebClient.create
        ("http://localhost:9000/");
        Category categoryBooks = clientBook.path(
              bookString).accept("application/xml")
              .get(Category.class);

        Iterator<Book> iterator = categoryBooks.getBooks().iterator();
        while (iterator.hasNext()) {
           Book book = iterator.next();
           System.out.println("Book Name " + book.getBookName());
           System.out.println("Book ISBN " + book.getBookISBNnumber());
           System.out.println("Book ID " + book.getBookId());
           System.out.println("Book Author " + book.getAuthor());

        }
    }
}
```

The code carries out the following steps:

1. We start off by creating an instance of `WebClient`, by passing the base URI where the RESTful service is running.

   ```
   WebClient client = WebClient.create("http://localhost:9000/");
   ```

2. Next, we specify the URI path that we want to invoke, which updates the base URI, so the new URI becomes `http://localhost:9000/categoryservice/category/001`. The `accept` method on the client sets the Accept header for HTTP request and `get` method invokes the above URI. The response received from the RESTful service is mapped to the `Category` object.

   ```
   Category category = client.path("categoryservice/category/001").
   accept("application/xml").get(Category.class);
   ```

3. After getting the `Category` object from RESTFul service, we then create one more GET request to get books associated with the category. We create a URI as `http://localhost:9000/ categoryservice/category/001/books` and invoke the URI by calling the `get` method, and the response from the RESTful service is mapped to the `Category` object.

   ```
   String bookString = "categoryservice/category/"+
   category.getCategoryId() + "/books";
          WebClient clientBook = WebClient.create
          ("http://localhost:9000/");
          Category categoryBooks = clientBook.path(
                 bookString).accept("application/xml").
                 get(Category.class);
   ```

4. Next, we print out the book information associated with the category, as shown below:

   ```
   Iterator<Book> iterator = categoryBooks.getBooks().iterator();
          while (iterator.hasNext()) {
             Book book = iterator.next();
             System.out.println("Book Name " + book.getBookName());
             System.out.println("Book ISBN " + book.
             getBookISBNnumber());
             System.out.println("Book ID " + book.getBookId());
             System.out.println("Book Author " + book.getAuthor());
          }
   ```

   We have thus implemented a Client that invokes a GET operation for the `getCategory()` and `getBooks()` resource method. In the next chapter we will test the remaining resource methods and look at the HTTP request and response format which flows between the client and the RESTFul service.

Making RESTful service available over HTTP

Before testing the client, we need to make the `CategoryService` available over HTTP. The simplest way of doing this is by using the CXF `org.apache.cxf.jaxrs.JAXRSServerFactoryBean` class, which exposes the `CategoryService` over HTTP without the overhead of deploying the `CategoryService` in a web container. This is really helpful if you need to quickly test out your RESTful service and clients and can include this as part of your unit test before deploying the RESTful service in a web container. Deploying in a web container would require you to perform extra steps such as creating the web descriptor, JAX-RS configurations, and packaging your application as a web archive. In the next chapter we will look at these steps in detail when we will deploy the `CategoryService` in a web container.

We will now look at how to make the `CategoryService` available over HTTP using the CXF `JAXRSServerFactoryBean` class. We will name the class `CategoryServerStart`.

The following code listing shows the `CategoryServerStart.java` object:

```
package demo.restful.client;

import java.io.BufferedReader;
import java.io.IOException;
import java.io.InputStreamReader;
import org.apache.cxf.jaxrs.JAXRSServerFactoryBean;
import org.springframework.context.support.
ClassPathXmlApplicationContext;
import demo.restful.Category;
import demo.restful.CategoryService;

public class CategoryServerStart {

    public static void main(String[] args) {


            ClassPathXmlApplicationContext appContext = new
            ClassPathXmlApplicationContext(new String[] {
             "/demo/restful/restapp.xml"
           });

            CategoryService categoryService = (CategoryService)
        appContext.getBean("categoryService");

        // Service instance

        JAXRSServerFactoryBean restServer = new
JAXRSServerFactoryBean();
        restServer.setResourceClasses(Category.class);
        restServer.setServiceBeans(categoryService);
        restServer.setAddress("http://localhost:9000/");
        restServer.create();
BufferedReader br = new BufferedReader(new InputStreamReader(System.
in));

        try {
            br.readLine();
        } catch (IOException e) {
        }
        System.out.println("Server Stopped");
        System.exit(0);

    }

}
```

The following steps are executed as part of the code:

1. We start off by loading the Spring configuration files through the Spring `ClassPathXmlApplicationContext` method.

```
ClassPathXmlApplicationContext appContext =
new ClassPathXmlApplicationContext(new String[] {
       "/demo/restful/restapp.xml"
      });
```

2. After the Spring configuration file is loaded, all the beans defined will be instantiated and the references will be wired. We then access the `categoryService` bean through the `getBean()` method.

```
CategoryService categoryService = (CategoryService)
   appContext.getBean("categoryService");
```

3. Next, we create the `JAXRSServerFactoryBean` instance. We set the service bean to `CategoryService` instance, and set the address where the `CategoryService` needs to be deployed, which is `http://localhost:9000`, and invoke the `create` method on the `JAXRSServerFactoryBean` instance. The `create` method creates an embedded jetty service instance and deploys the `CategoryService`. The server instance will run until you hit enter on the console where this java program is executing.

```
JAXRSServerFactoryBean restServer = new JAXRSServerFactoryBean();
      restServer.setResourceClasses(Category.class);
      restServer.setServiceBeans(categoryService);
      restServer.setAddress("http://localhost:9000/");
      restServer.create();
```

Now, let's run the program and see our code in action.

Running the program

Before running the program, we will organize the code so far developed in the appropriate folder structure. You can create the folder structure, as shown below, and put the components in the respective subfolders.

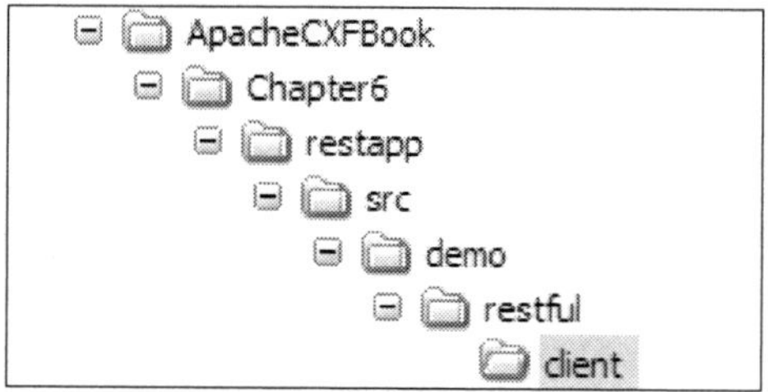

As you can see in previous screenshot, the `restapp` is the project folder for this chapter. The `restapp\src` is the location of our source code. Place the Java code into the respective package folders in the `restapp\src` folder and the Spring configuration file `restapp.xml` in the `src\demo\restful folder.`

Once the code is organized, we will build and deploy it in the Jetty embedded server. It will typically involve three steps:

- Building the code
- Deploying the code
- Executing the code

Building the code

Building the code means compiling the source java code. To build the code we will use the ANT tool. You need to create the CXF build scripts (`build.xml`) to build the code, as shown below. The `build.xml` the same as any build scripts shipped with CXF samples, but customized to our application. The build script for this example is provided in `Chapter6/restapp` folder. The following code illustrates the `build.xml` build script:

```
<?xml version="1.0" encoding="UTF-8"?>
<project name="CXF Book RESTFul App" default="build" basedir=".">
   <import file="common_build.xml"/>
    <target name="client" description=
    "run demo client" depends="build">
        <property name="param" value=""/>
        <cxfrun classname="demo.restful.client.CategoryServiceClient"
/>
    </target>
   <target name="server" description="run server" depends="build">
        <property name="param" value=""/>
        <cxfrun classname="demo.restful.client.CategoryServerStart" />
    </target>
    <property name="cxf.war.file.name" value="restapp"/>
      <target name="war" depends="build">
     <cxfwar filename="${cxf.war.file.name}.war" webxml=
     "webapp/WEB-INF/web.xml" />
    </target>
</project>
```

Alongside `build.xml`, you will also find `common_build.xml` which provides common CXF build functions. The `common_build.xml` is copied over from samples folder of Apache CXF distribution. Open the command prompt window, go to `restapp` folder, and run the **ant** command. It will build the code, and put the class files under the newly created `build` folder. The following screenshot shows the output generated on running the **ant** command:

```
Command Prompt
C:\ApacheCXFBook\Chapter6\restapp>ant
Buildfile: build.xml
    [mkdir] Created dir: C:\ApacheCXFBook\Chapter6\restapp\build
 [loadfile] Do not set property srcbuild.classpath as its length is 0.

maybe.generate.code:

compile:
    [mkdir] Created dir: C:\ApacheCXFBook\Chapter6\restapp\build\classes
    [mkdir] Created dir: C:\ApacheCXFBook\Chapter6\restapp\build\src
    [javac] Compiling 6 source files to C:\ApacheCXFBook\Chapter6\restapp\build\
classes

build:

BUILD SUCCESSFUL
Total time: 2 seconds
C:\ApacheCXFBook\Chapter6\restapp>
```

Deploying the code

After the code build is finished, we deploy it in the embedded jetty container for testing. To deploy our built code, navigate to the `restapp` folder and type the following command

```
ant server
```

This will execute the Java program `CategoryServerStart`, which starts the embedded jetty server, deploys the `CategoryService`, and makes it available over the URL `http://localhost:9000/catalogservice`

After running the above command, you will see the following output. Don't close this window as the server is running. After the client is invoked, you can hit enter on this console to stop the server.

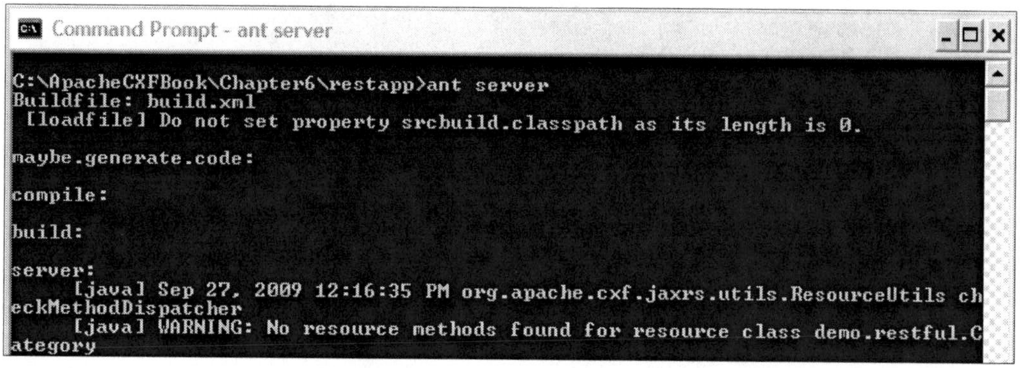

```
Command Prompt - ant server
C:\ApacheCXFBook\Chapter6\restapp>ant server
Buildfile: build.xml
 [loadfile] Do not set property srcbuild.classpath as its length is 0.

maybe.generate.code:

compile:

build:

server:
     [java] Sep 27, 2009 12:16:35 PM org.apache.cxf.jaxrs.utils.ResourceUtils ch
eckMethodDispatcher
     [java] WARNING: No resource methods found for resource class demo.restful.C
ategory
```

Executing the code

After the code deployment is finished, we are all set to run the Book Shop application. You execute the Java client program `CategoryServiceClient` to invoke the `CatalogService`. Run the client program by giving the following command on the command prompt window:

```
ant client
```

On executing this command, the `CategoryServiceClient` will invoke the `CategoryService getCategory` method using the URL `http://localhost:8080/categoryservice/category/001` followed by the `getBooks` method using the URL `http://localhost:8080/categoryservice/category/001/books` to get the books associated with the Category, as discussed in the *Creating the client* section. The following output will be printed on the console, which displays the category and book information for category ID `001`.

```
Command Prompt
C:\ApacheCXFBook\Chapter6\restapp>ant client
Buildfile: build.xml
 [loadfile] Do not set property srcbuild.classpath as its length is 0.

maybe.generate.code:

compile:

build:

client:
     [java] Category details from REST service.
     [java] Category Name Java
     [java] Category Id 001
     [java] Book details for Category 001 from REST service
     [java] Book Name Spring Series
     [java] Book ISBN ISB001
     [java] Book ID 001
     [java] Book Author Naveen Balani
     [java] Book Name CXF Series
     [java] Book ISBN ISB002
     [java] Book ID 002
     [java] Book Author Rajeev Hathi

BUILD SUCCESSFUL
Total time: 4 seconds
C:\ApacheCXFBook\Chapter6\restapp>
```

On the console where you executed the ant server, you will see the following response, denoting the `getCategory()` and `getBook()` request being executed for **category ID 001**.

```
server:
     [java] Sep 27, 2009 1:21:38 AM org.apache.cxf.jaxrs.utils.ResourceUtils che
ckMethodDispatcher
     [java] WARNING: No resource methods found for resource class demo.restful.C
ategory
     [java] getCategory called with category id: 001
     [java] getBooks called with category id : 001
```

You can also view the response of GET Category request in the browser by typing the URL `http://localhost:9000/categoryservice/category/001`. You will see the following response:

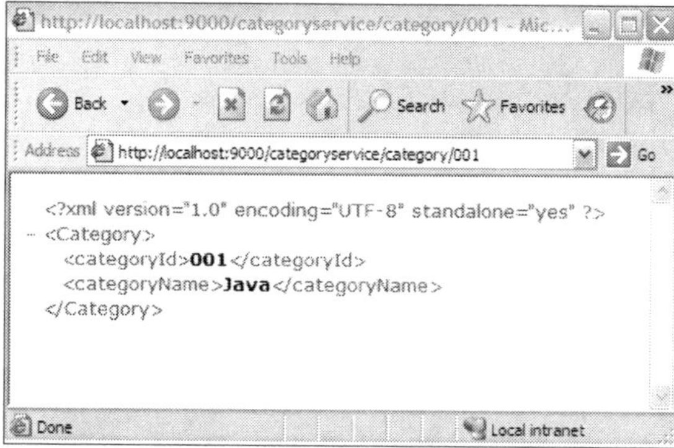

Similarly, to get the books' details for the category, type in URL `http://localhost:9000/categoryservice/category/001/books` in the browser, and you will see the following response:

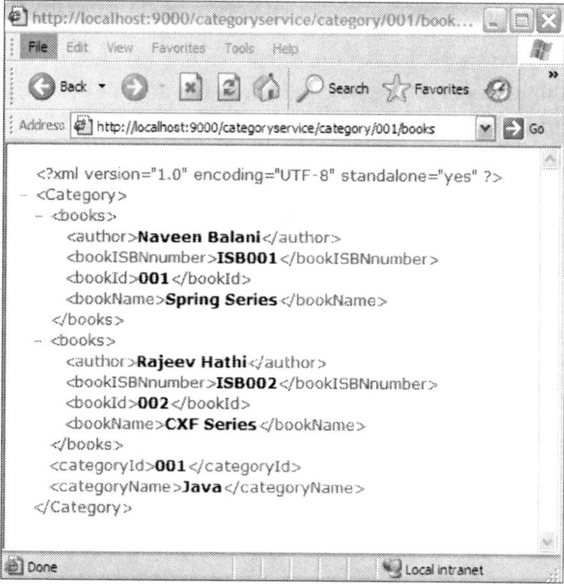

Thus we have successfully deployed and tested the RESTful service. In the next chapter we will look at how to deploy the Book Shop RESTful application in a Tomcat container and test out all the scenarios for the Book Shop application. With the RESTful service up and running, we next look at how to add exception handling to a RESTful service.

Adding exception handling to RESTful service

Let's take a scenario where a client sends a request to delete or update a category, and the category does not exist, so your implementation needs to return the correct error message back to the client.

To deal with exceptions, JAX-RS provides the `WebApplicationException`, which extends the Java `RuntimeException` class. The `WebApplicationException` can take an HTTP status code or `javax.ws.rs.core.Response` object as part of the constructor. The `Response` object can be used to set the entity information providing a user readable error message along with the HTTP status code.

Typically, exception handling for RESTful service would fall into one of the following categories:

- The implementation class can throw an unchecked `WebApplicationException` with the required HTTP Error code. The HTTP specification defines which HTTP response code should be used for unsuccessful requests, which can be interpreted by clients in a standard way. For example, Status code 4xx defines client error, such as Bad request, and 5xx defines the server request where server failed to fulfill a valid request.
- The implementation class can create a `javax.ws.rs.core.Response` object and send a custom error message to the client or send the required HTTP status code in the response.
- The implementation class can throw a checked exception, and you can wire an `Exception Resolver` implementation to convert the application exception to the `Response` object. The `ExceptionResolver` interface provides a contract for a provider that maps Java exception to a Response. For instance, if you are fetching information from the database, and a record does not exist, and your application throws a `RecordNotFound` exception, then you can map this exception to a `Response` object using your `ExceptionResolver` implementation. The `Response` object can be populated with a custom error message and sent back to the client, as mentioned in the second approach.

We will now modify the `CategoryService` class to add the exception handling capability. We use the first and second approach for exception handling to understand these concepts in detail. The following is the revised `CategoryService` class, we have only shown the code snippets which have changed.

```
package demo.restful;

//JAX-RS Imports ...

/*
 * CategoryService class - Add/Removes category for books
 */

@Path("/categoryservice")
@Produces("application/xml")
public class CategoryService{

    @GET
    @Path("/category/{id}")
    public Category getCategory(@PathParam("id") String id) {

        System.out.println("getCategory called with category id: " +
        id);

        Category cat = (Category) getCategoryDAO().getCategory(id);
        if (cat == null) {
            ResponseBuilder builder =
            Response.status(Status.BAD_REQUEST);
            builder.type("application/xml");
            builder.entity("<error>Category Not Found</error>");
            throw new WebApplicationException(builder.build());
        } else {
            return cat;
        }
    }

    @POST
    @Path("/category")
    @Consumes("application/xml")
    public Response addCategory(Category category) {

        System.out.println("addCategory called");

        Category cat = (Category) getCategoryDAO().getCategory(
                category.getCategoryId());

        if (cat != null) {
            return Response.status(Status.BAD_REQUEST).build();
        } else {
            getCategoryDAO().addCategory(category);
            return Response.ok(category).build();
```

```
        }
    }

    @DELETE
    @Path("/category/{id}")
    public Response deleteCategory(@PathParam("id") String id) {

        System.out.println("deleteCategory with category id : " + id);

        Category cat = (Category) getCategoryDAO().getCategory(id);
        if (cat == null) {
            return Response.status(Status.BAD_REQUEST).build();
        } else {
            getCategoryDAO().deleteCategory(id);
            return Response.ok().build();
        }
    }

    @PUT
    @Path("/category")
    public Response updateCategory(Category category) {

        System.out.println("updateCategory with category id : "
                + category.getCategoryId());

        Category cat = (Category) getCategoryDAO().getCategory(
                category.getCategoryId());
        if (cat == null) {
            return Response.status(Status.BAD_REQUEST).build();
        } else {
            getCategoryDAO().updateCategory(category);
            return Response.ok(category).build();
        }
    }

    @POST
    @Path("/category/book")
    @Consumes("application/xml")
    public Response addBooks(Category category) {

        System.out.println("addBooks with category id : "
                + category.getCategoryId());

        Category cat = (Category) getCategoryDAO().getCategory(
                category.getCategoryId());
        if (cat == null) {
            return Response.status(Status.NOT_FOUND).build();
        } else {
            getCategoryDAO().addBook(category);
            return Response.ok(category).build();
```

```
        }
    }
    @GET
    @Path("/category/{id}/books")
    @Consumes("application/xml")
    public Response getBooks(@PathParam("id") String id) {
        System.out.println("getBooks called with category id : " + id);
        Category cat = (Category) getCategoryDAO().getCategory(id);
        if (cat == null) {
            return Response.status(Status.NOT_FOUND).build();
        } else {
            cat.setBooks(getCategoryDAO().getBooks(id));
            return Response.ok(cat).build();
        }
    }
}
```

The code highlighted in the above code listing is the modification that we have made to add exception handling to the `CategoryService` implementation. The `getCategory` method uses the first approach, where we have used a `javax.ws.rs.core.Response.ResponseBuilder` to create a `Response` object, set the entity error message as xml `<error>Category Not Found</error>` and HTTP Status code as `BAD_REQUEST`. We then build the response and throw a `WebApplicationException` back to the client, as shown in above code listing. The CXF framework would convert the `WebApplicationException` into required HTTP format and send the response back to the client. We will look at HTTP response content in detail in the next chapter where we will look at various test scenarios for `CategoryService` implementation.

For the rest of the resource method implementation, we modify the output parameter to the `javax.ws.rs.core.Response` object. For instance , if you look at the `addBooks` implementation above, if we do not find a valid category ID in the client request, then we would sent the **HTTP STATUS NOT FOUND** message back to the client, and if the request is successfully processed, then we build the category response and send it back to the client using the `Response.ok(category).build()` method.

To test the exception handling code, follow the build and deploy steps mentioned in the *Running the program* section to rebuild and deploy the program. Once the Category Service is available over HTTP, type in `http://localhost:9000/categoryservice/category/003` in the browser, and you would get the **HTTP 400 BAD Request** message on the Internet Explorer browser, as shown in the next screenshot. Internet Explorer doesn't show the custom error message. If you open up the URL in Firefox browser, then you would see the custom error message "**<error>Category Not Found</error>**" in the browser. As you can see, depending on your client, the custom error message may not be shown. The standard method is to use HTTP status code for returning the status to the client. If your clients can interpret the error messages, then it's best to use a custom error message to give more information about the error.

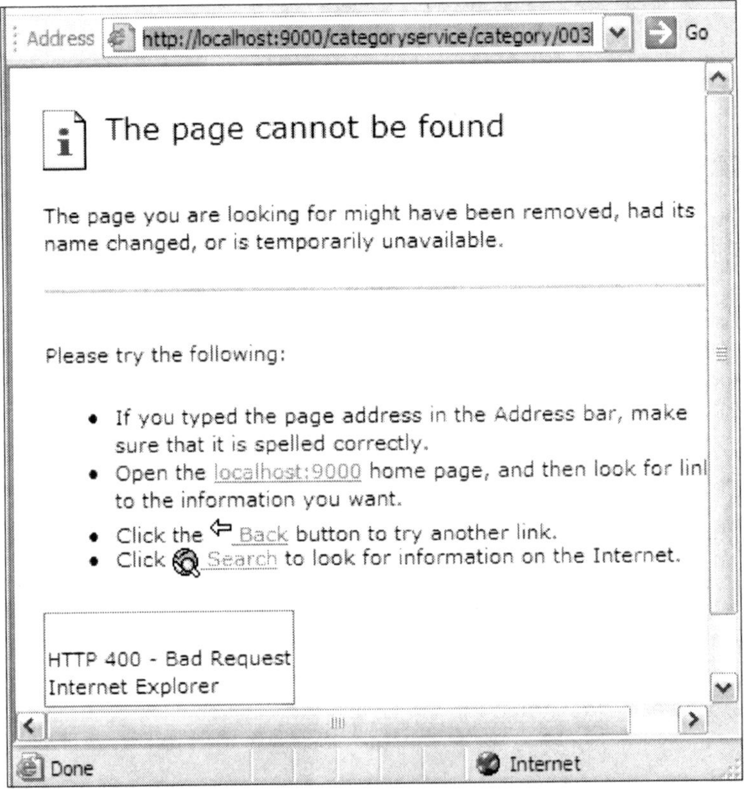

In the next chapter, we will look at the underlying request and response HTTP message in detail.

Summary

The chapter started by describing RESTful architecture and the REST based approach for developing web services. We looked at JAX-RS specifications and how CXF realizes the JAX-RS specification and provides additional features for developing enterprise RESTful services. We saw how to develop a RESTful web service with CXF by looking at the example of the Book Shop application in a step-by-step fashion. We also saw how to create clients to invoke the RESTful service and how to build, deploy, and execute the RESTful service using ANT and Tomcat.

RESTful HTTP provides a unique concept to the way resources are accessed and manipulated and simplifies overall web services development. In the next chapter we will look at how to deploy the RESTful service in various containers and execute the remaining test scenarios for the Book Shop application.

7
Deploying RESTful Services with CXF

In the last chapter we looked at how to develop RESTful services and test the service in an embedded jetty container. We also looked at how to handle exception scenarios for the RESTful service.

In this chapter we will look at how to package the Book Shop application and deploy it to the Tomcat container. We will then execute various test scenarios by invoking operations on the Book Shop RESTful application.

One of the features of the CXF framework is the support for a pluggable data binding mechanism in which different message formats such as XML, JSON, and XMLBeans can be plugged declaratively. We will look at how to extend the Book Shop application to support the JSON message format using CXF data binding support.

We will cover the following topics in this chapter:

- Packaging the Book Shop application.
- Invoking operations on the Book Shop RESTful application.
- Configuring JSON support for the Book Shop application.
- Intercepting messages for the Book Shop application.
- Deploying the Book Shop application on application servers.

Packaging the Book Shop application

Packaging the Book Shop application involves creating the web archive for deployment to a web container. So far we have created the Category Service RESTful bean as part of the Book Shop application, we now need to configure the bean and make this available over the HTTP address, which can then be invoked by clients.

We will carry out the following steps:

1. Configuring Category Service RESTful bean using Spring
2. Integrating Spring using `web.xml`
3. Building and deploying the WAR file

The source code of this chapter is available in the `Chapter7/restapp` folder of the source code distribution. Refer to *Appendix A* for detailed instructions on how to download the source code from the Packt site.

Configuring CategoryService RESTful bean using Spring

We will now expose the `CategoryService` bean as a RESTful resource over an endpoint address which clients invoke. CXF simplifies this configuration with the use of Spring-based configuration files. It is the use of such configuration files that makes development of RESTful services convenient and easy with CXF. Spring provides an Inversion of Control (IoC) container (also known as Dependency Injection) which simplifies configuration and wiring of the application objects. To find out more about the Spring framework and dependency injection, refer to *Appendix B*.

We will create a server side Spring-based configuration file and name it as `beans.xml`. The following code illustrates the `beans.xml` configuration file:

```
<?xml version="1.0" encoding="UTF-8"?>
<beans xmlns="http://www.springframework.org/schema/beans"
  xmlns:xsi="http://www.w3.org/2001/XMLSchema-instance"
  xmlns:jaxrs="http://cxf.apache.org/jaxrs"
  xsi:schemaLocation="
http://www.springframework.org/schema/beans
http://www.springframework.org/schema/beans/spring-beans.xsd
http://cxf.apache.org/jaxrs
http://cxf.apache.org/schemas/jaxrs.xsd">
```

```
    <import resource="classpath:META-INF/cxf/cxf.xml" />
    <import resource="classpath:META-INF/cxf/cxf-extension-jaxrs-
     binding.xml" />
    <import resource="classpath:META-INF/cxf/cxf-servlet.xml" />

   <jaxrs:server id="categoryRESTService" address="/">
      <jaxrs:features>
       <cxf:logging/>
  </jaxrs:features>
  <jaxrs:serviceBeans>
        <ref bean="categoryService" />
      </jaxrs:serviceBeans>
   </jaxrs:server>

  </beans>
```

Let's examine the above code and understand what it really means. We start off by defining the necessary namespaces. We then define a series of `<import>` statements, `cxf.xml`, `cxf-extension-soap.xml`, and `cxf-servlet.xml`. These files are Spring-based configuration files that define core components of CXF. These files are used to kick start CXF runtime and load the necessary CXF infrastructure objects such as WSDL manager, conduit manager, destination factory manager and so on.

The `<jaxrs:server>` element in the `beans.xml` file specifies the `CategoryService` as a RESTful resource over an address. The element is defined with the following attributes:

- `id`—specifies a unique identifier for a bean with value `categoryRESTService`.
- `address`—specifies the URL endpoint address where the RESTful resource will be available. The URL address must be relative to the web context. For our example, the endpoint will be published using the relative URL `/restapp`, where `/restapp` is the web context URL. So any request like `/restapp/categoryservice/category` would go to one of the resource classes in the given `jaxrs:server` endpoint, which is the `CategoryService` class.
- `serviceBeans`—specifies the actual RESTful implementation classes. In this case, we have only one implementor class `demo.restful.CategoryService`. The `serviceBeans` attribute wires the reference to `categoryService`, which provides the `CategoryService` bean definition. As you will recollect from an earlier chapter we specified the `CategoryService` bean definition in `restapp.xml`.

The `<jaxrs:server>` element publishes the `CategoryService` bean as a RESTful resource over address. A developer need not have to write any Java class to publish the RESTful service. Next we need to wire the CXF Controller Servlet (`CXFServlet`) in `web.xml` which directs the request to one of the matching RESTful resources defined in the `<jaxrs:server>` element.

Integrating Spring using web.xml

We will now wire CXF and Spring through `web.xml`. The following code illustrates the `web.xml` file:

```
<?xml version="1.0" encoding="ISO-8859-1"?>
<!DOCTYPE web-app
    PUBLIC "-//Sun Microsystems, Inc.//DTD Web Application 2.3//EN"
    "http://java.sun.com/dtd/web-app_2_3.dtd">
<web-app>
   <context-param>
      <param-name>contextConfigLocation</param-name>
      <param-value>
      WEB-INF/beans.xml
      classpath:demo/restful/restapp.xml
      </param-value>
   </context-param>
   <listener>
      <listener-class>
         org.springframework.web.context.ContextLoaderListener
      </listener-class>
   </listener>
   <servlet>
      <servlet-name>CXFServlet</servlet-name>
      <display-name>CXF Servlet</display-name>
      <servlet-class>
         org.apache.cxf.transport.servlet.CXFServlet
      </servlet-class>
      <load-on-startup>1</load-on-startup>
   </servlet>
   <servlet-mapping>
      <servlet-name>CXFServlet</servlet-name>
      <url-pattern>/*</url-pattern>
   </servlet-mapping>
</web-app>
```

Let's go through this piece of code. `web.xml`, as we know, is the web application configuration file that defines a servlet and its properties. The file defines `CXFServlet`, which acts as a front runner component that initiates the CXF environment. `web.xml` also defines the listener class `ContextLoaderListener`, which is responsible for loading the server-side configuration file `beans.xml` and `restapp.xml`. `restapp.xml` is the Spring configuration file that configures our RESTful application, which we discussed in one the earlier chapters. So on web server startup, the `CategoryService` RESTful service will be registered and available over the address, for example, `/restapp/categoryservice`.

Building and deploying the WAR file

The source code and build files for the example are available in the `Chapter7/restapp` folder of the downloaded source code. The following screenshot shows the folder layout:

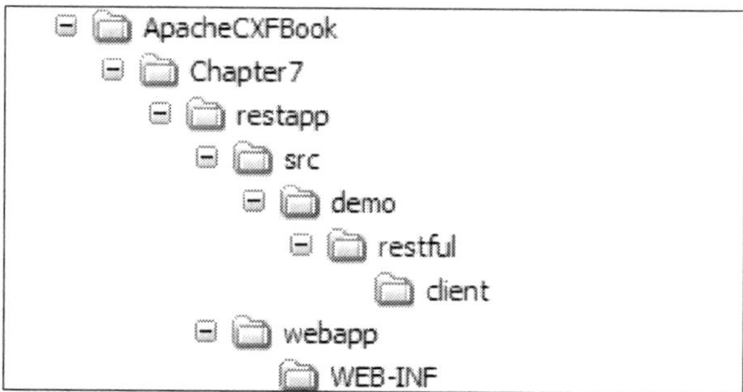

`beans.xml` and `web.xml` are available in the `webapp/WEB-INF` folder and the Java code is available in the relevant package folder. We will now build and deploy the code in the Tomcat server. We will carry out the following steps:

- Building the code
- Deploying the code

Building the code

Building the code means compiling the Java source code. To build the code we will use the ANT tool. The `build.xml` file is provided in the `Chapter 7/restapp` folder. `build.xml` is the same as other build scripts shipped with CXF samples, but customized to our application. The following code illustrates the `build.xml` build script:

```
<?xml version="1.0" encoding="UTF-8"?>
<project name="CXF Book RESTFul App" default="build" basedir=".">
   <import file="common_build.xml"/>
   <target name="runRESTClient" description="run demo client"
depends="build">
        <property name="param" value=""/>
        <cxfrun classname="demo.restful.client.
        CategoryServiceRESTClient"
      param1="${format}"
      />
    </target>
   <target name="server" description="run server" depends="build">
        <property name="param" value=""/>
        <cxfrun classname="demo.restful.client.CategoryServerStart" />
    </target>
    <property name="cxf.war.file.name" value="restapp"/>
    <target name="war" depends="build">
     <cxfwar filename="${cxf.war.file.name}.war" webxml="webapp/WEB-
     INF/web.xml" />
    </target>
</project>
```

Alongside `build.xml` you will also find `common_build.xml`. You will need to modify these build scripts to suit your environment. `common_build.xml` refers to the `CATILINA_HOME` environment variable for locating the Tomcat installation. Make sure that you have set up the environment as explained in *Appendix A*. Open the command prompt window, go to the `restapp` folder, and run the `ant` command. It will build the code and put the class files under the newly created `build` folder. The next screenshot shows the output generated upon running the `ant` command:

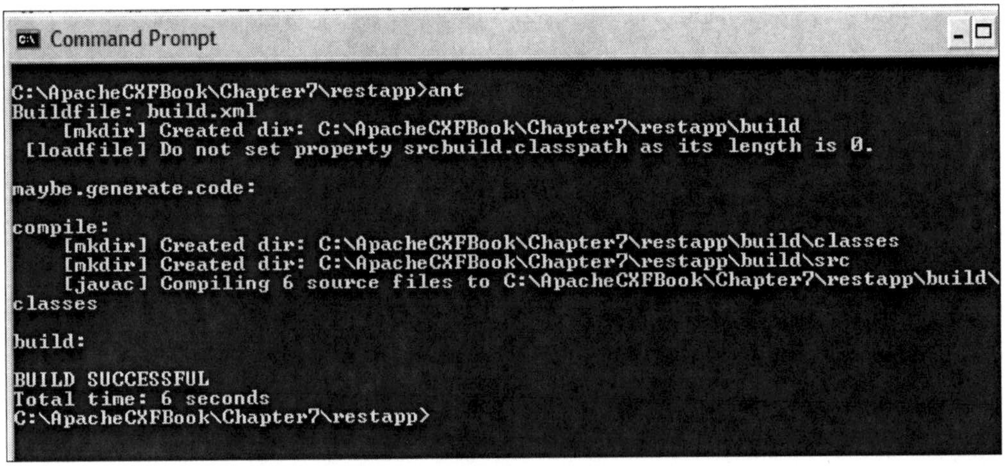

```
Command Prompt

C:\ApacheCXFBook\Chapter7\restapp>ant
Buildfile: build.xml
    [mkdir] Created dir: C:\ApacheCXFBook\Chapter7\restapp\build
 [loadfile] Do not set property srcbuild.classpath as its length is 0.

maybe.generate.code:

compile:
    [mkdir] Created dir: C:\ApacheCXFBook\Chapter7\restapp\build\classes
    [mkdir] Created dir: C:\ApacheCXFBook\Chapter7\restapp\build\src
    [javac] Compiling 6 source files to C:\ApacheCXFBook\Chapter7\restapp\build\
classes

build:

BUILD SUCCESSFUL
Total time: 6 seconds
C:\ApacheCXFBook\Chapter7\restapp>
```

Deploying the code

After the code build is finished, we deploy it. Deployment effectively means building and moving the code archive to the server deploy path. We will be using the Tomcat web container to deploy and run the application. To deploy our built code, navigate to the `restapp` folder and give the following command:

```
ant deploy
```

This will build the WAR file and put it under the Tomcat server `webapp` path. For example, if you have installed Tomcat in the `C:/Tomcat` folder, then the WAR file will be deployed to the `C:/Tomcat/webapp` folder.

The following screenshot shows the output generated upon running the `ant deploy` command:

```
Command Prompt
    [mkdir] Created dir: C:\ApacheCXFBook\Chapter7\restapp\libs
    [mkdir] Created dir: C:\ApacheCXFBook\Chapter7\restapp\config
 [loadfile] Do not set property srcbuild.classpath as its length is 0.

copy-war-libs:
     [copy] Copying 59 files to C:\ApacheCXFBook\Chapter7\restapp\libs
 [loadfile] Do not set property srcbuild.classpath as its length is 0.

copy-config-files:
     [copy] Copying 1 file to C:\ApacheCXFBook\Chapter7\restapp\config
      [war] Building war: C:\ApacheCXFBook\Chapter7\restapp\build\war\restapp.wa
r
   [delete] Deleting directory C:\ApacheCXFBook\Chapter7\restapp\libs
   [delete] Deleting directory C:\ApacheCXFBook\Chapter7\restapp\config
 [loadfile] Do not set property srcbuild.classpath as its length is 0.

deploy-tomcat:
 [loadfile] Do not set property srcbuild.classpath as its length is 0.

validate-tomcat:
     [copy] Copying 1 file to C:\Installed\Tomcat6\webapps

BUILD SUCCESSFUL
Total time: 22 seconds
C:\ApacheCXFBook\Chapter7\restapp>
```

When the deployment is finished, start the Tomcat server by navigating to the Tomcat install location and click on the `tomcat.exe` file. This starts the Tomcat server on the default port `8080`.

Invoking operations on the Book Shop RESTful application

In order to invoke operations on the Book Shop RESTful application, we need to create a client which will submit the HTTP request to the RESTful service. We first use the Poster development User Interface tool that provides a tooling environment to interact with web services and inspect the result. The tool is pretty useful as it is capable of working directly with the HTTP format, which allows us to understand how the actual messages are represented, and provides an environment for debugging raw HTTP messages. Next, we will look at how to use CXF APIs to create clients, hiding the complexity of dealing with raw HTTP messages.

Installing POSTER client

Poster is available as add-on extension for the Firefox browser. If you don't have the Firefox browser installed on your system, then install it from `http://www.mozilla.com/en-US/firefox/ie.html`. We used Firefox version 3.5.2. Follow these steps to install the Poster plug-in for Firefox:

1. Open up the URL `https://addons.mozilla.org/en-US/firefox/addon/2691` in the Firefox browser. The following screen comes up:

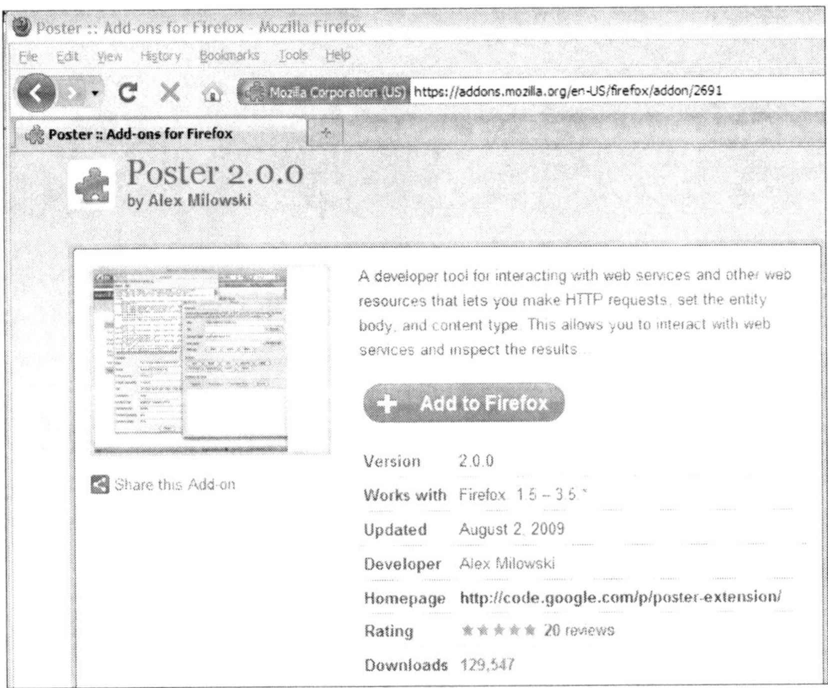

2. Click the **Add To Firefox** button. A pop-up screen will appear, as shown in the next screenshot. Click on the **Install** button. The **Poster** plug-in that we used is 2.0, which is compatible with Firefox 3.5.2.

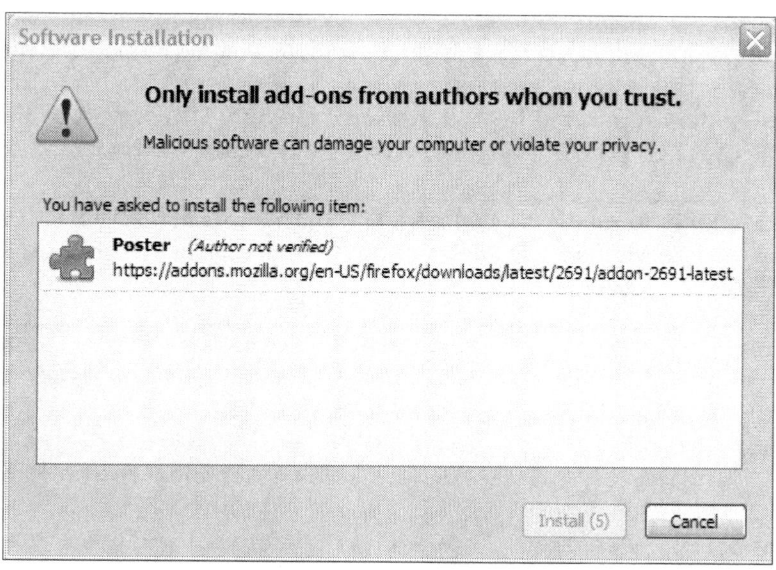

3. The Poster add-on will be installed, and you receive a confirmation screen. Click the **Restart Firefox** button.
4. Launch the Poster plug-in by clicking on the **P** icon, as shown in the next screenshot:

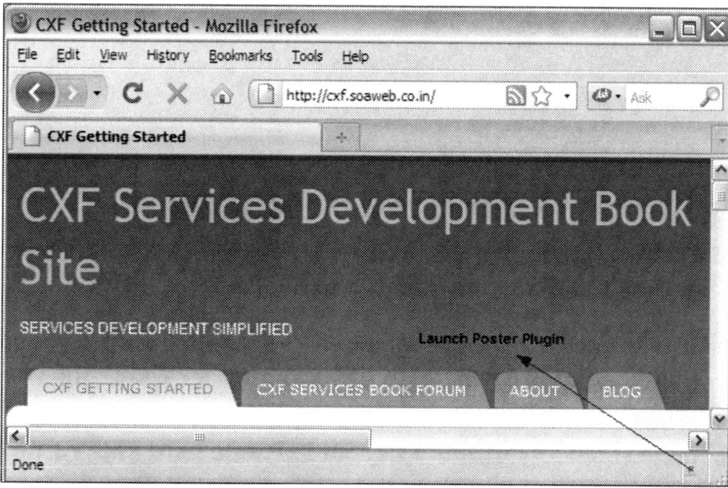

Invoking the Book Shop application using the the POSTER tool

We now invoke the various methods exposed by the `CategoryService` bean for our Book Shop application. To recap from a previous chapter, the following table provides the resource methods exposed by the `CategoryService` bean. Request method designators supported by each resource method, URI served by the methods and example of HTTP URL that would invoke the resource method.

Resource Method	Request Method Designators	@Path	Example of a HTTP URI request that matches the resource method
`getCategory`	@GET	`/category/{id}`	`http://localhost:8080/restapp/categoryservice/category/001`
`addCategory`	@POST	`/category`	`http://localhost:8080/restapp/categoryservice/category`
`deleteCategory`	@DELETE	`/category/{id}`	`http://localhost:8080/restapp/categoryservice/category/001`
`UpdateCategory`	@PUT	`/category`	`http://localhost:8080/restapp/categoryservice/category`
`AddBooks`	@POST	`/category/book`	`http://localhost:8080/restapp/categoryservice/category/book`
`getBooks`	@GET	`/category/{id"}/books`	`http://localhost:8080/restapp/categoryservice/category/001/books`

Invoking the Get Category operation

We now send a `GET Category` request to the `CategoryService`. Launch the poster plug-in, and enter the following information in the **Poster** screen

1. Enter **URL** as `http://localhost:8080/restapp/categoryservice/category/001` (replace 8080 with the port number where the web server is running)
2. Click on the **Headers** tab, enter **Accept** in **Name field** and **Value** as **application/xml**, as shown in the next screenshot, then click the **Add/change** button. The **Accept** header specifies that the client accepts only `application/xml` content type as a response.

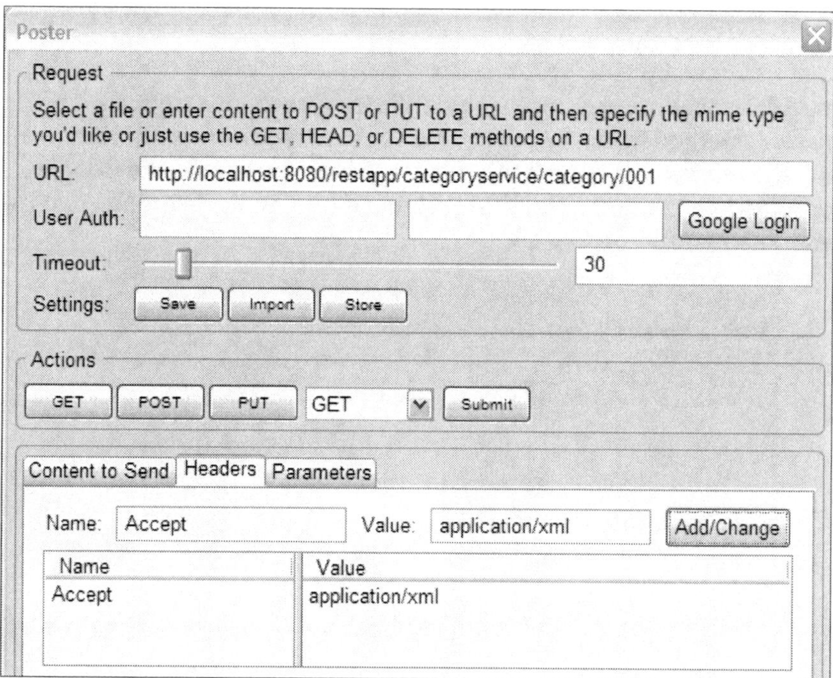

3. In the **Actions** tab, click **GET** method to issue HTTP GET request to the `CategoryService` with the above information.

The following `getCategory()` method code will be executed as highlighted in bold, retrieving the category information based on `category id`. Since we have populated category information with dummy data for category ID `001`, category information would be retrieved for category ID `001`. Next the CXF JSX-RS implementation converts the `Category` Java object to an XML format using JAXB binding. It also creates the HTTP response, sets the HTTP headers (status, content-type, content length), and Category XML in the HTTP message body data.

```
@GET
@Path("/category/{id}")
public Category getCategory(@PathParam("id") String id) {
  System.out.println("getCategory called with category id: " + id);
  Category cat = (Category) getCategoryDAO().getCategory(id);
  if (cat == null) {
    ResponseBuilder builder = Response.status(Status.BAD_REQUEST);
    builder.type("application/xml");
    builder.entity("<error>Category Not Found</error>");
    throw new WebApplicationException(builder.build());
  } else {
    return cat;
```

```
        }
    }
```

On successful invocation, you receive the following response from the `getCategory()` method of the `CategoryService`. As you can see in the next screenshot, the response is in an XML format, which represents the category information for category `001`. The HTTP Status is `200`, which signifies that the request was successfully processed.

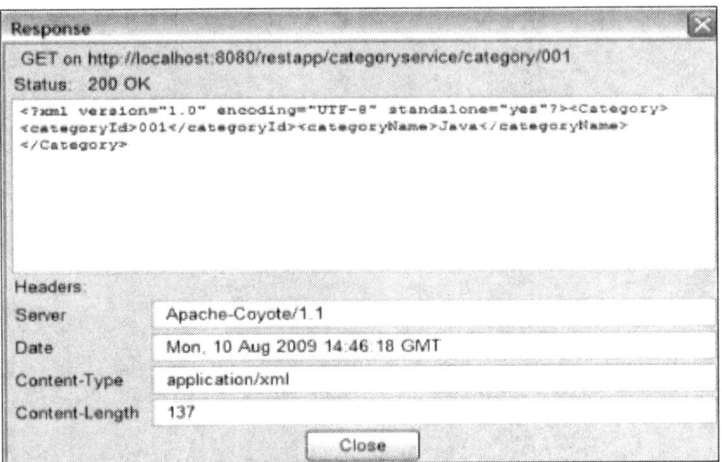

Invoking the Add Category operation

We will send an Add Category request to the `CategoryService`. Enter the following information in the **Poster** screen:

1. Enter **URL** as `http://localhost:8080/restapp/categoryservice/category` (Replace `8080` with the port number where the web server is running).
2. Enter **Content Type** as `application/xml`. The content type specifies the request format.
3. In the **Content to Send** field, enter the following Category information in an XML format:

   ```
   <Category><categoryName>.NET</categoryName><categoryId>002</
   categoryId></Category>
   ```

4. Click on the **Headers** tab, and check if the **Name** field contains **Accept** and if its **Value** is **application/xml**. If not, then add these values.

5. In the **Actions** tab, click **POST** method to issue HTTP POST request to the `CategoryService` with the above information.

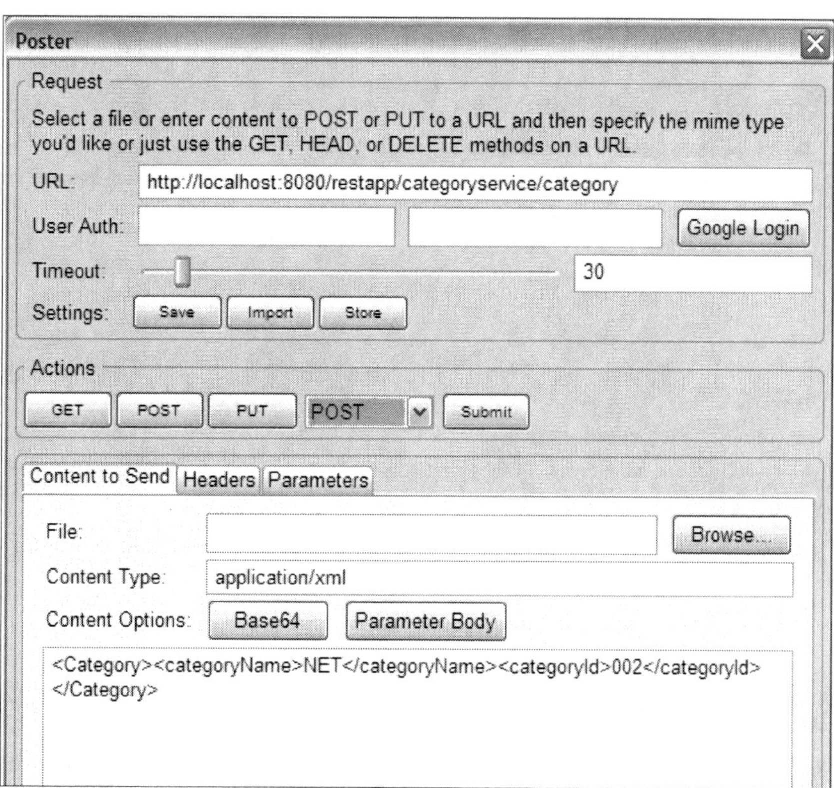

The following `addCategory()` method code, as highlighted in bold, will be executed in order to add the category information:

```
@POST
@Path("/category")
@Consumes("application/xml")
public Response addCategory(Category category) {
   System.out.println("addCategory called");
   Category cat = (Category) getCategoryDAO().getCategory(
         category.getCategoryId());
   if (cat != null) {
      return Response.status(Status.BAD_REQUEST).build();
   } else {
      getCategoryDAO().addCategory(category);
      return Response.ok(category).build();
   }
}
```

On successful invocation, you receive the following response from the `addCategory()` method of the `CategoryService`. You get the same XML request data resource as for the response data resource. The HTTP Status is `200`, which signifies that the request was successfully processed.

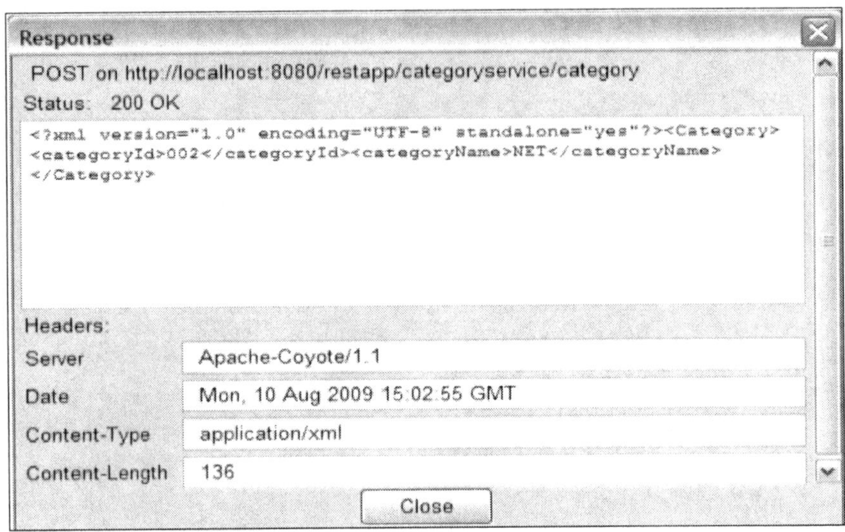

Invoking the Update Category operation

In this scenario, we will send an Update Category request to the `CategoryService` by entering the following information on the **Poster** screen:

1. Enter **URL** as `http://localhost:8080/restapp/categoryservice/category` (Replace 8080 with the port number where the web server is running).
2. Enter **Content Type** as **application/xml**. This specifies the request content type.
3. In the **Content to Send** field, enter the following Category information in XML format.

```
<Category><categoryName>Microsoft NET</
categoryName><categoryId>002</categoryId></Category>
```

4. Click on the **Headers** tab, and check if the **Name** field contains **Accept** and if its **Value** is **application/xml**. If not, then add these values.
5. In the **Actions** tab, click the **PUT** method to issue HTTP PUT request to the `CategoryService` with the above information.

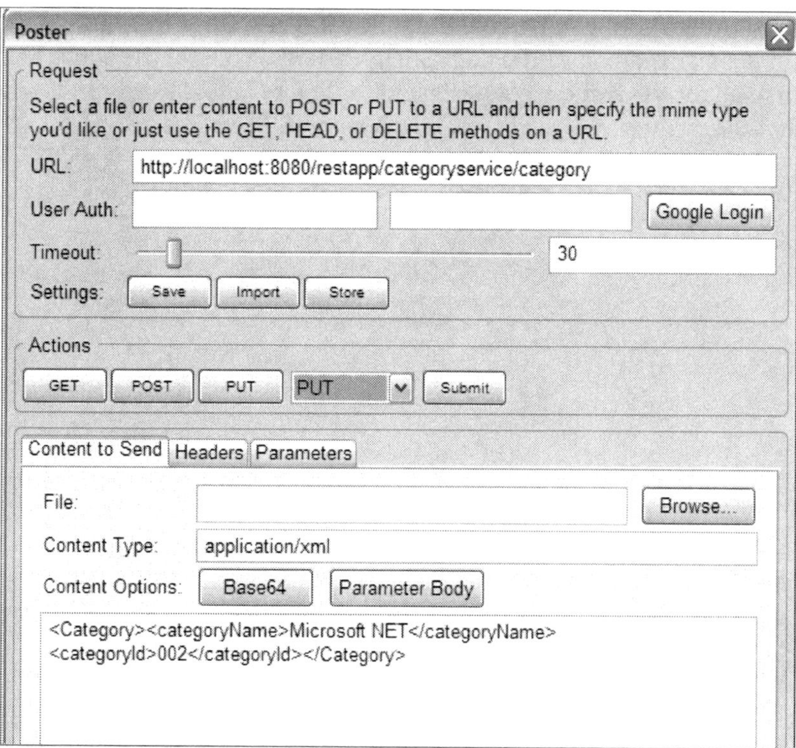

The following `updateCategory()` method code, as highlighted in bold, will be executed in order to update the category information for category ID `002`. Since the category ID `002` does exist, the update will be successful. If the category ID doesn't exist, then an error will be thrown back to the client. We will look at this scenario in the *Invoking the Update Category operation with Invalid request* section.

```
@PUT
@Path("/category")
public Response updateCategory(Category category) {
   System.out.println("updateCategory with category id : "
         + category.getCategoryId());

   Category cat = (Category) getCategoryDAO().getCategory(
         category.getCategoryId());
   if (cat == null) {
      return Response.status(Status.BAD_REQUEST).build();
   } else {
      getCategoryDAO().updateCategory(category);
      return Response.ok(category).build();
   }
}
```

On successful invocation, you receive the following response from the `updateCategory()` method of the `CategoryService`. You get the same XML request data resource as for the response data resource. The HTTP Status is `200`, which signifies that the request was successfully processed.

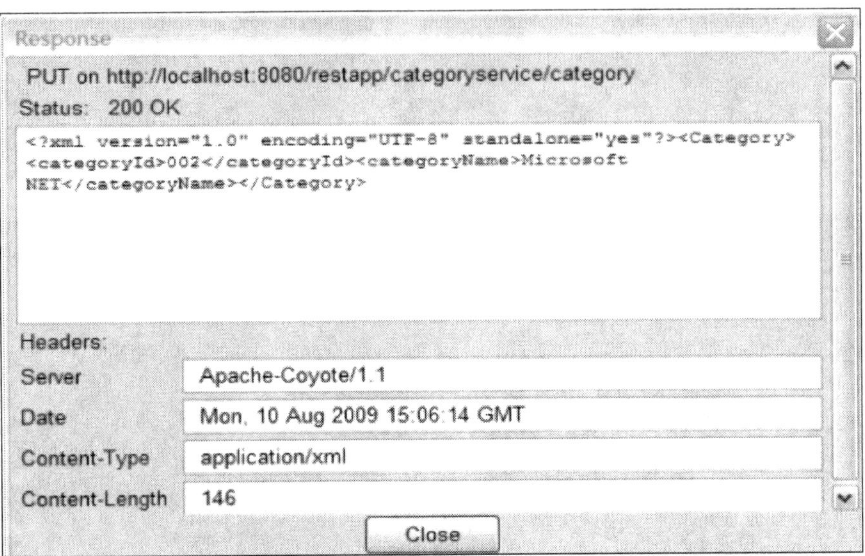

Invoking the Add Books operation

So far we have created a category Microsoft .NET with category ID `002`. We will now add books to the Category ID `002`. We send an Add Book request to the `CategoryService` by entering the following information in the **Poster** screen:

1. Enter **URL** as `http://localhost:8080/restapp/categoryservice/category/book` (Replace **8080** with the port number where the web server is running).
2. Enter **Content Type** as **application/xml**.
3. In the **Content to Send** field, enter the following Category information in an XML format. As you can see in the request below, we have specified the category ID as `002`.

```
<Category>
<books><author>Naveen Balani</author><bookISBNumber>ISB003</
bookISBNumber><bookId>003</bookId><bookName>Spring NET Series</
bookName></books>
<categoryName>Microsoft NET</categoryName><categoryId>002</
categoryId>
</Category>
```

4. Click on the **Headers** tab, and check if the **Name** field contains `Accept` and if its **Value** is **application/xml**. If not, then add these values.
5. In the **Actions** tab, click the **POST** method to issue HTTP POST request to the **CategoryService** with the above information.

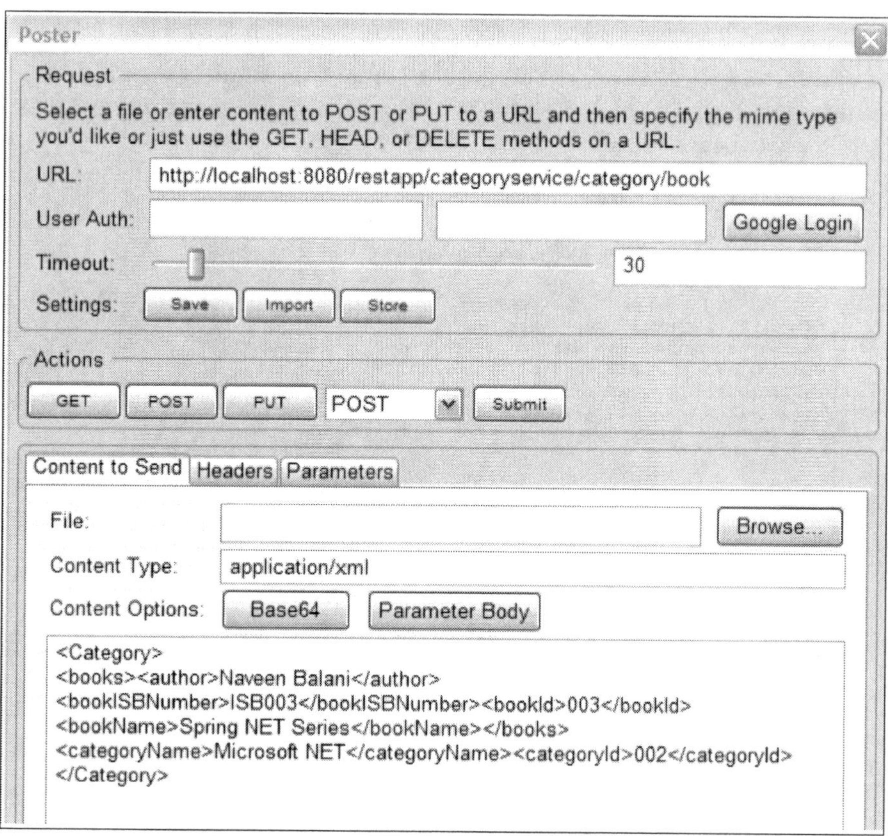

The following `addBook()` method code will be executed as highlighted in bold, adding the books information for category ID `002`.

```
@POST
@Path("/category/book")
@Consumes("application/xml")
public Response addBooks(Category category) {
   System.out.println("addBooks with category id : "
         + category.getCategoryId());
   Category cat = (Category) getCategoryDAO().getCategory(
         category.getCategoryId());
   if (cat == null) {
```

```
            return Response.status(Status.NOT_FOUND).build();
        } else {
            getCategoryDAO().addBook(category);
            return Response.ok(category).build();
        }
    }
```

On successful invocation, you receive the following response from the `addBooks()` method of the `CategoryService`. You get the same XML request message as the response message. The HTTP Status is `200`, which signifies the request was successfully processed.

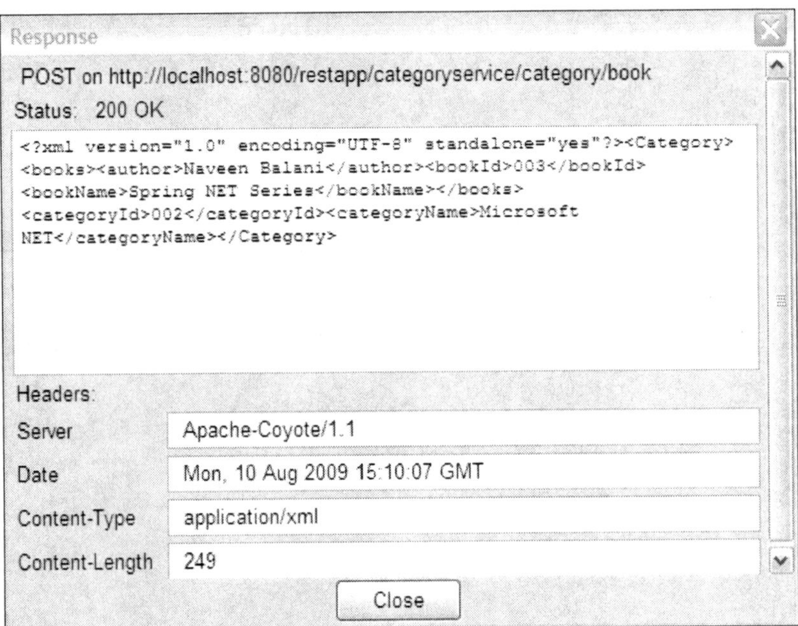

Invoking the Get Books operation

We will now retrieve the books information that we added by invoking the Get Book operations on the `CategoryService`. Enter the following information in the **Poster** screen:

1. Enter **URL** as `http://localhost:8080/restapp/categoryservice/category/002/books` (Replace 8080 with the port number where the web server is running).
2. Click on the **Headers** tab, and check if the **Name** field contains **Accept** and if its **Value** is **application/xml**. If not, then add these values.

3. In the **Actions** tab, click the **GET** method to issue HTTP GET request to the `CategoryService` with the above information.

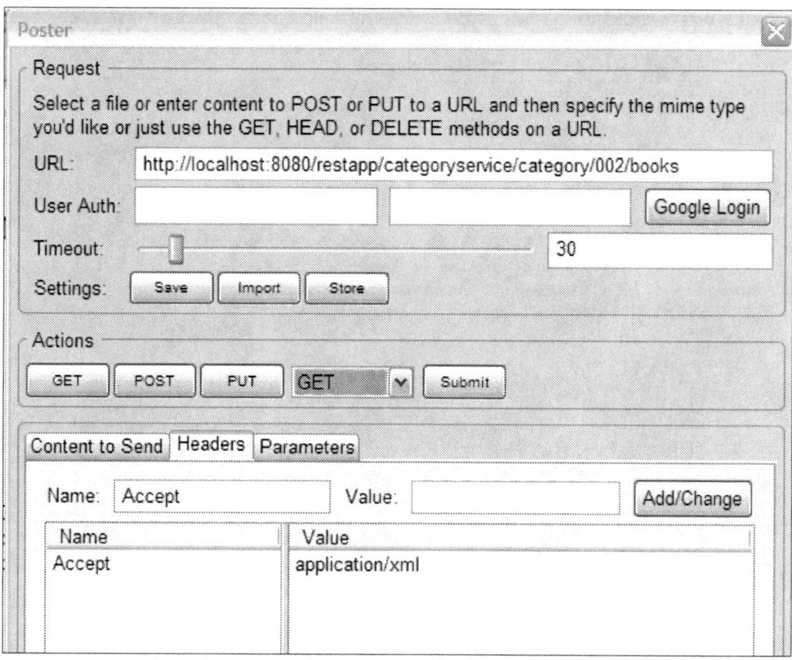

The following `getBooks()` method code will be executed as highlighted in bold, retrieving all books information associated with the category ID.

```
@GET
@Path("/category/{id}/books")
@Consumes("application/xml")
public Response getBooks(@PathParam("id") String id) {
    System.out.println("getBooks called with category id : " + id);
    Category cat = (Category) getCategoryDAO().getCategory(id);
    if (cat == null) {
        return Response.status(Status.NOT_FOUND).build();
    } else {
        cat.setBooks(getCategoryDAO().getBooks(id));
        return Response.ok(cat).build();
    }
}
```

On successful invocation, you receive the following response from the `getBooks()` method of the `CategoryService`. As you can observe in the screenshot below the response is in XML format, which represents the books information for category `001`. The HTTP Status is `200`, which signifies that the request was successfully processed:

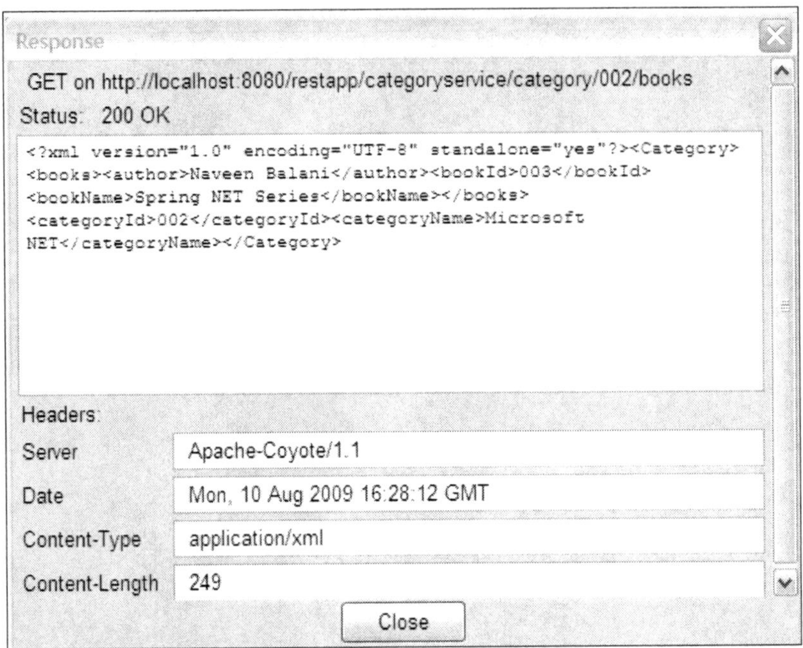

Invoking the Update Category operation with invalid request

We will now test out exception scenarios for `CategoryService`. We will send an Update Category request to the `CategoryService` with a category ID that does not exist in the system. Enter the following information in the **Poster** screen.

1. Enter **URL** as `http://localhost:8080/restapp/categoryservice/category` (Replace 8080 with the port number where the web server is running).
2. Enter **Content Type** as **application/xml**.
3. Click on the **Headers** tab, and check if the **Name** field contains **Accept** and if **Value** is **application/xml**. If not, then add these values.

4. In the **Content to Send** field, enter the following Category information in an XML format. Note that we specify the `categoryId` as `003`, which does not exist.

   ```
   <Category><categoryName>Microsoft NET</
   categoryName><categoryId>003</categoryId></Category>
   ```

5. In the **Actions** tab, click the **PUT** method to issue HTTP PUT request to the `CategoryService` with the above information.

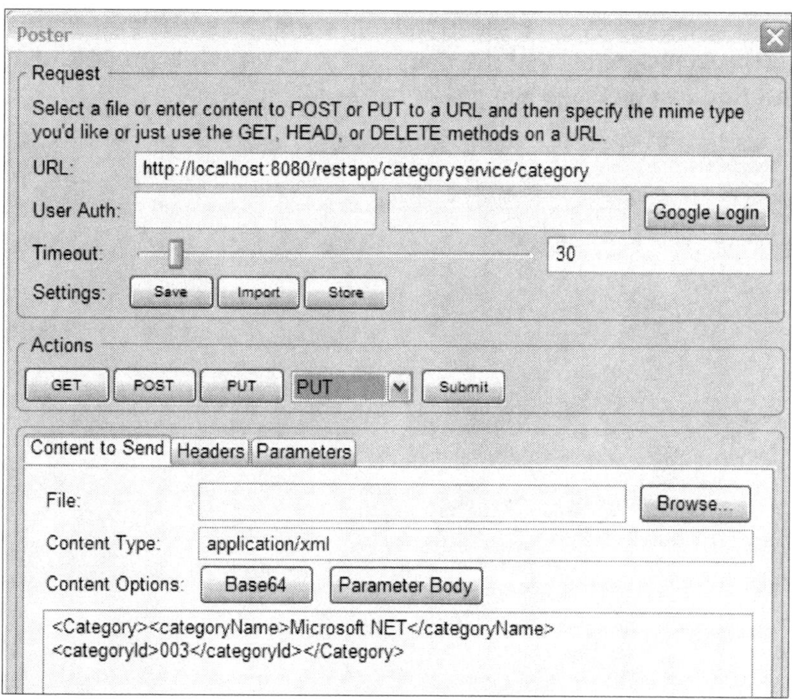

The following `updateCategory()` method code will be executed as highlighted in bold. As the category ID `003` doesn't exist, we set the Response Status as `BAD_REQUEST` denoting an error. The CXF JSX RS implementation then creates an HTTP response with status code as `400` (`BAD_REQUEST`) denoting an error back to the client. Apart from HTTP status code, you can also send a custom error message back to the client. We will look at this scenario in the next invocation request.

```
@PUT
@Path("/category")
public Response updateCategory(Category category) {
   System.out.println("updateCategory with category id : "
         + category.getCategoryId());
   Category cat = (Category) getCategoryDAO().getCategory(
```

```
            category.getCategoryId());
      if (cat == null) {
         return Response.status(Status.BAD_REQUEST).build();
      } else {
         getCategoryDAO().updateCategory(category);
         return Response.ok(category).build();
      }
   }
```

You would receive the following response from the `updateCategory()` method of the `CategoryService`. As you see in the following screenshot, the Status is **400 Bad Request**, which signifies that the there was an error while processing the request due to a **Bad Request** message being sent by the client.

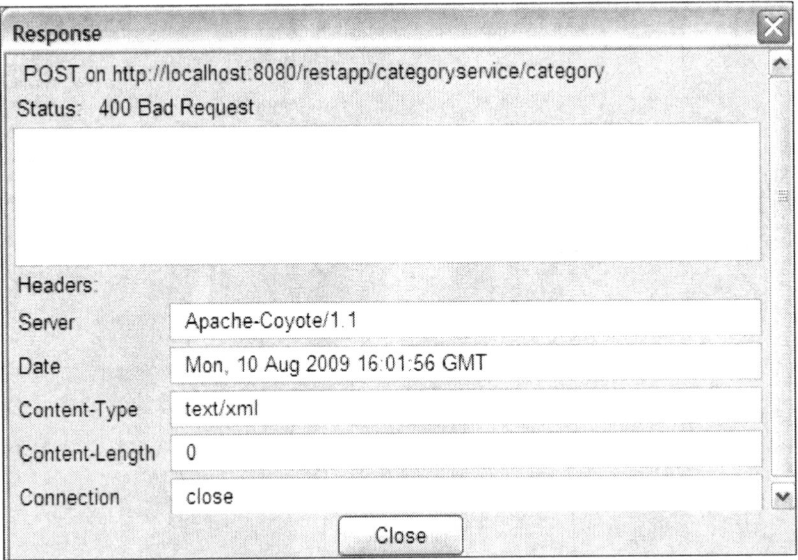

Invoking the Get Category operation with invalid request

In this scenario, we will send a Get Category request to the `CategoryService` where category ID does not exist. Enter the following information in the **Poster** screen:

1. Enter **URL** as `http://localhost:8080/restapp/categoryservice/category/003` (Replace 8080 with the port number where the web server is running). Here we can see that category ID is specified as 003.
2. Click on the **Headers** tab, and check if the **Name** field contains **Accept** and **Value is application/xml**. If not, then add these values.

3. In the **Actions** tab, click the **GET** method to issue HTTP GET request to the `CategoryService` with the above information.
4. The following `getCategory()` method code will be executed, as highlighted in bold. Since the category ID doesn't exist, we create a custom error message `"<error>Category Not Found</error>"` and set it in `Response` object and throw a `WebApplicationException`. Next, the CXF JSX-RS implementation creates the HTTP response, sets the HTTP Status code as `400`, and sets the exception message in HTTP body.

```
@GET
@Path("/category/{id}")
public Category getCategory(@PathParam("id") String id) {

        System.out.println("getCategory called with category id: "
        + id);

        Category cat = (Category) getCategoryDAO().getCategory(id);
        if (cat == null) {
           ResponseBuilder builder = Response.status(Status.BAD_
           REQUEST);
           builder.type("application/xml");
           builder.entity("<error>Category Not Found</error>");
           throw new WebApplicationException(builder.build());
    } else {
        return cat;
    }
}
```

You would receive the following error response from the `getCategory()` service:

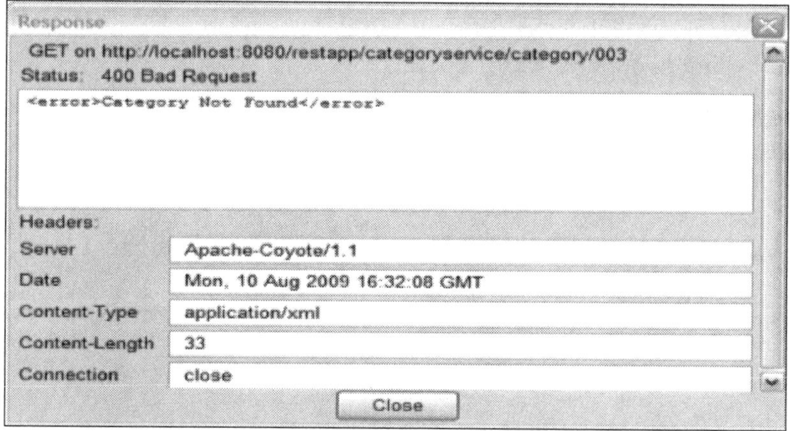

Invoking the Delete Category operation

We will now delete the category information by sending a delete category request to the `CategoryService`. Enter the following information in the **Poster** screen

1. Enter **URL** as `http://localhost:8080/restapp/categoryservice/category/002` (replace `8080` with the port number where the web server is running). Here we can see that the category ID is specified as `002`.
2. In the **Actions** tab, select the **DELETE** method and click submit to issue an HTTP DELETE request to the `CategoryService` with the above information.

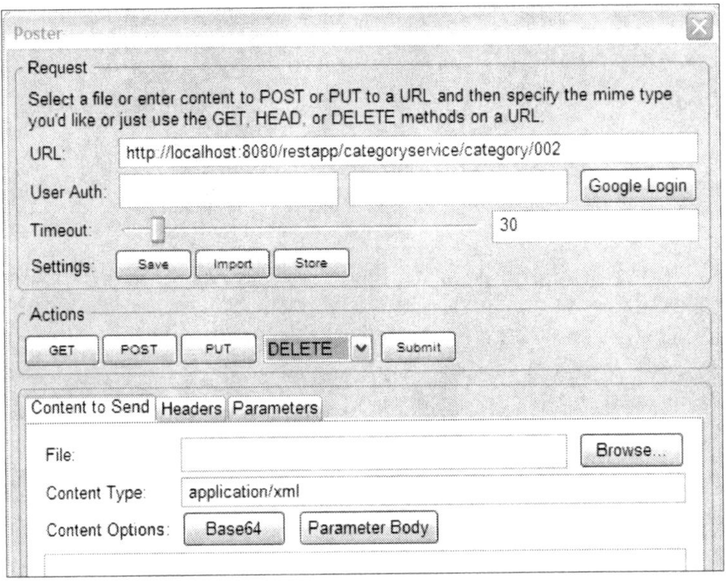

The following `deleteCategory()` method code will be executed as highlighted in bold. If the category is deleted, then we build the response for successful confirmation using `Response.ok().build()`:

```
@DELETE
@Path("/category/{id}")
public Response deleteCategory(@PathParam("id") String id) {

   System.out.println("deleteCategory with category id : " + id);

   Category cat = (Category) getCategoryDAO().getCategory(id);
   if (cat == null) {
      return Response.status(Status.BAD_REQUEST).build();
   } else {
      getCategoryDAO().deleteCategory(id);
```

```
            return Response.ok().build();
        }
    }
```

You will receive the following response from the `deleteCategory()` service. The HTTP status code is `200` denoting a successful invocation.

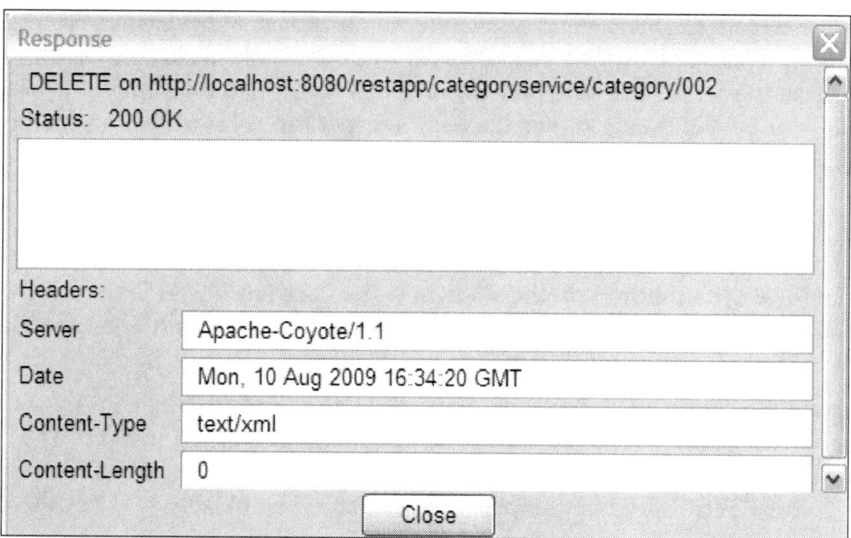

You can verify if the category ID is successfully deleted, by invoking the `GET` Category operation with the category ID `002`.

Invoking the Book Shop application using CXF APIs

We will now look at how to invoke the Book shop application using CXF APIs. The source code for the client, which is `CategoryServiceRESTClient.java`, is available in the `Chapter7/restapp/demo/restful/client` folder of the downloaded source code. The `CategoryServiceRESTClient` class is a standalone class, which provides a test method for testing out the various `CategoryService` RESTful methods. We can break down the code into code snippets for better understanding.

- The `testAddCategory()` method

  The `testAddCategory()` method invokes the `addCategory()` method of the `CategoryService`.

  We start off by creating an instance of `WebClient` by passing the base `URI` where the RESTful service is running. We looked at the `WebClient` API in an earlier chapter. The following code snippet shows the `WebClient` API:

```
WebClient client = WebClient.create(CATEGORY_URL)
```

The `CATEGORY_URL` is defined as one of the constants in the `CategoryServiceRESTClient` class. Change the value to point it to the `URL` where the Category Service is running:

```
private static final String CATEGORY_URL="http://localhost:8080";
```

Next, we specify the `URI` path that we want to invoke in `client.path()` method, so the actual `URI` to invoke becomes `CATEGORY_URL + categoryservice/category`. Following shows the code snippet for `client.path()` method:

```
client.path("categoryservice/category").accept(
      format).type(format);
```

The `accept` method on the client sets the `Accept` header for HTTP request, and the `type` method on the client sets the `Content Type`. Since we are dealing with XML messages, we would pass the `type` and `accept` values as `application/xml` while running the program.

- Next we create an instance of `Category` object and call the `client.post(cat, Category.class)`. The `client` post method invokes an HTTP POST request with the `Category` object as input. The response received back from RESTful service is mapped to the `Category` object.

  The following shows the code snippet:

  ```
  Category cat = new Category();
  cat.setCategoryId(CATEGORY_ID);
  cat.setCategoryName("Fiction");
  Category catResponse = client.post(cat, Category.class);
  System.out.println("Category Id retreived for format " + format
  + "
     is "+ catResponse.getCategoryId());
  ```

  Here we can see how the `WebClient` abstracts out the underlying low level implementation details, and we directly work with the Java object. The conversion of Java objects to XML messages and the creation of an HTTP request, as specified in *Invoking the Add Category operation* section, would be carried out by the CXF framework.

- The `testUpdateCategory()` method

  The `testUpdateCategory()` method invokes the `updateCategory()` method of the `CategoryService`.

We start off by creating an instance of the `Category` object and call the `client.put(cat)` method. The `client put` method invokes an HTTP PUT request with the `Category` object as input. The response received back from the RESTful service is mapped to the `Response` object. We then print the status of PUT operation using the `response.getStatus()` method, which should be 200 in the case of a successful update. We looked at the `Response` object in an earlier chapter while dealing with exception handling. The following shows the code snippet:

```
Category cat = new Category();
cat.setCategoryId(CATEGORY_ID);
cat.setCategoryName("Fiction Series");
Response response = client.put(cat);
System.out.println("Status retreived for update category for
format "   + format + " is " + response.getStatus());
```

- The `testGetCategory()` method

  The `testGetCategory()` method invokes the `getCategory()` method of the `CategoryService`.

  We invoke the `get` method on the `client` using the `get(Category.class)` method. The input to the `get` method is a class name. The CXF framework maps the response received from the RESTful service to the `Category` class. The `get` method would invoke an HTTP GET method with the required `URL`.

  The following shows the code snippet:

```
WebClient client = WebClient.create(CATEGORY_URL);
Category category = client.path("/categoryservice/
category/"+CATEGORY_ID).accept(
            format).type(format).get(Category.class);
System.out.println("Category details retreived from service with
format "+ format);
System.out.println("Category Name " + category.getCategoryName());
System.out.println("Category Id " + category.getCategoryId());
```

- The `testAddBooksForCategory()` method

  The `testAddBooksForCategory()` method invokes the `addBooks()` method on the `CategoryService`.

We start off by creating an instance of `Category` and `Book` object, and add the `Book` object to the Category instance. We specify a category ID which exists in the system. A similar exception would be thrown, as discussed in *Invoking the Get Category operation with Invalid request* section, if category ID passed does not exist in the system. We then invoke the `post(cat, Category.class)` method on the `client`. The `client post` method invokes an HTTP POST request with the `Category` object as input. The response received back from the RESTful service is mapped to the `Category` object. The following shows the code snippet:

```
WebClient client = WebClient.create(CATEGORY_URL);
        client.path("/categoryservice/category/book").type(format).
                accept(format);
        Category cat = new Category();
        cat.setCategoryId(CATEGORY_ID);
        cat.setCategoryName("Fiction Series");
        Book book1 = new Book();
        book1.setAuthor("Naveen Balani");
        book1.setBookId("NB001");
        book1.setBookISBNnumber("ISBNB001");
        book1.setBookName("Fiction Book1");

        Collection<Book> booksList = new ArrayList<Book>();
        booksList.add(book1);
        cat.setBooks(booksList);
        client.post(cat, Category.class);
```

- The `testGetBooksForCategory()` method

  The `testGetBooksForCategory()` method invokes the `getBooks()` method on the `CategoryService`.

  We invoke the `get` method on the client using the `get(Category.class)` method. The input to the `get` method is the class name. CXF framework maps the response received from the RESTful service to the `Category` class. We then retrieve the books associated with the `Category` object and print the output on the console.

  The following code snippet explains how to retrieve the books information and prints out the book details:

```
WebClient clientBook = WebClient.create(CATEGORY_URL);
Category categoryBooks = clientBook.path(
"/categoryservice/category/"+CATEGORY_ID +"/books")
.type(format).accept(format)
```

```
.get(Category.class);
System.out.println("Book details retreived from service
with format "+ format);

assertEquals(String.valueOf(categoryBooks.getBooks().size()),
"1");

Iterator<Book> iterator = categoryBooks.getBooks().iterator();
while (iterator.hasNext()) {
Book book = iterator.next();
 System.out.println("Book Name " + book.getBookName());
 System.out.println("Book ISBN " + book.getBookISBNnumber());
 System.out.println("Book ID " + book.getBookId());
 System.out.println("Book Author " + book.getAuthor());
}
```

Next, we will run the client. To run the client, navigate to the `Chapter7/restapp/demo/restful/client` folder of the downloaded source code, and type in the following `ant` command. Before running the client, make sure that the Tomcat server is running.

```
ant runRESTClient -Dformat=application/xml
```

This command will run the `CategoryServiceRESTClient` class. We pass the **format** argument to the `CategoryServiceRESTClient` class with value as `application/xml`. The `application/xml` value is set as the `type` and `accept` value on the `WebClient` object instance, as discussed earlier. The `type` maps to HTTP Content-Type and `accept` maps to HTTP `Accept` tag, denoting the request format is `application/xml` and the client is expecting the response in an `application/xml` format.

After running the client you see the following output at the console. Each of the test methods listed above gets executed, which invokes the required methods on the RESTful service and prints out the response at the console.

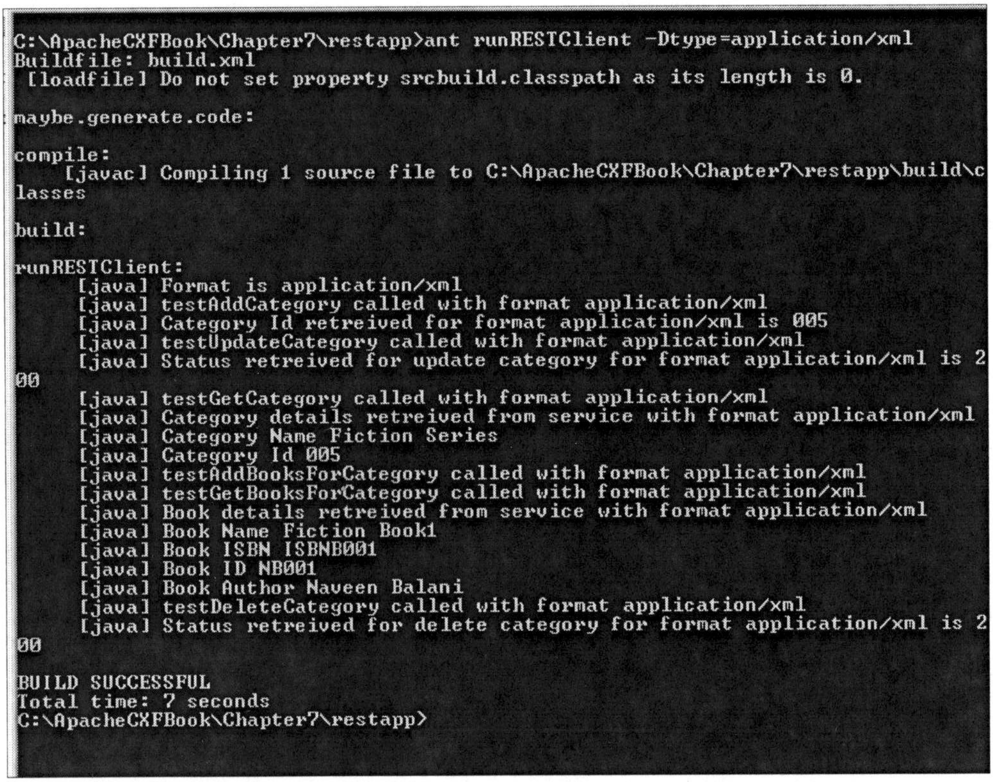

```
C:\ApacheCXFBook\Chapter7\restapp>ant runRESTClient -Dtype=application/xml
Buildfile: build.xml
 [loadfile] Do not set property srcbuild.classpath as its length is 0.

maybe.generate.code:

compile:
    [javac] Compiling 1 source file to C:\ApacheCXFBook\Chapter7\restapp\build\c
lasses

build:

runRESTClient:
     [java] Format is application/xml
     [java] testAddCategory called with format application/xml
     [java] Category Id retreived for format application/xml is 005
     [java] testUpdateCategory called with format application/xml
     [java] Status retreived for update category for format application/xml is 2
00
     [java] testGetCategory called with format application/xml
     [java] Category details retreived from service with format application/xml
     [java] Category Name Fiction Series
     [java] Category Id 005
     [java] testAddBooksForCategory called with format application/xml
     [java] testGetBooksForCategory called with format application/xml
     [java] Book details retreived from service with format application/xml
     [java] Book Name Fiction Book1
     [java] Book ISBN ISBNB001
     [java] Book ID NB001
     [java] Book Author Naveen Balani
     [java] testDeleteCategory called with format application/xml
     [java] Status retreived for delete category for format application/xml is 2
00

BUILD SUCCESSFUL
Total time: 7 seconds
C:\ApacheCXFBook\Chapter7\restapp>
```

Configuring JSON support for the Book Shop application

For the Book Shop application, we used XML as the message format for interaction between clients and RESTful services. Based on applications requirements, you may want to use JSON as the message format. JSON is a light weight data-interchange format and is being widely used with **AJAX (Asynchronous JavaScript and XML)** based applications.

CXF simplifies handling of multiple message formats through its support for Pluggable Binding mechanism, where the same RESTful resource can support multiple message formats, for instance, JSON as the message format.

We will now look at how to support JSON message format for the Book Shop application.

Incorporating JSON message format for the Book Shop application

We will now change the `CategoryService` bean to handle the JSON message format. The following code highlighted in bold illustrates the modification for `CategoryService` for handling JSON message format:

```
package demo.restful;
//JAX-RS Imports
import javax.ws.rs.Consumes;
import javax.ws.rs.DELETE;
import javax.ws.rs.GET;
import javax.ws.rs.POST;
import javax.ws.rs.PUT;
import javax.ws.rs.Path;
import javax.ws.rs.PathParam;
import javax.ws.rs.Produces;
import javax.ws.rs.WebApplicationException;
import javax.ws.rs.core.Response;
import javax.ws.rs.core.Response.ResponseBuilder;
import javax.ws.rs.core.Response.Status;
/*
 * CategoryService class - Add/Removes category for books
 */
@Path("/categoryservice")
@Produces({"application/json","application/xml"})
public class CategoryService {
   private CategoryDAO categoryDAO = new CategoryDAO();
   public CategoryDAO getCategoryDAO() {
      return categoryDAO;
   }
   public void setCategoryDAO(CategoryDAO categoryDAO) {
      this.categoryDAO = categoryDAO;
   }
   @GET
   @Path("/category/{id}")
   @Produces({"application/json","application/xml"})
   public Category getCategory(@PathParam("id") String id) {
      System.out.println("getCategory called with category id: " + id);
      Category cat = (Category) getCategoryDAO().getCategory(id);
      if (cat == null) {
         ResponseBuilder builder = Response.status(Status.BAD_REQUEST);
         builder.type("application/xml");
```

```
        builder.entity("<error>Category Not Found</error>");
        throw new WebApplicationException(builder.build());
    } else {
        return cat;
    }
}
@POST
@Path("/category")
@Consumes({"application/json","application/xml"})
public Response addCategory(Category category) {
    System.out.println("addCategory called");
    Category cat = (Category) getCategoryDAO().getCategory(
            category.getCategoryId());
    if (cat != null) {
        return Response.status(Status.BAD_REQUEST).build();
    } else {
        getCategoryDAO().addCategory(category);
        return Response.ok(category).build();
    }
}
@DELETE
@Path("/category/{id}")
public Response deleteCategory(@PathParam("id") String id) {
    System.out.println("deleteCategory with category id : " + id);
    Category cat = (Category) getCategoryDAO().getCategory(id);
    if (cat == null) {
        return Response.status(Status.BAD_REQUEST).build();
    } else {
        getCategoryDAO().deleteCategory(id);
        return Response.ok().build();
    }
}
@PUT
@Path("/category")
@Consumes({"application/json","application/xml"})
public Response updateCategory(Category category) {
    System.out.println("updateCategory with category id : "
            + category.getCategoryId());
    Category cat = (Category) getCategoryDAO().getCategory(
            category.getCategoryId());
    if (cat == null) {
        return Response.status(Status.BAD_REQUEST).build();
    } else {
        getCategoryDAO().updateCategory(category);
        return Response.ok(category).build();
    }
}
```

```
    @POST
    @Path("/category/book")
    @Consumes({"application/json","application/xml"})
    public Response addBooks(Category category) {
       System.out.println("addBooks with category id : "
             + category.getCategoryId());
       Category cat = (Category) getCategoryDAO().getCategory(
             category.getCategoryId());
       if (cat == null) {
          return Response.status(Status.NOT_FOUND).build();
       } else {
          getCategoryDAO().addBook(category);
          return Response.ok(category).build();
       }
    }
    @GET
    @Path("/category/{id}/books")
    @Consumes("application/xml,application/json")
    public Response getBooks(@PathParam("id") String id) {
       System.out.println("getBooks called with category id : " + id);
       Category cat = (Category) getCategoryDAO().getCategory(id);
       if (cat == null) {
          return Response.status(Status.NOT_FOUND).build();
       } else {
          cat.setBooks(getCategoryDAO().getBooks(id));
          return Response.ok(cat).build();
       }
    }
}
```

The above code shows that we have modified only the `@Produces` and `@Consumes` annotations to add support for `application/json` type, which specifies the `CategoryService` accepts and produces `application/json` type in addition to `application/xml`. The CXF runtime would handle the conversion of HTTP JSON request to Java objects, and map the response from Java objects to HTTP JSON response format. Based on the content type associated with the HTTP request, the JSON or XML request would be serialized to Java objects and the appropriate methods which serve those request types would be called. For the `CategoryService`, all resource methods accept and produce XML as well as JSON formats.

We have thus enabled JSON support for `CategoryService`. Follow the steps in the *Building the code* and *Deploying the code* sub sections mentioned in the *Building and deploying the WAR file* section to deploy the latest code. Before running the deploy command on the console, carry out the following steps:

1. Stop the Tomcat server
2. Undeploy the web application by running the following command on the command prompt from the `Chapter7/restapp` folder

   ```
   ant undeploy
   ```

3. Start the Tomcat server

We would next invoke the `CategoryService` RESTful resource using JSON as the message format.

Invoking the Get Category operation with JSON as the message format

We now send a Get Category request to the `CategoryService` and receive the output response in JSON format. Launch the poster plug-in, and enter the following information in the **Poster** screen:

1. Enter **URL** as `http://localhost:8080/restapp/categoryservice/category/001` (Replace `8080` with the port number where the web server is running).
2. Click on the **Headers** tab, and in the **Name** field enter **Accept,** in the **Value** field enter **application/json**, and click **Add/Change**. This will overwrite any existing values for the **Accept** parameter.
3. In the **Actions** tab, click **GET** to issue a HTTP GET request to the `CategoryService`.

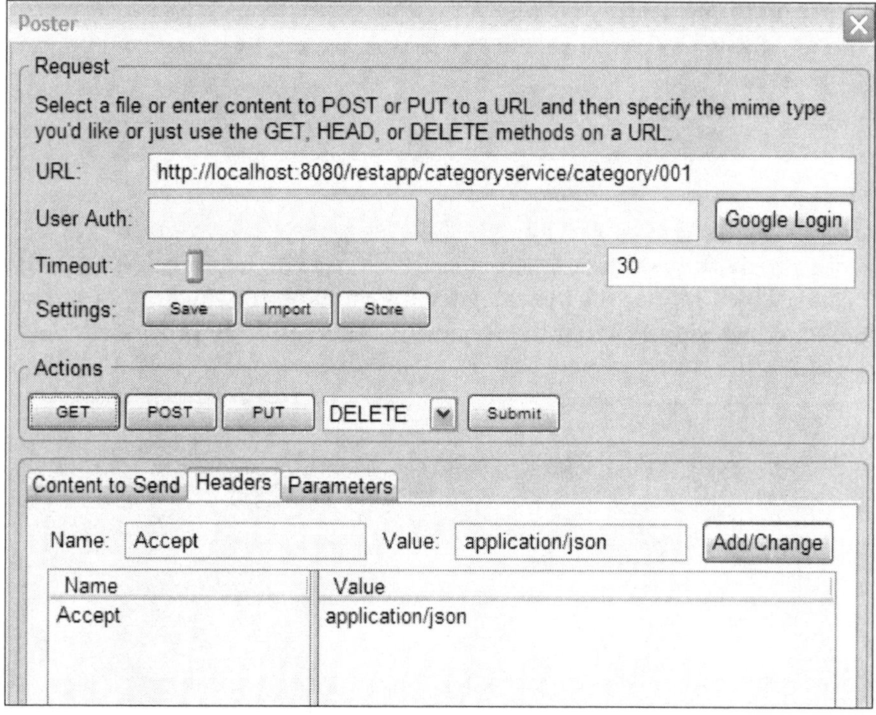

The `getCategory()` method code will be executed, as shown in the next code snippet. We had analyzed this code earlier in the *Invoking the Get Category operation* section. There is no change in the implementation, the only thing that we added was the `@Produces` annotation which specifies that `geCategory()` accepts `application/xml` and `application/json` as the message format. If you remove the `application/json` value, build and redeploy the application, and fire the same request, then CXF runtime will throw an error as it can't find a resource that accepts the `application/json` message type. The CXF implementation converts the `Category` Java object to the JSON format using default JSON binding. It also creates the HTTP response, and sets the HTTP headers (status, content-type, content length) and Category JSON format as the HTTP body data.

```
@GET
   @Path("/category/{id}")
   @Produces({"application/json","application/xml"})
   public Category getCategory(@PathParam("id") String id) {
      System.out.println("getCategory called with category id: " + id);
      Category cat = (Category) getCategoryDAO().getCategory(id);
      if (cat == null) {
         ResponseBuilder builder = Response.status(Status.BAD_REQUEST);
         builder.type("application/xml");
```

```
            builder.entity("<error>Category Not Found</error>");
            throw new WebApplicationException(builder.build());
        } else {
            return cat;
        }
    }
```

On successful invocation, you receive the following response from the `getCategory()` method of the `CategoryService`. As you can see, the response is in JSON format, which represents the category information for category `001`. The HTTP Status is `200`, which signifies that the request was successfully processed.

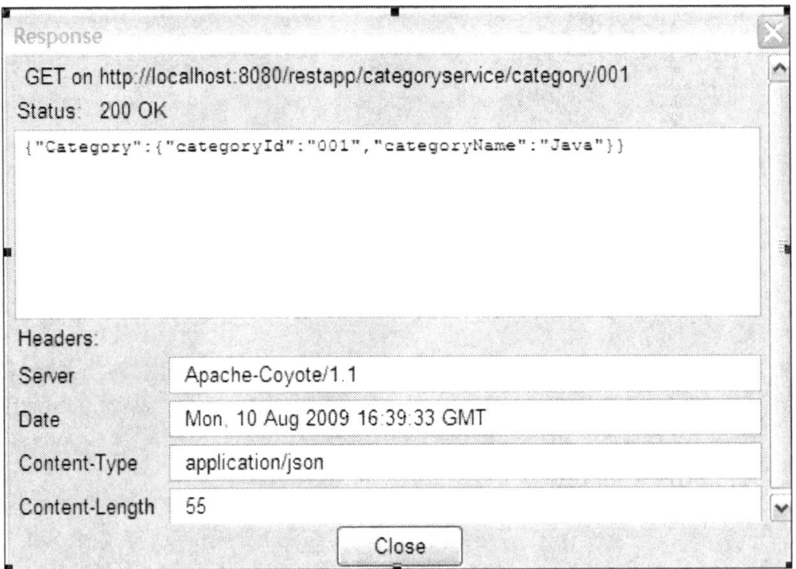

Invoking the Add Category operation with JSON as the message format

We will send an Add Category request to the `CategoryService` using JSON as the message format. Enter the following information in the **Poster** screen, as shown in the next screenshot:

1. Enter **URL** as `http://localhost:8080/restapp/categoryservice/category` (Replace 8080 with the port number where the web server is running).
2. Enter **Content Type** as **application/json**. This specifies the request content type.

3. Click on the **Headers** tab, and in the **Name** field enter **Accept,** in the **Value** field enter **application/json**, and click **Add/Change**. This will overwrite any existing values for the **Accept** parameter.
4. In the **Content to Send** field, enter the following Category information in a JSON format.

```
{"Category":{"categoryId":"003","categoryName":"WebSphere"}}
```

5. In the **Actions** section, click on the **POST** method, which will issue an HTTP POST request to the `CategoryService` with the above information.

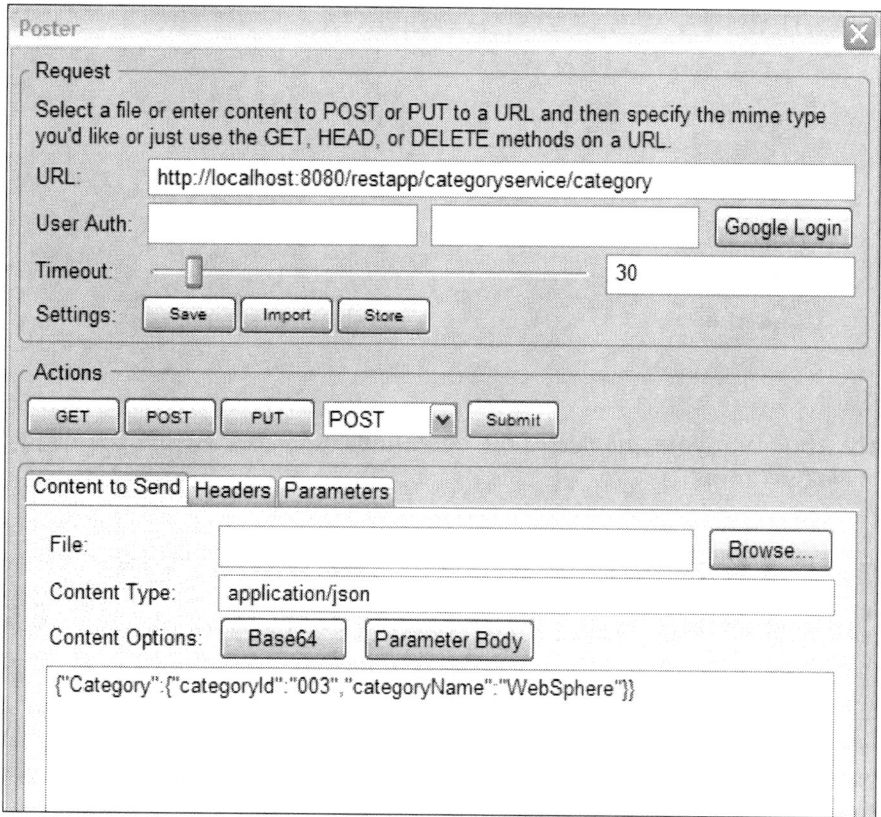

The `addCategory()` method is executed for the above request, which now consumes `application/json` as the message format. The code is the same as the one we analyzed earlier in the *Invoking the Add category* section.

On successful invocation you receive the following response from the `addCategory()` method of the `CategoryService`. You get the same JSON request message as for the response message. The HTTP Status is `200`, which signifies that the request was successfully processed.

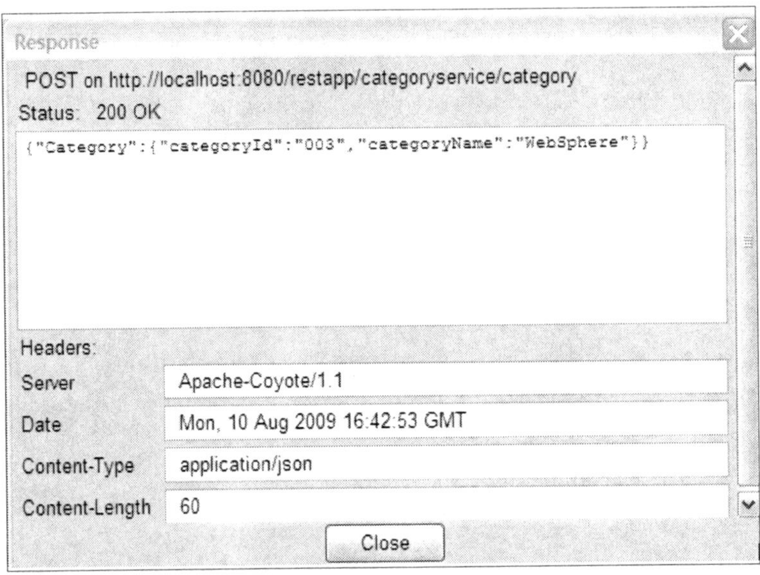

Similarly, you can invoke the rest of the operations of `CategoryService` using JSON as the message format.

Invoking the Book Shop application with JSON as the message format using CXF APIs

We will use the same client, discussed earlier in the *Invoking the Book Shop application using CXF APIs* section. To run the client, navigate to the `Chapter7/restapp/demo/restful/client` folder of the downloaded source code, and type in the following `ant` command. Before running the client, please make sure that the Tomcat server is running.

```
ant runRESTClient -Dformat=application/json
```

This command will run the `CategoryServiceRESTClient` class. As you can see, we now pass the `format` argument as `application/json`. The `application/json` value will be set as the `type` and `accept` value on the `WebClient` object instance, as discussed earlier in the *Invoking the Book Shop application using CXF APIs* section. The `type` maps to HTTP Content-Type and `accept` maps to HTTP `Accept` tag denotes the request format is `application/json` and that the client is expecting the response in `application/json` format.

The important point to note is there is no change in the client code, except that we now set `application/json` as the message format. CXF handles the conversion of JSON format to Java objects transparently behind the scenes. CXF handles this conversion transparently through its data-binding framework.

After running the above command you will see the following output at the console. Each of the test methods, as discussed earlier in the *Invoking the Book Shop application using CXF APIs* section, gets executed, and this invokes the required methods on the RESTful service and prints out the response at the console. As you can see in the following screenshot, we are now using **application/json** as the message format.

```
C:\ApacheCXFBook\Chapter7\restapp>ant runRESTClient -Dformat=application/json
Buildfile: build.xml
 [loadfile] Do not set property srcbuild.classpath as its length is 0.

maybe.generate.code:

compile:

build:

runRESTClient:
     [java] Format is application/json
     [java] testAddCategory called with format application/json
     [java] Category Id retreived for format application/json is 005
     [java] testUpdateCategory called with format application/json
     [java] Status retreived for update category for format application/json is
200
     [java] testGetCategory called with format application/json
     [java] Category details retreived from service with format application/json

     [java] Category Name Fiction Series
     [java] Category Id 005
     [java] testAddBooksForCategory called with format application/json
     [java] testGetBooksForCategory called with format application/json
     [java] Book details retreived from service with format application/json
     [java] Book Name Fiction Book1
     [java] Book ISBN ISBNB001
     [java] Book ID NB001
     [java] Book Author Naveen Balani
     [java] testDeleteCategory called with format application/json
     [java] Status retreived for delete category for format application/json is
200

BUILD SUCCESSFUL
Total time: 5 seconds
C:\ApacheCXFBook\Chapter7\restapp>
```

Intercepting messages for the Book Shop application

Based on application requirements you may want to intercept the request and response messages to log the messages or do pre or post processing of the messages. For instance, you may want to check if security headers are present in the request, authenticate the information, and then invoke the JAX-RS resource. CXF provides Interceptors and Custom Invokers to pre or post process the message. In Chapter 5 we looked at how to use Interceptors to intercept SOAP requests. If your application requires you to merely log the messages, then you can use the `<cxf:logging>` configuration in association with `<jaxrs:server>` definition to log inbound and outbound messages.

For the Book Shop application, we would go with simplified logging capability. To enable logging, we modify `beans.xml`. The following highlighted code shows the modification made to `bean.xml` to enable logging:

```
<?xml version="1.0" encoding="UTF-8"?>
<beans xmlns="http://www.springframework.org/schema/beans"

  xmlns:xsi="http://www.w3.org/2001/XMLSchema-instance"

  xmlns:jaxrs="http://cxf.apache.org/jaxrs"

  xmlns:cxf="http://cxf.apache.org/core"
  xsi:schemaLocation="
http://www.springframework.org/schema/beans
http://www.springframework.org/schema/beans/spring-beans.xsd
http://cxf.apache.org/jaxrs
http://cxf.apache.org/schemas/jaxrs.xsd
http://cxf.apache.org/core http://cxf.apache.org/schemas/core.xsd">

  <import resource="classpath:META-INF/cxf/cxf.xml" />
  <import resource="classpath:META-INF/cxf/cxf-extension-jaxrs-
  binding.xml" />
  <import resource="classpath:META-INF/cxf/cxf-servlet.xml" />


 <jaxrs:server id="categoryService" address="/">
    <jaxrs:features>
     <cxf:logging/>
</jaxrs:features>
<jaxrs:serviceBeans>
```

```
        <ref bean="categoryServiceBean" />
      </jaxrs:serviceBeans>
    </jaxrs:server>

    <bean id="categoryServiceBean" class="demo.restful.CategoryService"/>

  </beans>
```

As you can see in the above configuration, we have added an `<jaxrs:features>` definition tag along with `<cxf:logging>`, which tells the CXF runtime to enable logging for `categoryService`.

Thus we have enabled logging for `CategoryService`. Follow the steps in the *Building the code* and *Deploying the code* subsection mentioned in the *Building and deploying the WAR file* section to deploy the latest code. Before running the deploy command on the console, carry out the following steps:

1. Stop the Tomcat server
2. Undeploy the web application by running the following command on the command prompt from the source code build location `C:\ApacheCXFBook\restapp`

   ```
   ant undeploy
   ```

3. Start the Tomcat server

Fire a sample `GET` request with category ID `001`, as mentioned in *Invoking the Get Category operation* and the *Invoking the Get Category operation with JSON message format* section.

You will see the following messages being logged in the `tomcat_install/logs/catalina.xxxx-xx-xx.log` file:

```
INFO: Inbound Message
----------------------------
ID: 1
Address: /restapp/categoryservice/category/001
Encoding: UTF-8
Content-Type:
Headers: {connection=[keep-alive], accept-language=[en-us,en;q=0.5],
host=[localhost:8080], keep-alive=[300], user-agent=[Mozilla/5.0
(Windows; U; Windows NT 5.1; en-US; rv:1.9.0.13) Gecko/2009073022
Firefox/3.0.13 (.NET CLR 3.5.30729)], accept-encoding=[gzip,deflate],
Content-Type=[null], Accept=[application/xml], accept-charset=[ISO-
8859-1,utf-8;q=0.7,*;q=0.7]}
Payload:
```

```
--------------------------------------
Aug 10, 2009 10:40:05 PM org.apache.cxf.interceptor.LoggingOutIntercep
tor$LoggingCallback onClose
INFO: Outbound Message
---------------------------
ID: 1
Encoding:
Content-Type: application/xml
Headers: {Date=[Mon, 10 Aug 2009 17:10:04 GMT]}
Payload: <?xml version="1.0" encoding="UTF-8" standalone="yes"?><Cate
gory><categoryId>001</categoryId><categoryName>Java</categoryName></
Category>
--------------------------------------
```

The above message specifies the `GET Category` request with the response type as `application/xml`. As you can see above, the response Content-Type is set as `application/xml`, denoting XML as response format.

The following messages specify the `GET Category` request with the response type as `application/json`:

```
Aug 10, 2009 10:40:13 PM org.apache.cxf.interceptor.
LoggingInInterceptor logging
INFO: Inbound Message
----------------------------
ID: 2
Address: /restapp/categoryservice/category/001
Encoding: UTF-8
Content-Type:
Headers: {connection=[keep-alive], accept-language=[en-us,en;q=0.5],
host=[localhost:8080], keep-alive=[300], user-agent=[Mozilla/5.0
(Windows; U; Windows NT 5.1; en-US; rv:1.9.0.13) Gecko/2009073022
Firefox/3.0.13 (.NET CLR 3.5.30729)], accept-encoding=[gzip,deflate],
Content-Type=[null], Accept=[application/json], accept-charset=[ISO-
8859-1,utf-8;q=0.7,*;q=0.7]}
Payload:
--------------------------------------
Aug 10, 2009 10:40:13 PM org.apache.cxf.interceptor.LoggingOutIntercep
tor$LoggingCallback onClose
INFO: Outbound Message
---------------------------
ID: 2
Encoding:
Content-Type: application/json
Headers: {Date=[Mon, 10 Aug 2009 17:10:13 GMT]}
Payload: {"Category":{"categoryId":"001","categoryName":"Java"}}
--------------------------------------
```

As you can see above, the response Content-Type is set as `application/json`, denoting JSON as response format.

Thus, we have successfully deployed and tested the RESTful service which utilizes the CXF logging feature.

Deploying the Book Shop application in the application servers

So far we have deployed the Book Shop application web archive in the Tomcat web server. You might want to deploy the Book Shop application in various other application servers. The steps to deploy the Book Shop application web archive remains more or less the same for all application servers, where the application servers provide some kind of administration console or administrative command to deploy the applications. The war file (`restapp.war`) for the Book Shop application is available inside the `/restapp/build/war` folder where you built the source code. You need to import this war file during deployment. Once the web archive is deployed, you can test your deployment by invoking various operations, as mentioned in the *Invoking the Book Shop Application* section.

Summary

In this chapter we looked at how to deploy a RESTful service in a Tomcat web container. We then executed various operations on the RESTful service using the Poster development tool.

We also looked at how to enable JSON support for the existing `CategoryService` implementation and how CXF framework enables the JSON data-binding mechanism seamlessly. To follow up, we executed sample invocation scenarios for the `CategoryService` with JSON as the message format. We thus enabled support for XML as well as JSON for the Book Shop RESTful application.

Finally, we looked at how to enable logging using the CXF features declaratively, and touched upon procedures to deploy the Book Shop application to various application servers.

Using the CXF JAX-RS features greatly simplified the RESTful service development and provided various capabilities such as logging interceptors, multiple data-binding supports, and simplified configuration using integration with the Spring framework.

8
Working with CXF Tools

The CXF framework provides various tools that assist developers in creating and invoking web services. CXF provides tools to create web service clients and web service implementations from WSDL files, to create SOAP binding and service definition from WSDL interfaces, to validate WSDL files, and to integrate with the popular Apache Maven software tool for build management.

In this chapter we will look at some of the commonly used CXF tools that assist in web service development. We will cover the following topics in this chapter:

- Invoking web services using a Java client
- Invoking web services using JavaScript
- Creating web service implementation from a WSDL file
- Using the WSDLValidator tool to validate the WSDL file

Invoking a web service using the Java client

A web service exposes a set of operations over the network, typically via HTTP protocol. In order to invoke the web services, the web service client needs to know the following information:

- What operations are exposed by the web service
- The input and output message formats required to access the service operations
- What protocol, for instance HTTP or JMS, to use to invoke the web service
- The URL location of the web service

All of the above information is contained in the standard XML descriptor called **WSDL (Web Service Description Language)**. The WSDL file provides a format contract between the web service provider and the web service client. In earlier chapters we looked at the formats of the WSDL file. The web service client typically inspects the WSDL file to determine what operations are exposed by the web service, what parameters need to be supplied to invoke the web service operation and to formulate the request, and invokes the web service over the supported protocol. Similarly, the web service clients need to write the code to inspect the response and convert it into the required format. CXF hides the complexity of creating web service clients by providing the WSDL to Java command line tool, which takes a WSDL file and generates client code. The client code can be used by developers with no changes to invoke the web services.

In Chapter 3 we looked at the **Contract First development** approach where we used the `WSDL2Java` tool to generate SEI classes from WSDL. In order to create clients, we reused the server-side SEI interface and input classes. Often this might not be the case as you wouldn't have access to the actual SEI interface and input classes and you would generate client code from the WSDL file and use this for creating clients. In this section, we will look at how to generate client code from an existing WSDL. For this example, we will take a real world scenario, where we will invoke a **.NET** service located over the Web using the Java client generated by the WSDL to Java tool. This shows the true power of web service interoperability, where applications implemented in different languages can communicate with each other.

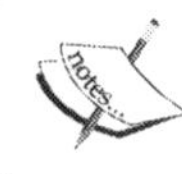

The process of generating web service clients does not differ for web services implemented in different languages, as you generate web service clients from WSDL and XML Schema definitions.

Before invoking the .NET service, let's examine the WSDL to determine which operations are exposed by the web service.

Analyzing the service WSDL definition

We will invoke a publicly available .NET web service located at `http://www.ignyte.com/webservices/ignyte.whatsshowing.webservice/moviefunctions.asmx?wsdl`. This web service retrieves US Theaters and Movie Showtime information based on a valid US zip code and a radius supplied by the web service clients.

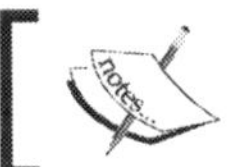

The .NET web service is a **WS-I** compliant web service.

The **Web Services Interoperability Organization** (**WS-I**), an open industry organization, was formed to promote web services interoperability across platforms, operating systems, and programming languages. One concrete product of WS-I is the **Basic Profile**. Basic Profile narrows the scope of specifications to a reasonable set of rules and guidelines that are best suited to help interoperability.

If you type in the given URL in the browser, you see the WSDL definition, as shown in the following screenshot:

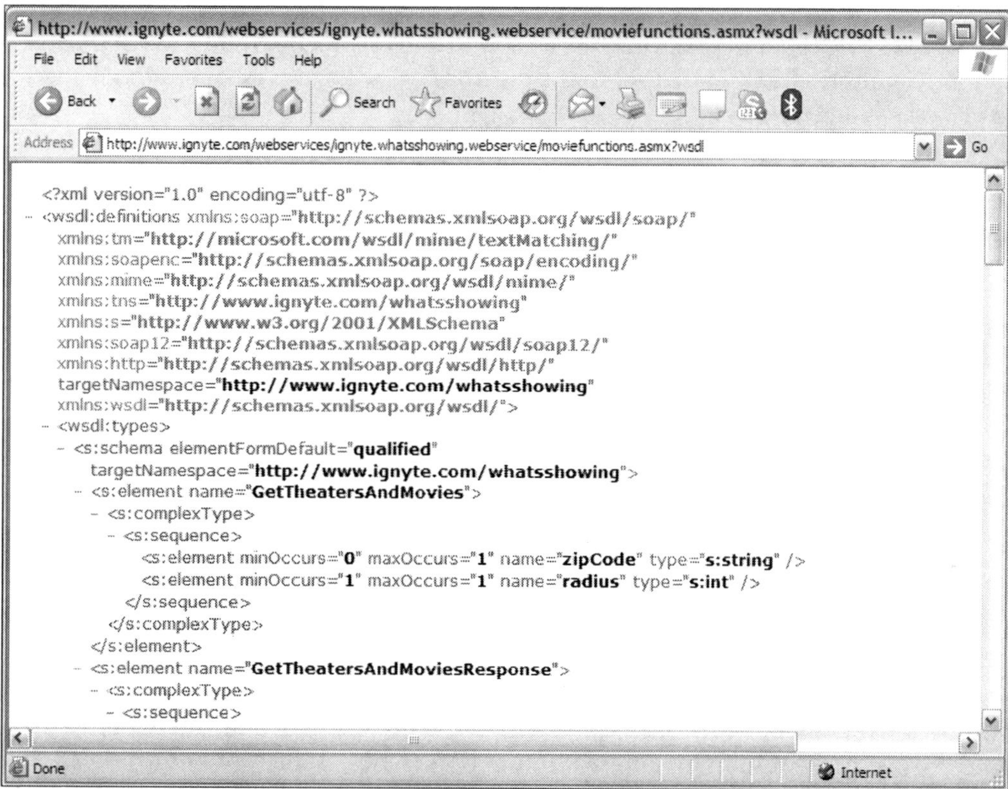

Let's analyze the important sections of the WSDL file to get an understanding of which operations are exposed by the movie information web service and which message formats are required to invoke the web service.

The web service provides two operations, `GetTheatersAndMovies` and `GetUpcomingMovies`, as shown in listing below. For this chapter, we will focus on how to invoke the `GetTheatersAndMovies` operation. The `GetTheatersAndMovies` takes the `GetTheatersAndMoviesSoapIn` message as the input and provides `GetTheatersAndMoviesSoapOut` as the output message.

```
<wsdl:portType name="MovieInformationSoap">
    <wsdl:operation name="GetTheatersAndMovies">
      <wsdl:documentation xmlns:wsdl="http://schemas.xmlsoap.org/
wsdl/">This method will retrieve a list of all theaters and the movies
playing today.</wsdl:documentation>
      <wsdl:input message="tns:GetTheatersAndMoviesSoapIn" />
      <wsdl:output message="tns:GetTheatersAndMoviesSoapOut" />
    </wsdl:operation>
  </wsdl:portType>
```

The web service client invokes the `GetTheatersAndMovies` operation to get theater and movie information. The input to the `GetTheatersAndMovies` operation is the `GetTheatersAndMoviesSoapIn` XML message.

The `GetTheatersAndMoviesSoapIn` message references the `GetTheatersAndMovies` element, which defines the actual XML schema definition for the input message. The following is the code listing of `GetTheatersAndMovies` schema definition:

```
<s:element name="GetTheatersAndMovies">
        <s:complexType>
          <s:sequence>
            <s:element minOccurs="0" maxOccurs="1"
            name="zipCode" type="s:string" />
            <s:element minOccurs="1" maxOccurs="1"
            name="radius" type="s:int" />
          </s:sequence>
        </s:complexType>
      </s:element>
```

The `GetTheatersAndMovies` contains an element `zipCode` of type `String` and `radius` which is of type `integer` that needs to be passed as input by the web services client as an input to the `GetTheatersAndMoviesSoapIn` operation. The **minOccurs** and **maxOccurs** attribute associated with `zipCode` and `radius` is used to specify the minimum and maximum occurrence of the element inside a `GetTheatersAndMovies` element. The `zipCode` and `radius` element can appear only once inside a `GetTheatersAndMovies` element as it specifies the value of `maxOccurs="1"`. If `maxOccurs` has the value `Unbounded`, then it implies that multiple occurrences of the element can exist.

Similarly, the `GetTheatersAndMoviesResponse` specifies the output message format for the response. The following is the code listing of the `GetTheatersAndMoviesResponse` schema definition. We will break down the schema for better understanding:

- The `GetTheatersAndMoviesResponse` schema

  The following shows the definition of `GetTheatersAndMoviesResponse`. The `GetTheatersAndMoviesResponse` contains an element `ArrayOfTheater`.

```
<s:element name="GetTheatersAndMoviesResponse">
        <s:complexType>
          <s:sequence>
            <s:element minOccurs="0" maxOccurs="1"
            name="GetTheatersAndMoviesResult" type=
            "tns:ArrayOfTheater" />
          </s:sequence>
        </s:complexType>
</s:element>
```

- The `ArrayOfTheater` Schema

  The following shows the definition of `ArrayOfTheater` schema. The `ArrayOfTheater` is an array which consists of `Theatre` elements. The `maxOccurs="unbounded"` specifies that multiple occurrences of `Theatre` elements can exist in an `ArrayOfTheater` element.

```
   <s:complexType name="ArrayOfTheater">
        <s:sequence>
          <s:element minOccurs="0" maxOccurs=
          "unbounded" name="Theater" nillable=
          "true" type="tns:Theater" />
        </s:sequence>
   </s:complexType>
```

- The `Theatre` Schema

  The `Theater` elements consist of the `Name` and `Address` elements of type `String`, which specifies the name and address of the `Theatre` and an array of `ArrayOfMovie` element.

```
<s:complexType name="Theater">
        <s:sequence>
          <s:element minOccurs="0" maxOccurs="1"
          name="Name" type="s:string" />
          <s:element minOccurs="0" maxOccurs="1"
          name="Address" type="s:string" />
          <s:element minOccurs="0" maxOccurs="1"
          name="Movies" type="tns:ArrayOfMovie" />
        </s:sequence>
</s:complexType>
```

- The `ArrayOfMovie` Schema

  The following is the `ArrayOfMovie` definition. The `ArrayOfMovie` is an array which consists of `Movie` elements. The `maxOccurs="unbounded"` specifies that multiple occurrences of `Movie` elements can exist in an `ArrayOfMovie` element.

```
<s:complexType name="ArrayOfMovie">
        <s:sequence>
          <s:element minOccurs="0" maxOccurs=
          "unbounded" name="Movie" nillable=
          "true" type="tns:Movie" />
        </s:sequence>
      </s:complexType>
```

- The `Movie` Schema

  The `Movie` element contains details of movies such as ratings, names of the movies, running times and show times represented as `String` type.

```
<s:complexType name="Movie">
        <s:sequence>
          <s:element minOccurs="0" maxOccurs="1"
          name="Rating" type="s:string" />
          <s:element minOccurs="0" maxOccurs="1"
          name="Name" type="s:string" />
          <s:element minOccurs="0" maxOccurs="1"
          name="RunningTime" type="s:string" />
          <s:element minOccurs="0" maxOccurs="1"
          name="ShowTimes" type="s:string" />
        </s:sequence>
      </s:complexType>
```

Based on the Schema definitions above, the CXF **WSDL2Java** tool generates Java code that maps to these XML elements. The web service clients communicate with the web services using these generated Java objects to invoke a Java method representing the `GetTheatersAndMoviesoperation` and leave the SOAP XML to Java conversion and low level implementation details with the CXF framework.

The SOAP address in the WSDL file specifies the location of the service, which is `http://www.ignyte.com/webservices/ignyte.whatsshowing.webservice/moviefunctions.asmx`, as shown in the listing below:

```
<wsdl:service name="MovieInformation">
    <wsdl:port name="MovieInformationSoap" binding=
    "tns:MovieInformationSoap">
      <soap:address location="http://www.ignyte.com/webservices/
      ignyte.whatsshowing.webservice/moviefunctions.asmx" />
    </wsdl:port>
```

```
    <wsdl:port name="MovieInformationSoap12" binding=
    "tns:MovieInformationSoap12">
      <soap12:address location="http://www.ignyte.com/webservices/
      ignyte.whatsshowing.webservice/moviefunctions.asmx" />
    </wsdl:port>
  </wsdl:service>
</wsdl:definitions>
```

We will now look at how to generate the web service client code for the Movie information web service.

Building and running the Java web service clients

The source code and build files for the example are available in the `Chapter8/wsdl2Java` folder of the downloaded source code. We will follow the steps below to build and execute the web service client:

- Generate the web service clients
- Analyze the generated artifacts
- Modify the generated code
- Build the web service client
- Run the web service client

Generate the web service clients

We will use the Ant build script (`build.xml`) for generating the web service client code and building the project code as shown below. Navigate to the `Chapter8/wsdl2java` folder of the downloaded source code. Execute the `cxfWSDLToJava` target by navigating to the `wsdl2java` folder and running the following command:

```
ant cxfWSDLToJava
```

The following figure shows the output generated upon running the `ant command`:

```
Command Prompt - cmd

C:\ApacheCXFBook\wsdl2Java>ant cxfWSDLToJava
Buildfile: build.xml

cxfWSDLToJava:

BUILD SUCCESSFUL
Total time: 15 seconds
C:\ApacheCXFBook\wsdl2Java>
```

The **cxfWSDLToJava** ant target calls the CXF tool **apache.cxf.tools.wsdlto.WSDLToJava** to generate web service client code based on the URL `http://www.ignyte.com/webservices/ignyte.whatsshowing.webservice/moviefunctions.asmx?wsdl`

The following is a code snippet of ant target `cxfWSDLToJava` in `build.xml`:

```
<target name="cxfWSDLToJava">
   <java classname="org.apache.cxf.tools.wsdlto.WSDLToJava"
   fork="true">
      <arg value="-client"/>
      <arg value="-d"/>
      <arg value="src"/>
      <arg value="http://www.ignyte.com/webservices/ignyte.
      whatsshowing.webservice/moviefunctions.asmx?wsdl"/>
      <classpath>
         <path refid="cxf.classpath"/>
      </classpath>
   </java>
</target>
```

`WSDLToJava` generates JAX-WS compliant Java code for the services defined in the WSDL document. Based on the parameters passed, it can generate the starting point of the code for developing the web service client and service. The `client` option, as shown in above snippet, generates the client code. The following is a list of augments and descriptions supported by the `WSDLToJava` tool extracted as it is from the CXF website—`http://cwiki.apache.org/CXF20DOC/wsdl-to-java.html`.

Option	Description
`-?`	Displays the online help for this utility.
`-help`	Displays the online help for this utility.
`-h`	Displays the online help for this utility.
`-fe frontend-name`	Specifies the frontend technology to use for generating code. Default is JAXWS. Currently supports only JAXWS frontend.
`-db databinding-name`	Specifies the data binding mechanism. Default is `jaxb`. Currently supports `jaxb` and `xmlbeans` databinding. `sdo` (`sdo-static` and `sdo-dynamic`) supported in 2.3.
`-wv wsdl-version`	Specifies the WSDL version. Default is WSDL1.1. Currently supports only WSDL1.1 version.
`-p [ wsdl-namespace= ] PackageName`	Specifies zero or more package names to use for the generated code. Optionally specifies the WSDL namespace to package name mapping.
`-sn service-name`	The WSDL service name to use for the generated code.
`-b binding-name`	Specifies JAXWS or JAXB binding files or `XMLBeans` context files. Use multiple `-b` flags to specify multiple entries.
`-catalog catalog-file-name`	Specify catalog file to map the imported wsdl/schema
`-d output-directory`	Specifies the directory into which the generated code files are written.
`-compile`	Compiles generated Java files.
`-classdir complile-class-dir`	Specifies the directory into which the compiled class files are written.
`-client`	Generates starting point code for a client mainline.
`-server`	Generates starting point code for a server mainline.
`-impl`	Generates starting point code for an implementation object.
`-all`	Generates all starting point code—types, service proxy, service interface, server mainline, client mainline, implementation object, and an Ant `build.xml` file.
`-ant`	Generates the Ant `build.xml` file.
`-autoNameResolution`	Automatically resolve naming conflicts without requiring the use of binding customizations.

Option	Description
`-defaultValues=[DefaultValueProvider impl]`	Specifies that default values are generated for the `impl` and client. You can also provide a custom default value provider. The default provider is `RandomValueProvider`.
`-nexclude schema-namespace [=java-packagename]`	Ignore the specified WSDL schema namespace when generating code. This option may be specified multiple times. Also, it optionally specifies the Java package name used by types described in the excluded namespace(s).
`-exsh (true/false)`	Enables or disables processing of implicit SOAP headers (that is, SOAP headers defined in the `wsdl:binding` but not the `wsdl:portType` section). Default is `false`.
`-dns (true/false)`	Enables or disables the loading of the default namespace package name mapping. Default is true and `http://www.w3.org/2005/08/addressing=org.apache.cxf.ws.addressing` namespace package mapping will be enabled.
`-dex (true/false)`	Enables or disables the loading of the default excludes namespace mapping. Default is `true`.
`-validate`	Enables validating the WSDL before generating the code.
`-keep`	Specifies that the code generator will not overwrite any pre-existing files. You will be responsible for resolving any resulting compilation issues.
`-wsdlLocation wsdlLocation`	Specifies the value of the `@WebServiceClient` annotation's `wsdlLocation` property.
`-xjc<xjc args>`	Specifies a comma separated list of arguments that are passed directly to the XJC processor when using the JAXB databinding. A list of available XJC plugins can be obtained using -xjc-X.
`-noAddressBinding`	For compatibility with CXF 2.0, this flag directs the code generator to generate the older CXF proprietary WS-Addressing types instead of the JAX-WS 2.1 compliant WS-Addressing types.
`-v`	Displays the version number for the tool.
`-verbose`	Displays comments during the code generation process.
`-quiet`	Suppresses comments during the code generation process.
`wsdlfile`	The path and name of the WSDL file to use in generating the code.

After executing the command, the generated code is created in the `wsdl2java/src` folder.

Analyzing the JAX-WS and client generated artifacts

The following artifacts are generated in the `wsdl2Java/src/com/ignite/whatsshowing` folder:

- JAXB classes—these are generated by reading the schema definitions defined in the Movie information WSDL. The classes generated for the Movie information web service are `ArrayOfMovie`, `ArrayOfTheater`, `ArrayOfUpcomingMovie`, `Movie`, `Theater` `UpcomingMovie`, and `ObjectFactory`.
- The `RequestWrapper` and `ResponseWrapper` classes—as the Movie information web service uses the document-literal web service style, the `Request` and `Response` wrapper objects are generated for input and output message formats for the operations `GetTheatersAndMovies` and `GetUpcomingMovies`. The `Request` and `Response` Wrapper objects wrap the input and output for document-literal wrapped style web services. The `GetTheatersAndMovies` (Request Wrapper) and `GetTheatersAndMoviesResponse` (Response Wrapper) are generated for the `getTheatersAndMovies` operation.
- The next code snippet shows the generated `GetTheatersAndMovies.java`. As you can see below, the class has JAXB annotations that are defined to map Java to an XML element. The JAXB annotations are similar to one that was defined in earlier chapters. The `@XmlRootElement` defines the root element of the input request which has the name `GetTheatersAndMovies`. The attributes `zipCode` and `radius` are contained in the `GetTheatersAndMovies` XML element. The annotations are used to map Java to an XML request.

  ```
  @XmlAccessorType(XmlAccessType.FIELD)
  @XmlType(name = "", propOrder = {
      "month",
      "year"
  })
  @XmlRootElement(name = "GetTheatersAndMovies")
  public class GetTheatersAndMovies {
      protected String zipCode;
      protected int radius;
      public String getZipCode() {
          return zipCode;
  ```

```
        }
        public void setZipCode(String value) {
            this.zipCode = value;
        }
        public int getRadius() {
            return radius;
        }
        public void setRadius(int value) {
            this.radius = value;
        }
    }
```

- Service Interface—this class contains the service interface for the Movie information web service. The service interface generated for the Movie information web service is `MovieInformationSoap.java`.
- Service class—this is the class that web service clients will use to make requests to the web service. The service class generated for the Movie information web service is `MovieInformation.java`. The service class contains the `@WebServiceClient` annotation and lookup methods to retrieve the Service Interface.
- Client code—the standalone web service client code that provides a starting point for the client code, which calls various operations of the web service. You need to modify the client code to provide the input for each of the operations being invoked. The client code generated for the Movie information web service is `MovieInformationSoap_MovieInformationSoap12_Client.java` and `MovieInformationSoap_MovieInformationSoap_Client.java`. Two client codes are generated as there are two ports defined for the Movie information service, `MovieInformationSoap` and `MovieInformationSoap12`. You can use any of the client code. There are two port types provided to support SOAP 1.1 and SOAP 1.2 request.

Modifying the generated client

We will now modify the generated client `MovieInformationSoap_MovieInformationSoap12_Client.java` to provide input to the `getTheatersAndMovies` operations method. Open the `MovieInformationSoap_MovieInformationSoap12_Client.java` in any text editor, and modify the generated code, as highlighted in bold.

```
package com.ignyte.whatsshowing;
import java.io.File;
```

```
//Other imports.....
import java.util.List;
public final class MovieInformationSoap_MovieInformationSoap12_Client
{
    public static void main(String args[]) throws Exception {
        //Refer to generated code for compete listing
          System.out.println("Invoking getTheatersAndMovies...");
          java.lang.String _getTheatersAndMovies_zipCode = "78750";
          int _getTheatersAndMovies_radius = 2;
com.ignyte.whatsshowing.ArrayOfTheater _getTheatersAndMovies__
return = port.getTheatersAndMovies(_getTheatersAndMovies_zipCode, _
getTheatersAndMovies_radius);
System.out.println("getTheatersAndMovies.result=" + _
getTheatersAndMovies__return);
      System.out.println("Theater List is : "
            + _getTheatersAndMovies__return.getTheater().size());
List<Theater> theatreList = _getTheatersAndMovies__return.
getTheater();
      for (int i = 0; i < theatreList.size(); i++) {
         System.out.println("Theatre Name : " +
         theatreList.get(i).getName());
         List<Movie> movieList =
         theatreList.get(i).getMovies().getMovie();
           for (int j = 0; j < movieList.size(); j++) {
         System.out.println("Movie Name : " +
               movieList.get(j).getName());
         System.out.println("Movie Rating : " +
         movieList.get(j).getRating());
         }
         System.out.println("End of Movies for Theatre :"
         + theatreList.get(i).getName());
      }
//Remaining code block
```

As you can see in the previous code, we specify the zip code as `78750` and radius as `2`. Next, the operation `getTheatersAndMovies(_getTheatersAndMovies_zipCode, _getTheatersAndMovies_radius)` is invoked. The operation returns the `com.ignyte.whatsshowing.ArrayOfTheater` response. We then get the list of theatres from `com.ignyte.whatsshowing.ArrayOfTheater` object by calling the `_getTheatersAndMovies__return.getTheater()` method. Next we iterate through the `theatreList` and print the name, `theatreList.get(i).getName()`. For each theatre, we retrieve the list of movies running in that theatre, by calling `theatreList.get(i).getMovies().getMovie()`. We then iterate through the set of movies and print the name, `movieList.get(j).getName()` and rating, `movieList.get(j).getRating()` for each movie.

Building the client

To build the client, navigate to the `wsld2java` folder, and run the following command to build the code:

```
ant build
```

The following screenshot shows the output generated on running the `ant` command:

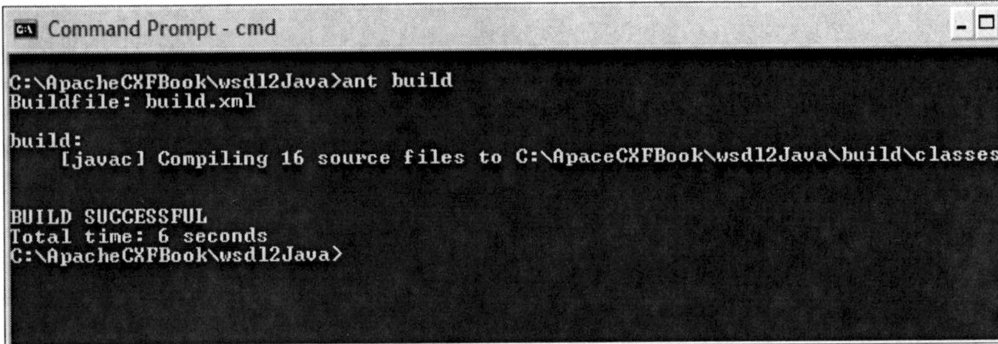

Running the client

To run the client, navigate to the `wsld2java` folder, and run the following command to build the code:

```
ant runClient
```

This command calls the target `runClient` in `build.xml`, and executes the `MovieInformationSoap_MovieInformationSoap_Client` class

The following output will be printed on the console. Look for the **Theater List is** system output message to determine how many theatres are retrieved for that area code. For each theatre you see the movie information being printed on the console. Look for the **Movie Name** and **Movie Rating** system output message, as shown in the next screenshot. Note that this information is retrieved at runtime, so the value of **Theater List is** would vary from the one shown in the screenshot below:

```
Command Prompt
viceFactoryBean buildServiceFromWSDL
     [java] INFO: Creating Service {http://www.ignyte.com/whatsshowing}MovieInfo
rmation from WSDL: http://www.ignyte.com/webservices/ignyte.whatsshowing.webserv
ice/moviefunctions.asmx?wsdl
     [java] Invoking getUpcomingMovies...
     [java] getUpcomingMovies.result=null
     [java] Invoking getTheatersAndMovies...
     [java] getTheatersAndMovies.result=com.ignyte.whatsshowing.ArrayOfTheater@5
f1ae9
     [java] Theater List is : 18
     [java] Theatre Name : Alamo Drafthouse Lake Creek
     [java] Movie Name : District 9
     [java] Movie Rating : R
     [java] Movie Name : G.I. Joe: The Rise of Cobra
     [java] Movie Rating : PG-13
     [java] Movie Name : Harry Potter and the Half-Blood Prince
     [java] Movie Rating : PG
     [java] Movie Name : Inglourious Basterds
     [java] Movie Rating : R
     [java] Movie Name : Julie & Julia
     [java] Movie Rating : PG-13
     [java] Movie Name : Taking Woodstock
     [java] Movie Rating : R
     [java] Movie Name : The Goods: Live Hard. Sell Hard.
     [java] Movie Rating : R
     [java] Movie Name : The Hangover
     [java] Movie Rating : R
     [java] End of Movies for Theatre :Alamo Drafthouse Lake Creek
     [java] Theatre Name : Regal Arbor Cinema at Great Hills
     [java] Movie Name : (500) Days of Summer
     [java] Movie Rating : PG-13
     [java] Movie Name : Adam
```

We have thus successfully invoked the Movie information web service.

Invoking the web service using JavaScript

CXF provides a tool called *WSDL to JavaScript*, which generates JavaScript client code from the WSDL file that can be used to invoke the web service. The generated JavaScript code uses the `XMLHttpRequest` object, which provides scripted client functionality for transferring data between a client and a server. Most modern browsers support the `XMLHttpRequest` specification. You need a compatible browser supporting `XMLHttpRequest` APIs. The example has been tested on Internet Explorer version 6.x and above.

Building and running the Java web service clients

The source code and build files for the example are available in the `Chapter8/wsdl2Java` folder of the downloaded source code .We will follow the steps below to build and execute the JavaScript web service client:

- Generate the JavaScript web service client
- Analyze the generated JavaScript artifacts
- Modify the JavaScript code for execution
- Run the JavaScript client on the browser

Generating the JavaScript client

We will use the Ant build script (`build.xml`) to generate the JavaScript client code and build the project code, as shown below. Navigate to the `Chapter8/wsdl2JS` folder of the downloaded source code.

Execute the `cxfWSDLToJS` target by navigating to the `wsdl2JS` folder, and run the following command line:

```
ant cxfWSDLToJS
```

The following screenshot shows the output generated on running the ant command:

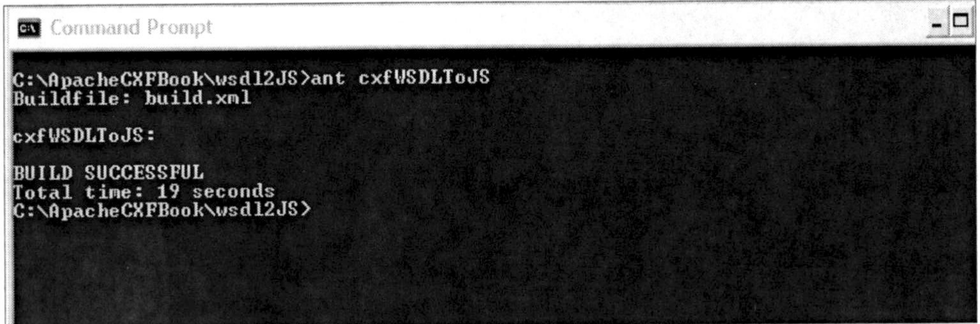

`cxfWSDLToJS` calls the CXF tool `org.apache.cxf.tools.wsdlto.javascript.WSDLToJavaScript` to generate JavaScript code based on the WSDL URL `http://www.ignyte.com/webservices/ignyte.whatsshowing.webservice/moviefunctions.asmx?wsdl`. The following shows the code snippet of the `cxfWSDLToJS` target.

```
<target name="cxfWSDLToJS">
```

```
        <java classname="org.apache.cxf.tools.wsdlto.javascript.
        WSDLToJavaScript" fork="true">
         <arg value="-d"/>
           <arg value="src"/>
           <arg value="http://www.ignyte.com/webservices/ignyte.
           whatsshowing.webservice/moviefunctions.asmx?wsdl"/>
           <classpath>
              <path refid="cxf.classpath"/>
           </classpath>
        </java>
     </target>
```

The `-d` option in the above code snippet specifies the directory for the generated code. After running the `cxfWSDLToJS` target, the JavaScript code will be generated in the `src` folder. The `WSDLToJavaScript` generates JavaScript for the services defined in the WSDL document. The following is the list of arguments and descriptions supported by the `WSDLToJS` tool, extracted as it is from the CXF website—`http://cwiki.apache.org/CXF20DOC/wsdl-to-javascript.html`

Option	Description
`-?`	Displays the online help for this utility.
`-help`	Displays the online help for this utility.
`-h`	Displays the online help for this utility.
`-p`	Specifies a mapping between the namespaces used in the WSDL document and the prefixes used in the generated JavaScript. This argument can be used more than once.
`-catalog`	Specifies the URL of an XML catalog to be used for resolving imported schemas and WSDL documents.
`-d`	Specifies the directory into which the generated code is written.
`-validate`	Instructs the tool to validate the WSDL document before attempting to generate any code.
`-v`	Displays the version number for the tool.
`-verbose`	Displays comments during the code generation process
`-quiet`	Suppresses comments during the code generation process.
`wsdlUrl`	Specifies the location of the WSDL document from which the code is generated.

After executing the command, the generated code is created in the `src` folder of the `wsdl2JS` folder.

Analyzing the generated artifacts

JavaScript `MovieInformation.js` gets generated from the WSDL document in the `wsdl2JS/src` folder. The JavaScript code is organized as follows:

- Schema functions—these are generated by reading the schema definitions defined in Movie information WSDL. For each of the schemas defined in WSDL, a corresponding JavaScript function is generated. The code for each schema starts with a comment, such as

  ```
  Definitions for schema: http://www.ignyte.com/whatsshowing
  Constructor for XML Schema item {http://www.ignyte.com/
  whatsshowing}Movie
  ```

  The Following is an example of the generated Movie schema:

  ```
  //
  // Definitions for schema: http://www.ignyte.com/whatsshowing
  //  http://www.ignyte.com/webservices/ignyte.whatsshowing.
  webservice/moviefunctions.asmx?wsdl#types1
  //
  // Constructor for XML Schema item {http://www.ignyte.com/
  whatsshowing}Movie
  //
  function www_ignyte_com_whatsshowing_Movie () {
      this.typeMarker = 'www_ignyte_com_whatsshowing_Movie';
      this._Rating = null;
      this._Name = null;
      this._RunningTime = null;
      this._ShowTimes = null;
  }
  ```

  For the Movie Information web service, we would have the JavaScript functions code generated for `Movie`, `UpcomingMovie`, `ArrayOfMovie`, `Theater`, `ArrayOfUpcomingMovie`, `ArrayOfTheater`, `GetUpcomingMovies-Response`, `GetTheatersAndMoviesResponse`, `GetTheatersAndMovies`, and `GetUpcomingMovies`.

- Serialization and Deserialization functions—For each of the Schema code generated, corresponding Serialization and Deserialization functions are generated. The serialize function is used to convert the JavaScript schema object to an XML request format and the deserialize function converts the XML response to the corresponding JavaScript object. The following code snippet shows the generated function handling the serializing and deserializing of the `Movie` object:

```
//
// Serialize {http://www.ignyte.com/whatsshowing}Movie
//
function www_ignyte_com_whatsshowing_Movie_serialize(cxfjsutils,
elementName, extraNamespaces) {
    var xml = '';
    if (elementName != null) {
     xml = xml + '<';
     xml = xml + elementName;
     xml = xml + ' ';
     xml = xml + 'xmlns:jns0=\'http://www.ignyte.com/
     whatsshowing\' ';
     if (extraNamespaces) {
      xml = xml + ' ' + extraNamespaces;
     }
     xml = xml + '>';
    }
    // block for local variables
    {
     //Converts Rating object to XML Object
     if (this._Rating != null) {
      xml = xml + '<jns0:Rating>';
      xml = xml + cxfjsutils.escapeXmlEntities(this._Rating);
      xml = xml + '</jns0:Rating>';
     }

     //Look at the generated code, remaining code not
    //included...
    }
```

As you can see in the above code snippet, the `www_ignyte_com_whatsshowing_Movie_serialize` function serializes the `www_ignyte_com_whatsshowing_Movie` object to XML. It creates the XML request for the `Movie` and `Rating` element.

```
function www_ignyte_com_whatsshowing_Movie_deserialize
(cxfjsutils, element) {
    var newobject = new www_ignyte_com_whatsshowing_Movie();
    cxfjsutils.trace('element: ' + cxfjsutils.
traceElementName(element));
    var curElement = cxfjsutils.getFirstElementChild(element);
    var item;
    cxfjsutils.trace('curElement: ' + cxfjsutils.
traceElementName(curElement));
    cxfjsutils.trace('processing Rating');
    //Converts Rating XML element to Rating object
    if (curElement != null &&
    cxfjsutils.isNodeNamedNS(curElement,
   'http://www.ignyte.com/whatsshowing', 'Rating')) {
     var value = null;
     if (!cxfjsutils.isElementNil(curElement)) {
      value = cxfjsutils.getNodeText(curElement);
      item = value;
     }
     newobject.setRating(item);
     if (curElement != null) {
      curElement = cxfjsutils.getNextElementSibling(curElement);
     }
    }
    //For complete listing, look at the generated code,
    //remaining code not included here.

    return newobject;
}
```

The `www_ignyte_com_whatsshowing_Movie_deserialize` function, as shown above, does the opposite of converting the XML Response received from the Movie information web service into the `www_ignyte_com_whatsshowing_Movie` object. The rating information is retrieved from `XMLResponse` and set in the `Movie` object by calling the `newobject.setRating(item)` method.

The function uses the methods from the `cxf-utils.js` JavaScript file. `cxf-utils.js` is part of the CXF distribution, available at `CXF_Install/etc/cxf-utils.js` location. `cxf-utils.js` provides code for invoking the web service and retrieving the XML response, common XML conversion code, and browser compatibility support.

- Service function—this function is generated by reading the service definition from the WSDL. The generate service function code starts with a comment such as:

```
// Definitions for service: {http://www.ignyte.com/whatsshowing}
MovieInformation
//

// Javascript for {http://www.ignyte.com/whatsshowing}
MovieInformationSoap

   The following is an example of the generated MovieInformation
service definition.

// Javascript for {http://www.ignyte.com/whatsshowing}
MovieInformationSoap

function www_ignyte_com_whatsshowing_MovieInformationSoap () {
    this.jsutils = new CxfApacheOrgUtil();
    this.jsutils.interfaceObject = this;
    this.synchronous = false;
    this.url = null;
    this.client = null;
    this.response = null;
    //For complete listing, look at the generated code,
    //remaining code not included here.
}
```

  The generated code defines the synchronous property, which specifies the interaction between the JavaScript client and the web service. By default, the `synchronous` property is set to `false` for asynchronous style interaction. In case of asynchronous style interaction, you need to provide a callback function which is executed when the response is received from the web service. Setting this property to `true`, implies that the JavaScript client code (that calls the operations) would wait till the response is received from the web service. The URL property specifies the URL of the web service. You need to set the URL before calling the web service.

- Operation functions—these are generated by reading the service operations defined in the WSDL. The generated service operation code starts with a comment like the following:

```
//
// Operation {http://www.ignyte.com/whatsshowing}
GetTheatersAndMovies
```

```
// Wrapped operation.
// parameter zipCode

   The following is an example of the generated code for
GetTheatersAndMovies operation

//
// Operation {http://www.ignyte.com/whatsshowing}
GetTheatersAndMovies
// Wrapped operation.
// parameter zipCode
// - simple type {http://www.w3.org/2001/XMLSchema}string//
parameter radius
// - simple type {http://www.w3.org/2001/XMLSchema}int//
function www_ignyte_com_whatsshowing_GetTheatersAndMovies_
op(successCallback, errorCallback, zipCode, radius) {
    this.client = new CxfApacheOrgClient(this.jsutils);
    var xml = null;
    var args = new Array(2);
    args[0] = zipCode;
    args[1] = radius;
    //Calls corresponding Serialize Function
    //Invoke the web service
 //For complete listing, look at the generated code,
    //remaining code not included here.

}
```

We invoke the `www_ignyte_com_whatsshowing_GetTheatersAndMovies_op` operation to retrieve the `Theatre` and `Movies` information.

Creating the client

In this section we will create an HTML page, which will include the generated JavaScript. You need to write a few lines of JavaScript code to invoke the operations defined in the generated JavaScript code and provide a callback function that will be called after a response is received from the web service.

We have provided a reference HTML file named `MovieInformation.html` in the `Chapter8/wsdl2Java/src folder` of the downloaded source code. `MovieInformation.html` uses the CXF JavaScript Utility `cxf-utils.js` file. Copy this file from `CXF_Install/etc` to the `src` folder. The following shows the code listing of the `MovieInformation.html` page. We will break down the HTML file into code snippets as follows:

1. We start off by including the `cxf-utils.js` and generated `MovieInformation.js` file.

```
<head>
<script type="text/javascript" src="cxf-utils.js"></script>
<script type="text/javascript" src="MovieInformation.js"></script>
```

2. Next, we create a JavaScript function `addDataTable` to add results retrieved from the Movie web service. Since we retrieve the Movie information at runtime, we call this function recursively to display the Movie information retrieved in a tabular format. The following code snippet adds rows to a table dynamically:

```
<script language="JavaScript" type="text/javascript">

function addDataTable(name,value)
{
  var tbl = document.getElementById('tblResults');
  var lastRow = tbl.rows.length;
  var row = tbl.insertRow(lastRow);

  // left cell
  var cellLeft = row.insertCell(0);
  var textNodeLeft = document.createTextNode(name);
  cellLeft.appendChild(textNodeLeft);

  // right cell
  var cellRight = row.insertCell(1);
  var textNodeRight = document.createTextNode(value);
  cellRight.appendChild(textNodeRight);

}
</script>
```

3. Next, we define a `function invokeMovieInformation`(), which invokes the operation `GetTheatersAndMovies` by calling the function `MovieService.GetTheatersAndMovies(sucessResponse,errorResponse,zipCode, radius)`.We retrieve the zip code and radius values from the input form element. We also pass the functions `sucessResponse` and `errorResponse` as input.

```
function invokeMovieInformation()
{
  var zipCode = document.movieinfoform.zipCode.value;
  var radius = document.movieinfoform.radius.value;
MovieService.
GetTheatersAndMovies(sucessResponse,errorResponse,zipCode,radius);
}
```

4. The `sucessResponse` function is called after a successful response is retrieved from the Movie information web service. `sucessResponse` is a callback function which retrieves the response object and calls the `addDataTable` function to display the Theatre and Movie information retrieved from the web service. We first display the length of Theatre received by calling the method `response.getGetTheatersAndMoviesResult().getTheater().length`). Next we display the first Theater Name and Address by calling the methods `response.getGetTheatersAndMoviesResult().getTheater()[0].getName()` and `response.getGetTheatersAndMoviesResult().getTheater()[0].getAddress()`. We then display the count of movies running in that theatre by calling the method `response.getGetTheatersAndMoviesResult().getTheater()[0].getMovies().getMovie().length`, and we display all movie names running in that theatre by calling the `addDataTable()` recursively.

   The `sucessResponse` function is shown in the following code snippet:

```
<!-- This is the function called for a sucessResponse. -->
function sucessResponse(response)
{
   addDataTable("Length of Theatres " , response.
   getGetTheatersAndMoviesResult().getTheater().length);
   addDataTable("First Theatre name " ,  response.
   getGetTheatersAndMoviesResult().getTheater()[0].getName());
   addDataTable("First Theatre address  " , response.
   getGetTheatersAndMoviesResult().getTheater()[0].getAddress())
   addDataTable("Count of Movies running in Fisrt Theatre - "
   , response.getGetTheatersAndMoviesResult().getTheater()[0].
   getMovies().getMovie().length)
   var movieLength = response.getGetTheatersAndMoviesResult().
   getTheater()[0].getMovies().getMovie().length;
   var i=0;
   for (i=0;i<movieLength;i++)
   {
```

```
        addDataTable( i+1 + " Movie Name" , response.
getGetTheatersAndMoviesResult().getTheater()[0].getMovies().
getMovie()[i].getName())
    }
}
```

5. The `errorResponse` function would be called in case of an unsuccessful web service invocation. The `errorResponse` function is shown in the following code snippet, which displays an error alert message in the browser:

```
<!-- This is the function called for an error. -->
function errorResponse(error)
{
        alert("Error message is " + error);
}
```

6. Next, we define the HTML form which calls the `invokeMovieInformation()` function. The form defines two text input elements for `zipCode` and `radius`. The form also defines a table element `tblResults` to display movie information retrieved from the web service. `invokeMovieInformation()` is shown in the following code snippet:

```
<form name="movieinfoform">
ZipCode: <input type="text" name ="zipCode" value="78759"/><br/>
Radius:  <input type="text" name ="radius" value="2"/><br/><br/>
Invoke Movie Information- <input type="button" value="Invoke"
name="Invoke Movie Information"
onClick="invokeMovieInformation()">

<br/><br/>

<table border="1" id="tblResults">
  <tr>
    <th colspan="2">Movie Results Web Service</th>
  </tr>
</table>
</form>
```

Running the client

Open up the `MovieInformation.html` page in the browser. You see the following screen. Click on **Invoke**.

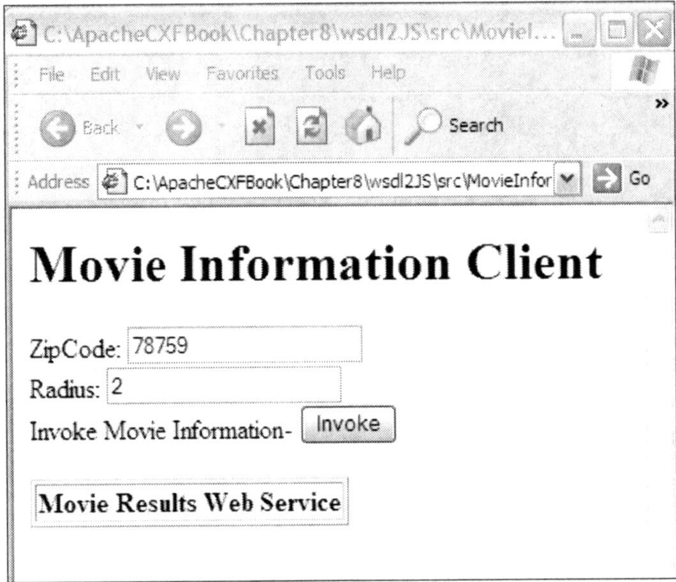

The **Invoke** button calls the `invokeMovieInformation()` JavaScript function, which invokes the Movie information web service. After a successful invocation, you see the following results displayed in the Movie Results web service table. Note that this information is retrieved at runtime, so the value would vary from the one shown in the next screenshot.

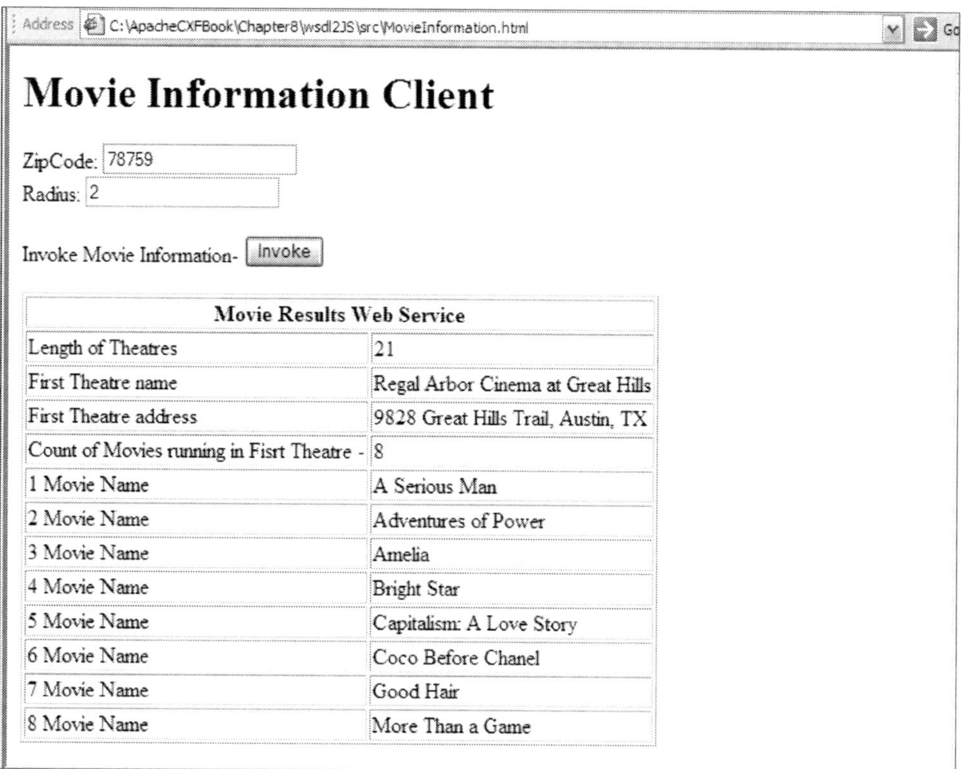

We have thus successfully invoked the Movie information web service using JavaScript.

Creating Service Implementation from the WSDL file

We looked at the `WSDLToJava` tool earlier, when we generated web service client code based on a WSDL file. Based on application requirements, you may want to create a replica of a web service being invoked by the web service client and deploy it in your local environment. This is typically beneficial when testing how your web service clients can connect to local web service implementation, rather than invoking the actual service over the Web. We created Service Implementation from a WSDL file in Chapter 3 where we looked at the Contract First development approach. The outlines of the procedure remain the same with the exception of using a real world .NET web service WSDL, and using it to create a Java Service Implementation. We will now look at how to create a service implementation from the Movie information WSDL file.

Generating and deploying the Service Implementation from the WSDL file

The source code and build files for the example are available in the `Chapter8/wsdl2JavaService` folder of the downloaded source code. We will follow the steps below to build and execute the web service client.

- Generate the web Service Implementation
- Analyze the generated artifacts
- Modify the web Service Implementation
- Build the web service project
- Deploy and publish the web service
- Invoke the web service

Generating the web Service Implementation

To generate the web Service Implementation, navigate to the `wsdl2JavaService` folder, and run the following command:

```
ant cxfWSDLToJava
```

The next screenshot shows the output generated on running the ant command:

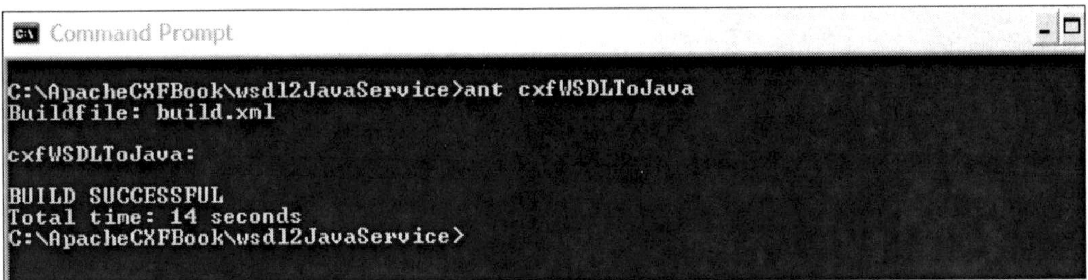

`cxfWSDLToJava` calls the CXF tool `org.apache.cxf.tools.wsdlto.WSDLToJava` to generate Java server code based on the WSDL URL `http://www.ignyte.com/webservices/ignyte.whatsshowing.webservice/moviefunctions.asmx?wsdl`. The following code snippet shows the `cxfWSDLToJava` target:

```
<target name="cxfWSDLToJava">
    <java classname="org.apache.cxf.tools.wsdlto.WSDLToJava"
    fork="true">
        <arg value="-server"/>
        <arg value="-impl"/>
        <arg value="-d"/>
```

```
        <arg value="src"/>
        <arg value="http://www.ignyte.com/webservices/ignyte.
        whatsshowing.webservice/moviefunctions.asmx?wsdl"/>
        <classpath>
           <path refid="cxf.classpath"/>
        </classpath>
    </java>
</target>
```

The `-server` option in the previous code snippet specifies the generation of the server code. After executing the command, the generated code is created in the `wsdl2JavaService/src` folder.

Analyzing the Service Implementation generated artifacts

The artifacts generated are the same as those mentioned in the *Analyzing the JAX-WS and Client Generated Artifacts* section with the addition of the Service Implementation classes and standalone server program. The client code is not generated as we have not specified the client option.

- Service Implementation class—this class provides a sample implementation which extends the `Service` interface. We would modify this class to add our implementation code. The service implementation generated for Movie Service is `MovieInformationSoapImpl.java`

  The following code snippet shows the generated `MovieInformationSoapImpl.java`:

```
@javax.jws.WebService(
                      serviceName = "MovieInformation",
                      portName = "MovieInformationSoap12",
                      targetNamespace = "http://www.ignyte.com/
whatsshowing",
                      wsdlLocation = "http://www.ignyte.com/
webservices/ignyte.whatsshowing.webservice/moviefunctions.
asmx?wsdl",
                      endpointInterface = "com.ignyte.
whatsshowing.MovieInformationSoap")

public class MovieInformationSoapImpl implements
MovieInformationSoap {

    private static final Logger LOG =
    Logger.getLogger(MovieInformationSoapImpl.class.getName());

    /* (non-Javadoc)
```

```
    * @see com.ignyte.whatsshowing.MovieInformationSoap#getUpcomi
ngMovies(int month ,)int year )*
    */
   public com.ignyte.whatsshowing.ArrayOfUpcomingMovie
getUpcomingMovies(int month,int year) {
  //For complete listing, look at the generated code,
   //remaining code not included here.
   }
   /* (non-Javadoc)
    * @see com.ignyte.whatsshowing.MovieInformationSoap#getTheate
rsAndMovies(java.lang.String zipCode ,)int radius )*
    */
   public com.ignyte.whatsshowing.ArrayOfTheater
getTheatersAndMovies(java.lang.String zipCode,int radius) {
  //For complete listing, look at the generated code,
   //remaining code not included here.
   }
}
```

As you can see from the previous code snippet, the generated web service implementation defines the `javax.jws.WebService` annotation which describes the Movie information web service. We looked at `WebService` annotations in earlier chapters. `MovieInformationSoapImpl.java` implements two methods, `getUpcomingMovies` and `getTheatersAndMovies`. In the next section, we will provide implementation for the `getTheatersAndMovies` method.

- Standalone server class—this class provides a standalone utility to publish and test the JAX-WS web service using an embedded server. The code generated for the Movie Information web service is `MovieInformationSoap_MovieInformationSoap12_Server.java`.

Modifying the generated Service Implementation

We will now modify the generated Service Implementation `MovieInformationSoapImpl.java` to add the implementation for the service methods.

1. Open `MovieInformationSoapImpl.java` in any text editor, and modify the generated code, as highlighted in bold.

```
//Imports commented out..
@javax.jws.WebService(
                      serviceName = "MovieInformation",
```

```
                     portName = "MovieInformationSoap",
                     targetNamespace = "http://www.ignyte.com/
whatsshowing",
                     endpointInterface = "com.ignyte.
whatsshowing.MovieInformationSoap")
public class MovieInformationSoapImpl implements
MovieInformationSoap {

//Code commented out.


    public com.ignyte.whatsshowing.ArrayOfTheater
getTheatersAndMovies(java.lang.String zipCode,int radius) {
        LOG.info("Executing operation getTheatersAndMovies");
        System.out.println(zipCode);
        System.out.println(radius);

     try {
   com.ignyte.whatsshowing.ArrayOfTheater _return = new
com.ignyte.whatsshowing.ArrayOfTheater();
        Theater theatre = new Theater();
           theatre.setName("Golden Gate Cinemas");
        theatre.setAddress("Golden Gate Lane");
        Movie movie = new Movie();
        movie.setName("Time changes movie");
        ArrayOfMovie movieArray =  new ArrayOfMovie();
        movieArray.getMovie().add(movie);
         theatre.setMovies(movieArray);
        _return.getTheater().add(theatre);
           return _return;
        } catch (Exception ex) {
           ex.printStackTrace();
           throw new RuntimeException(ex);
        }
    }

}
```

2. We first remove the generated `wsdlLocation` annotation property as we will deploy the web service locally. We provide a dummy implementation for the `getTheatersAndMovies` method.

3. We create an instance of the `Theater` object, which will be called as `theatre`, and set the name and address on the `Theater` object.
4. We then create the `Movie` object, set its name, and add the `Movie` to the `ArrayOfMovie` object (`movieArray`). Finally, we set the `movieArray` object in the `theatre` object, and add the `theatre` object to the `ArrayOfTheater` object.

Note that the `ArrayOfTheater`, `Theater`, `ArrayOfMovie`, and `Movie` objects are JAXB schema classes generated by the `WSDL2Java` tool, based on schema definitions in the Movie information web service.

5. Next, we modify the generated Standalone server class, `MovieInformationSoap_MovieInformationSoap12_Server.java` to publish it to the local address. Open `MovieInformationSoap_MovieInformationSoap12_Server.java` in any text editor. We should modify only the relevant code.

```
//Imports..
public class MovieInformationSoap_MovieInformationSoap12_Server{

    protected MovieInformationSoap_MovieInformationSoap12_Server()
    throws Exception {
        System.out.println("Starting Server");
        Object implementor = new MovieInformationSoapImpl();
        String address = "http://localhost:9082/MovieService";
        Endpoint.publish(address, implementor);
    }
}
```

We modify the address to `http://localhost:9082/MovieService`. The `Endpoint.publish()` method provides a convenient way to publish and test the JAX-WS web service. `publish()` takes two parameters, location of the web service, and the JAX-WS web service implementation class. The `publish()` method creates a lightweight web server at the specified URL, in this case `local host`, and `port 9082` deploys the web service to that location. After running the above program, the `MovieService` will be available at the following URL: `http://localhost:9082/MovieService`

Building the web service project

To build the web service project, navigate to the `wsld2JavaService` folder, and run the following command to build the code:

```
ant build
```

The following screenshot shows the output generated on running the `ant` command:

```
Command Prompt
C:\ApacheCXFBook\wsdl2JavaService>ant build
Buildfile: build.xml

build:
    [mkdir] Created dir: C:\ApacheCXFBook\wsdl2JavaService\build\classes
    [mkdir] Created dir: C:\ApacheCXFBook\wsdl2JavaService\build\src
    [javac] Compiling 17 source files to C:\ApacheCXFBook\wsdl2JavaService\build
classes

BUILD SUCCESSFUL
Total time: 6 seconds
C:\ApacheCXFBook\wsdl2JavaService>
```

Deploying and publishing the web service

To publish the web service, navigate to the `wsdl2JavaService` folder, and run the following command to build the code:

```
ant runServer
```

This command calls the target `runServer` in `build.xml`, and executes the `com.ignyte.whatsshowing.MovieInformationSoap_MovieInformationSoap12_Server` class

The following output is printed on the console, and you see the **Server ready...** message being displayed:

```
Mark Command Prompt - ant runServer
torProvider,org.apache.cxf.ws.rm.RMAssertionBuilder]; root of factory hierarchy
     [java] Sep 1, 2009 12:53:29 AM org.apache.cxf.service.factory.ReflectionSer
viceFactoryBean buildServiceFromWSDL
     [java] INFO: Creating Service {http://www.ignyte.com/whatsshowing}MovieInfo
rmation from WSDL: http://www.ignyte.com/webservices/ignyte.whatsshowing.webserv
ice/moviefunctions.asmx?wsdl
     [java] Sep 1, 2009 12:53:32 AM org.apache.cxf.endpoint.ServerImpl initDesti
nation
     [java] INFO: Setting the server's publish address to be http://www.ignyte.c
om:80/webservices/ignyte.whatsshowing.webservice/moviefunctions.asmx
     [java] Sep 1, 2009 12:53:32 AM org.mortbay.log.Slf4jLog info
     [java] INFO: Logging to org.slf4j.impl.JDK14LoggerAdapter(org.mortbay.log)
via org.mortbay.log.Slf4jLog
     [java] Sep 1, 2009 12:53:32 AM org.mortbay.log.Slf4jLog info
     [java] INFO: jetty-6.1.18
     [java] Sep 1, 2009 12:53:32 AM org.mortbay.log.Slf4jLog info
     [java] INFO: Started SelectChannelConnector@0.0.0.0:80
     [java] Server ready...
```

Once the web service ID is published, you can retrieve the WSDL by typing the URL `http://localhost:9082/MovieService?wsdl` at the browser. You get the following output in the browser:

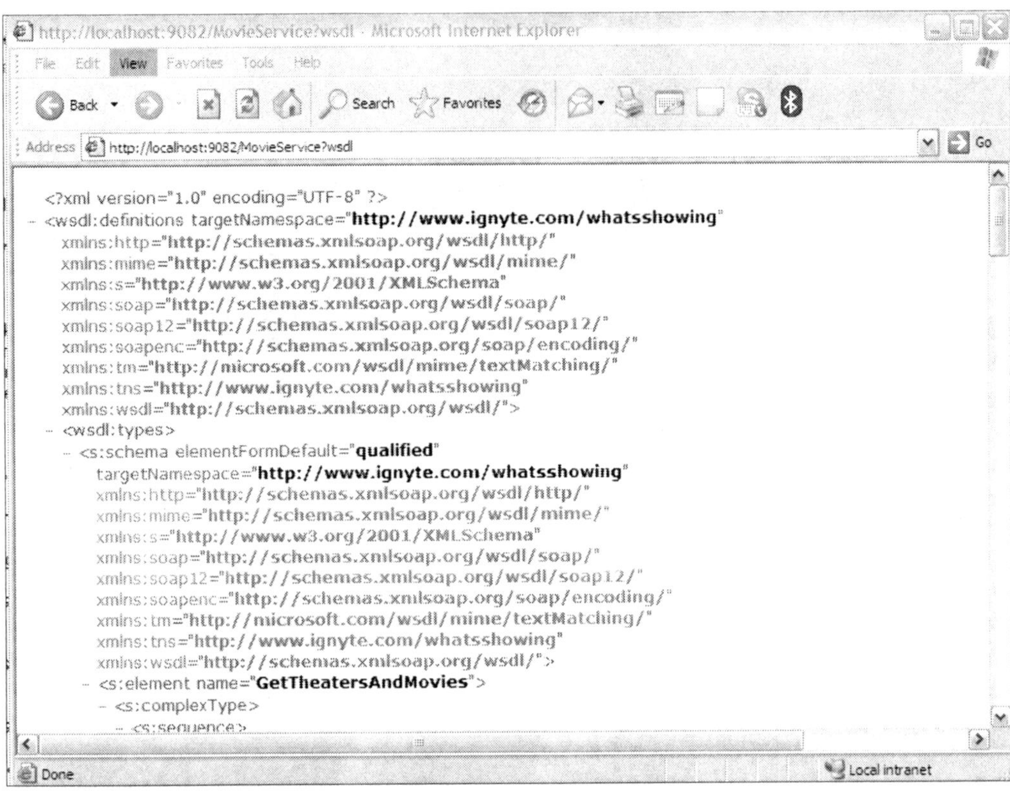

We have thus successfully deployed the Movie information web service. Next, we look at how to invoke the web service.

Invoking the web service

We will use the JavaScript client generated earlier to invoke the Movie web service. The only thing we need to change is the URL of the Movie web service in the HTML page. To do this, navigate to the `wsdl2JS/src` folder, edit the `MovieInformation.html` page, replace `http://www.ignyte.com/webservices/ignyte.whatsshowing.webservice/moviefunctions.asmx` with the address `http://localhost:9082/MovieService` as shown below, and save the HTML page.

```
MovieService.url = " http://www.ignyte.com/webservices/ignyte.
whatsshowing.webservice/moviefunctions.asmx";
by
MovieService.url = "http://localhost:9082/MovieService";
```

Open the `MovieInformation.html` page, and click on the **Invoke button**. You will see the following results being displayed in **Movie Results Web Service table**. As you can see, the information displayed is what we have implemented in the **MovieInformationSoapImpl** service.

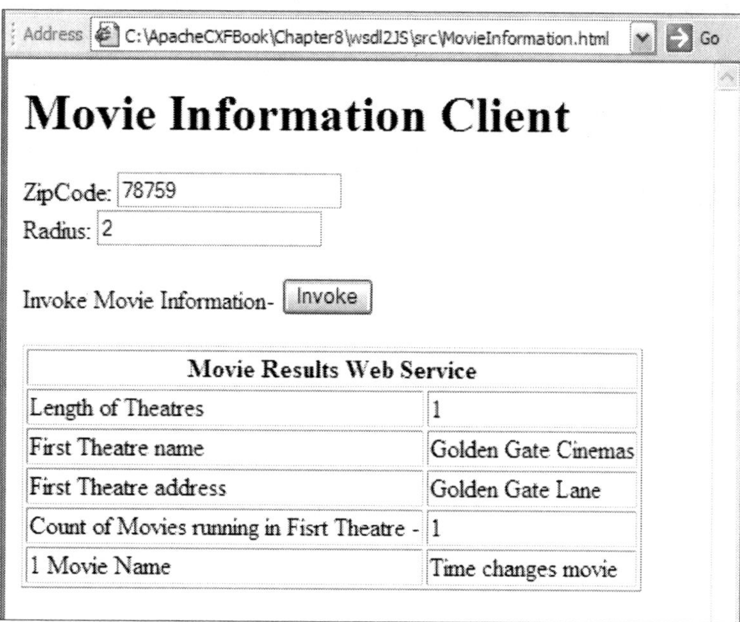

We have thus successfully published and invoked the Movie information web service.

Validating WSDL files

CXF provides a `WSDLValidator` tool to validate the WSDL file and to ensure schemas are well defined. This tool is helpful if you have created the WSDL file from scratch and want to validate it for correctness.

The build file for the example is available in the `Chapter8/WSDLValidator` folder of the downloaded source code. To run the example, navigate to `Chapter8/WSDLValidator`, and run the following command. Before running the target, make sure that you have published the Movie Service, as mentioned in the *Deploying and publishing the web service* section.

```
ant cxfWSDLValidator
```

This will validate the Movie Service WSDL file available at `http://localhost:9082/MovieService?wsdl`.

The next screenshot shows the output that should appear at the console. The **Valid WSDL** output will be displayed if the WSDL was successfully validated:

```
C:\ApacheCFXBookToolsFinal\WSDLValidator>ant cxfWSDLValidator
Buildfile: build.xml

cxfWSDLValidator:
     [java] Passed Validation : Valid WSDL

BUILD SUCCESSFUL
Total time: 7 seconds
C:\ApacheCFXBookToolsFinal\WSDLValidator>
```

The following code snippet shows the `cxfWSDLValidator` target in `build.xml.cxfWSDLValidator` calls the Apache CXF utility `org.apache.cxf.tools.validator.WSDLValidator` to validate the WSDL file whose URL is `http://localhost:9082/MovieService?wsdl`. You can also change the WSDL file location to actual .NET URL at `http://www.ignyte.com/webservices/ignyte.whatsshowing.webservice/moviefunctions.asmx?wsdl`

```
<target name="cxfWSDLValidator">
      <java classname="org.apache.cxf.tools.validator.WSDLValidator"
      fork="true">
          <arg value="http://localhost:9082/MovieService?wsdl"/>
        <classpath>
           <path refid="cxf.classpath"/>
        </classpath>
      </java>
   </target>
```

Summary

In this chapter we looked at how to:

- Utilize CXF tools for web services development
- Create Java and JavaScript web service clients from WSDL and invoke real world web services
- Create and deploy web service implementations from WSDL files and validate WSDL files

We also learnt that CXF tools come in very handy when you want to integrate and invoke third-party system functionality, exposed as web services.

A

Getting Ready with Code Examples

You need to follow these steps to run the code examples in this book:

- Download the source code for this book from the Packt website
- Download the software required for the book
- Set up the environment

In the course of chapters we explained how to use the ANT tool to build and execute the source code examples. If you plan to use Maven instead of the ANT tool, refer to the *Using Maven for Build management* section below on how to use Maven to build CXF examples.

Downloading the source code

The source code of the CXF book is available from the Packt website `http:/packtpub.com/files/code/5401_Code.zip`. Download the `cxf-5401.zip` file to a directory of your choice, such as `c:\`, and you will see the following structure:

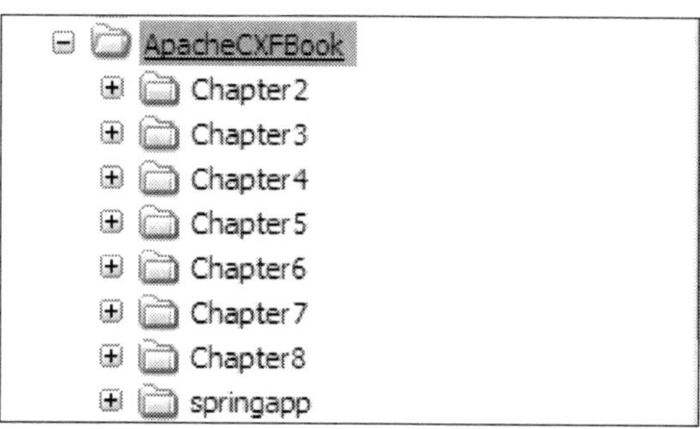

Each chapter provides the ANT build files (`build.xml` and `common_build.xml`) to run the examples using the ANT tool. In each chapter we have explained in detail how to create the examples from scratch, and build using the ANT tool. The source code and ANT build files are provided as a reference.

Chapter 2 provides a Maven build file (`pom.xml`) that can be used to run the examples with Maven. You can refer to the said `pom.xml` file to replicate build for other chapters for use with Maven.

The next screenshot shows the sample code structure from Chapter 2. In each chapter we have provided the layout of the folder structure. Here the **orderapp** folder contains the source code for Chapter 2.

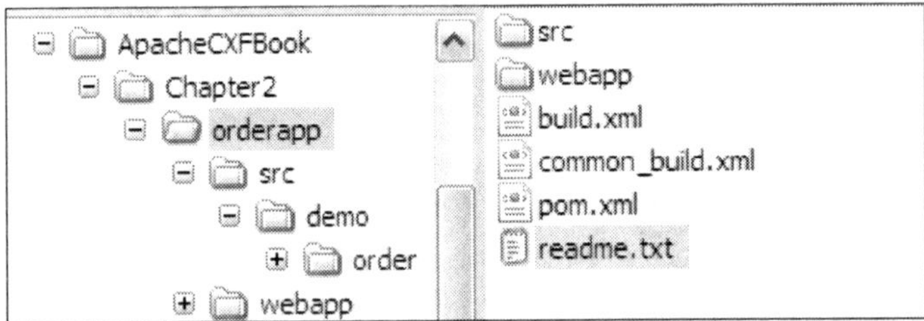

Downloading the software required for the book

You need the following software to be installed before running the code example:

- Java 5 or higher. Apache CXF requires JDK 5 or a later version. JDK 5 can be downloaded from the following site: `http://java.sun.com/j2se/1.5.0/download.jsp`
- Tomcat 6.0 or higher. There is no strict requirement for Tomcat for CXF. Any servlet container that supports Java 5 or higher can be used with CXF. For our illustrations, we use Tomcat as our servlet container. Tomcat version 6.0 can be downloaded from the following site: `http://tomcat.apache.org/download-60.cgi`
- Apache Ant 1.7.1 or higher (for building the code with Ant). Ant is used to build and deploy the code. The build utility can be downloaded from the following site: `http://ant.apache.org/bindownload.cgi`
- CXF binary distribution 2.2.3 or latest. CXF binary distribution can be downloaded from the site: `http://cxf.apache.org/download.html`

- Maven 2.x or higher (for building the code with Maven). If you plan to use Maven for build management, refer to the *Using Maven for Build management* section. Maven can be downloaded from the following site: `http://maven.apache.org/`

Setting up the environment

Once the the software is installed, we go about setting up the following environment variables:

Environment Variable	Description
`JAVA_HOME`	Set this to point to JDK 1.5 installation root folder, for example `C:\jdk1.5.0_12`
`CATALINA_HOME`	Set this to point to Tomcat installation root folder, for example `C:\Program Files\Tomcat 6.0`
`ANT_HOME`	Set this to point to ANT installation root folder, for example `C:\apache-ant-1.7.1`
`CXF_HOME`	Set this to point to CXF installation root folder, for example `C:\apache-cxf-2.2.3`
`MAVEN_HOME`	Set this to point to Maven installation root folder, for example. `C:\apache-maven-2.2.1`
`PATH`	Set this to point to the above respective '`HOME`' bin folder, for example `%JAVA_HOME%\bin`. Make sure that you do not overwrite the existing `PATH` variable content. You will need to add to the existing PATH.

The environment setup can also be automated using batch script. The script, under Windows environment, might look like the following:

```
@echo off
rem -----------------------------------------------------------
rem CXF Environment Setup script
rem -----------------------------------------------------------
set JAVA_HOME=C:\jdk1.5.0_12
set CATALINA_HOME=C:\Program Files\Tomcat 6.0
set ANT_HOME=C:\apache-ant-1.7.1
set CXF_HOME=C:\apache-cxf-2.2.3
set MAVEN_HOME= C:\apache-maven-2.2.1
set PATH=%PATH%;%JAVA_HOME%\bin;%CATALINA_HOME%\bin;%ANT_HOME%\
bin;%CXF_HOME%\bin;%MAVEN_HOME%\bin
rem -----------------------------------------------------------
```

Alternatively, Windows users can make use of **Control Panel** to set up the environment variable. From **Control Panel**, select **System Properties** and select the **Advanced** tab. Under the **Advanced** tab, click on the **Environment Variables** button, and set the appropriate environment variable.

Once the environment is set up, refer to the relevant chapter on how to develop, build and run the source code.

Using Maven for Build management

Maven is a software tool for build and project management. It uses a construct known as the **Project Object Model** (**POM**), which describes the components of your project and dependency to build the project in an XML format. Maven provides various pre-defined tasks, which facilitate build management and allow extensions to add more specific build tasks. Understanding and using Maven effectively is a vast topic, and there are a lot of books dedicated to using Maven effectively. We intend to provide a very short overview on Maven for readers who are not familiar with the tool.

A key concept in Maven is that of artifacts, a packaged archive like a JAR or WAR, which is created by the build and stored in a repository. Maven maintains artifacts in a repository, indexed by Group ID which specifies the group, Artifact ID which specifies the name of the artifact, and Version which specifies the version number of the artifact. For instance, in the case of the CXF JAX-WS component, the group ID is `org.apache.cxf`, artifact ID is `cxf-rt-frontend-jaxws`, and the version is `2.2.3` (or the latest). When you build using the Maven tool, a local repository is created for you, typically in your home drive, that is, `C:\Documents and Settings\userName\.m2\repository` and all the dependent artifacts required for building the project are copied in their respective `groups\artifacts\version` folder in the local repository. Note that while building the project, the Maven tool first checks if the required artifact exists in the local repository and then looks up the Maven central repository (or the repository specified) to download the artifact from the Internet.

Apache CXF also supports Maven-based build and installation and provides various tasks which simplify CXF application management. The CXF artifacts can be accessed from the Maven central repository itself. The complete release is available at the following location: `http://repo1.maven.org/maven2/org/apache/cxf/`

The following shows an example of POM, and how dependencies are declared to build applications which use the CXF framework using Maven:

```
<properties>
  <!-- CXF Version -->
  <cxf.version>2.2.3</cxf.version>
</properties>


<dependencies>
   <dependency>
      <groupId>org.apache.cxf</groupId>
      <artifactId>cxf-rt-frontend-jaxws</artifactId>
      <version>${cxf.version}</version>
   </dependency>
   <dependency>
      <groupId>org.apache.cxf</groupId>
      <artifactId>cxf-rt-transports-http</artifactId>
      <version>${cxf.version}</version>
   </dependency>
   <dependency>
```

Each dependency is listed as the `<dependency>` tag, with the `<groupId>`, `<artifactId>`, and `<version>`

Building chapter source code using Maven

We will show how to use Maven for building the source code as part of Chapter 2. The following shows the `pom.xml` from the `Chapter2\orderapp` folder of the source code download. Please refer to the inline comments, which are highlighted in bold for an explanation of the tags.

```
<project xmlns="http://maven.apache.org/POM/4.0.0" xmlns:xsi=
"http://www.w3.org/2001/XMLSchema-instance"
   xsi:schemaLocation="http://maven.apache.org/POM/4.0.0
   http://maven.apache.org/maven-v4_0_0.xsd">
   <modelVersion>4.0.0</modelVersion>
   <!-- Defines group id for cxfbook -->
   <groupId>com.packtpub.cxfbook</groupId>
   <!-- Name of the artifact -->
   <artifactId>orderapp</artifactId>
   <!-- Packing format. We want to pakacge this as a WAR archive -->
   <packaging>war</packaging>
   <!-- Version for the oderapp arifact -->
   <version>1.0-SNAPSHOT</version>
   <name>orderapp maven webapp</name>
```

```
    <properties>
       <!-- Version of CXF. Change this to latets version for building
against latest CXF distribution -->
       <cxf.version>2.2.3</cxf.version>
    </properties>
    <build>
          <!--Directory where the source code is located-->
          <sourceDirectory>src</sourceDirectory>
          <resources>
             <resource>
       <!-- Include properties and xml file from src folder-->
                <directory>src</directory>
                <includes>
                   <include>**/*.properties</include>
                   <include>**/*.xml</include>
                </includes>
             </resource>
             </resources>
      <plugins>
        <plugin>
       <!-- Maven Plugin used to build WAR archive-->
         <artifactId>maven-war-plugin</artifactId>
         <version>2.0</version>
         <configuration>
         <!-- Directory for Web application-->
         <webappDirectory>webapp</webappDirectory>
         <webResources>
           </webResources>
         </configuration>
       </plugin>
       <plugin>
        <!-- Plugin for compiling Java code -->
       <artifactId>maven-compiler-plugin</artifactId>
          <configuration>
             <!-- Java version for compiling the source code-->
           <source>1.5</source>
            <target>1.5</target>
          </configuration>
          </plugin>
       </plugins>
       <finalName>orderapp</finalName>
    </build>
    <dependencies>
       <dependency>
     <!-- Apache JAX-WS CXF Dependency for WAR and JAX-WS Client-->
          <groupId>org.apache.cxf</groupId>
          <artifactId>cxf-rt-frontend-jaxws</artifactId>
          <version>${cxf.version}</version>
       </dependency>
       <dependency>
```

```
        <!-- Apache JAX-WS CXF Dependency for HTTP transport-->
        <groupId>org.apache.cxf</groupId>
        <artifactId>cxf-rt-transports-http</artifactId>
        <version>${cxf.version}</version>
      </dependency>
    </dependencies>
  </project>
```

To build the Chapter 2 source code, navigate to the `Chapter2\orderapp` folder, and type in the following command:

```
mvn clean install
```

You will see the following build output, and the WAR file will be generated in the `orderapp/target` folder. You can then deploy the WAR file in the Tomcat server.

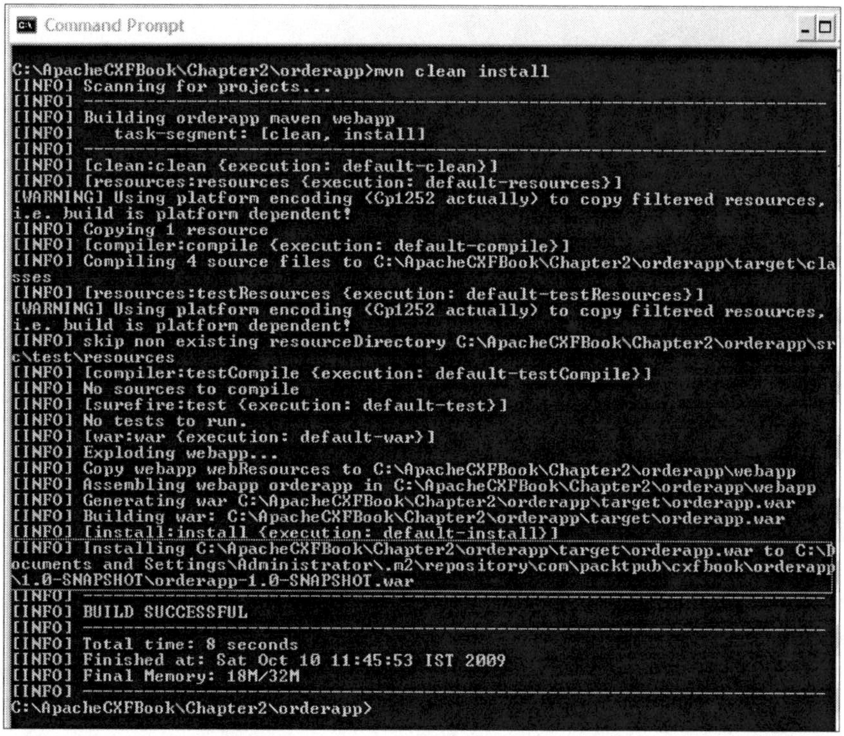

```
Command Prompt
C:\ApacheCXFBook\Chapter2\orderapp>mvn clean install
[INFO] Scanning for projects...
[INFO] ------------------------------------------------------------------------
[INFO] Building orderapp maven webapp
[INFO]    task-segment: [clean, install]
[INFO] ------------------------------------------------------------------------
[INFO] [clean:clean {execution: default-clean}]
[INFO] [resources:resources {execution: default-resources}]
[WARNING] Using platform encoding (Cp1252 actually) to copy filtered resources,
i.e. build is platform dependent!
[INFO] Copying 1 resource
[INFO] [compiler:compile {execution: default-compile}]
[INFO] Compiling 4 source files to C:\ApacheCXFBook\Chapter2\orderapp\target\cla
sses
[INFO] [resources:testResources {execution: default-testResources}]
[WARNING] Using platform encoding (Cp1252 actually) to copy filtered resources,
i.e. build is platform dependent!
[INFO] skip non existing resourceDirectory C:\ApacheCXFBook\Chapter2\orderapp\sr
c\test\resources
[INFO] [compiler:testCompile {execution: default-testCompile}]
[INFO] No sources to compile
[INFO] [surefire:test {execution: default-test}]
[INFO] No tests to run.
[INFO] [war:war {execution: default-war}]
[INFO] Exploding webapp...
[INFO] Copy webapp webResources to C:\ApacheCXFBook\Chapter2\orderapp\webapp
[INFO] Assembling webapp orderapp in C:\ApacheCXFBook\Chapter2\orderapp\webapp
[INFO] Generating war C:\ApacheCXFBook\Chapter2\orderapp\target\orderapp.war
[INFO] Building war: C:\ApacheCXFBook\Chapter2\orderapp\target\orderapp.war
[INFO] [install:install {execution: default-install}]
[INFO] Installing C:\ApacheCXFBook\Chapter2\orderapp\target\orderapp.war to C:\D
ocuments and Settings\Administrator\.m2\repository\com\packtpub\cxfbook\orderapp
\1.0-SNAPSHOT\orderapp-1.0-SNAPSHOT.war
[INFO] ------------------------------------------------------------------------
[INFO] BUILD SUCCESSFUL
[INFO] ------------------------------------------------------------------------
[INFO] Total time: 8 seconds
[INFO] Finished at: Sat Oct 10 11:45:53 IST 2009
[INFO] Final Memory: 18M/32M
[INFO] ------------------------------------------------------------------------
C:\ApacheCXFBook\Chapter2\orderapp>
```

Alternatively, if you wish to deploy using a standalone web server like Jetty, then you can add the following plugin in the `POM` file:

```
<plugins>
  <plugin>
    <groupId>org.mortbay.jetty</groupId>
    <artifactId>maven-jetty-plugin</artifactId>
```

```
        <version>6.1.19</version>
      </plugin>
```

You can run the server by giving the following command:

`mvn jetty:run`

The previous command will start the WAR on `localhost port 8080`

Once the WAR file is deployed, run the client, and this will invoke the Order Process web service by typing in the following command from the `Chapter2\orderapp` folder:

`mvn exec:java -Dexec.mainClass=demo.order.client.Client`

You will see the following output and "**order ID is ORD1234**" being printed at the console:

```
Command Prompt
INFO: No cxf.xml configuration file detected, relying on defaults.
Oct 10, 2009 11:53:04 AM org.springframework.context.support.AbstractApplication
Context obtainFreshBeanFactory
INFO: Bean factory for application context [org.apache.cxf.bus.spring.BusApplica
tionContext@136c55]: org.springframework.beans.factory.support.DefaultListableBe
anFactory@52eef4
Oct 10, 2009 11:53:04 AM org.springframework.beans.factory.support.DefaultListab
leBeanFactory preInstantiateSingletons
INFO: Pre-instantiating singletons in org.springframework.beans.factory.support.
DefaultListableBeanFactory@52eef4: defining beans [cxf,org.apache.cxf.bus.spring
.BusApplicationListener,org.apache.cxf.bus.spring.BusWiringBeanFactoryPostProces
sor,org.apache.cxf.bus.spring.Jsr250BeanPostProcessor,org.apache.cxf.bus.spring.
BusExtensionPostProcessor,org.apache.cxf.resource.ResourceManager,org.apache.cxf
.configuration.Configurer,org.apache.cxf.binding.BindingFactoryManager,org.apach
e.cxf.transport.DestinationFactoryManager,org.apache.cxf.transport.ConduitInitia
torManager,org.apache.cxf.wsdl.WSDLManager,org.apache.cxf.phase.PhaseManager,org
.apache.cxf.workqueue.WorkQueueManager,org.apache.cxf.buslifecycle.BusLifeCycleM
anager,org.apache.cxf.endpoint.ServerRegistry,org.apache.cxf.endpoint.ServerLife
CycleManager,org.apache.cxf.endpoint.ClientLifeCycleManager,org.apache.cxf.trans
ports.http.QueryHandlerRegistry,org.apache.cxf.endpoint.EndpointResolverRegistry
,org.apache.cxf.headers.HeaderManager,org.apache.cxf.catalog.OASISCatalogManager
,org.apache.cxf.endpoint.ServiceContractResolverRegistry,org.apache.cxf.jaxws.co
ntext.WebServiceContextResourceResolver,org.apache.cxf.jaxws.context.WebServiceC
ontextImpl,org.apache.cxf.binding.soap.SoapBindingFactory,org.apache.cxf.binding
.soap.SoapTransportFactory,org.apache.cxf.binding.soap.customEditorConfigurer,or
g.apache.cxf.binding.xml.XMLBindingFactory,org.apache.cxf.ws.addressing.policy.A
ddressingAssertionBuilder,org.apache.cxf.ws.addressing.policy.AddressingPolicyIn
terceptorProvider,org.apache.cxf.ws.addressing.policy.UsingAddressingAssertionBu
ilder,org.apache.cxf.transport.http.policy.HTTPClientAssertionBuilder,org.apache
.cxf.transport.http.policy.HTTPServerAssertionBuilder,org.apache.cxf.transport.h
ttp.policy.NoOpPolicyInterceptorProvider,org.apache.cxf.transport.http.ClientOnl
yHTTPTransportFactory]; root of factory hierarchy
Oct 10, 2009 11:53:04 AM org.apache.cxf.service.factory.ReflectionServiceFactory
Bean buildServiceFromClass
INFO: Creating Service {http://order.demo/}OrderProcessService from class demo.o
rder.OrderProcess
Order approved; order ID is ORD1234
C:\ApacheCXFBook\Chapter2\orderapp>
```

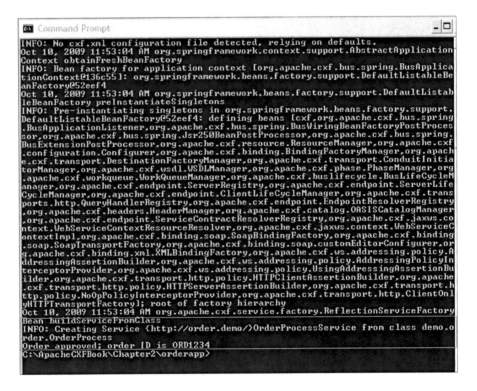

We have thus successfully built, deployed, and executed the code using the Maven tool.

B

Getting Started with Spring

Spring is an open source framework created to simplify the complexity of enterprise application development. The Spring framework addresses all tiers of application development in a consistent manner. The Spring framework provides a layered architecture comprised of well defined modules, where each module can be used independently to simplify some area of enterprise development. Spring functionality can be used in a non managed environment, for instance an eclipse-based application running in J2SE environment or in Java EE server.

To learn more about the latest developments in the Spring framework, visit the Spring website at `http://www.springsource.org/about`

Understanding all the modules and features provided by the Spring framework is a vast topic in itself and there are numerous books dedicated to Spring. In this appendix chapter our attempt is to cover the basic understanding of Spring framework to get you acquainted with the Spring capabilities used in the context of CXF web services development for this book. The following topics will be covered in this appendix chapter:

- Concept of POJO-based development
- Understanding **Inversion of Control** (**IoC**)
- Overview of aspect-oriented programming
- Introduction to Spring framework
- Creating a Spring IoC application

Concept of POJO-based development

A POJO is simply a Java object that does not implement any infrastructure framework-specific interfaces. The POJO-based development model is all about using Plain Old Java objects for designing and developing applications and concentrating on business logic, without worrying about external dependency, such as adding code to POJO for transaction handling, dealing with message queues and connections in the case of **JMS** (**Java Message Service**) applications, and so on. The POJO programming model enables you to unit test the code without requiring an external dependency like an EJB container or an application server, making the whole programming experience simplified.

Once you start creating applications comprised of POJO, the next thing you need to determine is how you would assemble the application out of these POJOs in a loosely coupled and consistent manner, as ultimately your goal is to run your application in J2SE or a Java EE environment. If you are planning to deploy your application in Java EE environment, you will also want to leverage container capabilities like distributed transaction management, persistence support, or JMS support. For your unit testing, you will want to run POJO without these external container dependencies. In short, we want various services to be applied to POJO in a consistent manner, so it can work in any environment. This is where the Spring framework comes in, whose aim is to provide a consistent programming model for POJO-based development, apply various services to POJO transparently, and to enable enterprise application development using POJO.

Two of the most important features you need to be aware of before understanding the Spring framework are IoC and AOP.

Note that the Spring framework offers many more capabilities than IoC and AOP.

Understanding Inversion of Control

The basic concept of the Inversion of Control pattern (also known as dependency injection) is that you do not create your objects but describe how they should be created.

Take the following example of a loan processing application. For simplicity the Loan process system carries out three steps—Customer Address verification, Credit verification, and Loan assessment. Each of these steps is implemented as Java classes, `VerifyAddress`, `VerifyCredit`, and `LoanAssessment`, respectively. Now, in traditional application development without IoC, the following code snippet would be used by the Loan processing application to carry out the loan processing as part of the `appyLoan()` method shown below:

```
package demo.spring;

public class LoanProcessImpl {

   public Loan
 applyLoan(Loan loan) {

      VerifyAddress verifyAddress = new VerifyAddressImpl();
      VerifyCredit verifyCredit = new VerifyCreditImpl();
      LoanAssessment loanAssessment = new LoanAssessmentImpl();

      //Step one - verify address
      boolean validAddress = verifyAddress.
      verifyAddress(loan.getCustomer().getAddress());
      if(!validAddress){
         throw new RuntimeException("Address for Customer SSN "+
         loan.getCustomer().getSSN() + " is not valid");
      }
      //Step two -verify credit
      String status = verifyCredit.verifyCredit(loan.getCustomer());
      if(status.equalsIgnoreCase(VerifyCredit.BAD_CREDIT)){
         //If bad credit, disapprove Loan
         loan.setLoanStatus(LoanAssessment.LOAN_REJECTED);
         return loan;
      }else {
         return loanAssessment.assessLoan(loan);
      }

   }

}
```

As you see in the previous code, in the `applyLoan()` method we have created an instance of `VerifyAddress`, `VerifyCredit`, and `LoanAssessment` objects. If any of these objects is dependant on other objects, then it needs to be instantiated in that scope (that is, in that class or method). These dependencies can grow based on our application, and manageability could become a difficult task. You may not realize that most of the time your object would be stateless and would eventually require one shared instance of object in your application, rather than creating a creating a new object for every request. Apart from object creation, you could also have configuration in your code, such as looking up the Data source connection factory using JNDI.

Applying IoC principles would make your design modular and move the object creation code and configuration outside of the application code and manage these dependency in an external configuration file. A container (like the Spring framework's IoC container) then uses the external configuration file to create the beans, manage the dependency and assemble the application from these loosely coupled beans. In the Spring IoC application section, we will look at how to apply IoC principles using Spring by taking the example of the Loan application that we discussed above.

Overview of aspect-oriented programming

Aspect-oriented programming, or AOP, is a programming technique that allows modularization of software by minimizing crosscutting concerns, or behavior that cuts across multiple modules (or classes) in a system, such as logging, security and transaction management. AOP and IoC are complementary technologies in that both apply a modular approach to complex problems in enterprise application development.

In order to understand the concept of AOP, let's take a simple example of logging functionality used in applications. In a typical object-oriented development approach you might implement logging functionality by putting logger statements in all your methods and Java classes. In an AOP approach you would instead modularize the logging concern and apply it declaratively to the components that require logging functionality, without the component knowing about the existence of the logging concern itself. In AOP terminology, the modular unit for crosscutting concern like logging, which is applied dynamically to modules, is referred to as Aspect.

Introduction to Spring framework

Spring framework is a light weight open source layered application framework created to simplify the complexity of enterprise application development. Spring has become the de facto framework for creating Java based enterprise applications.

The Spring framework provides the following functionality:

- Light weight IoC container for lifecycle and dependency management of objects.
- AOP functionality for modularizing cross-cutting concerns and providing services to POJO in a declarative fashion, like transaction management, logging, messaging, exposing POJO using one of the remote technology like RMI, HTTP, web services, and so on.
- Consistent abstraction layer which provides integration with various standards like **JPA (Java Persistence API)**, JDBC, JMS, and third party APIs like Hibernate, Top Link, and JDO.
- MVC framework which provides a highly configurable Model View Controller implementation via strategy interfaces, and accommodates numerous view technologies including JSP, Velocity, Tiles, iText, and POI implementation.

Spring framework assists in POJO development where all the features described above can be applied to POJO and the Spring IoC container provides the necessary infrastructure to assemble POJOs to create the required application.

The Spring IoC container

The core of Spring's design is the `org.springframework.beans` package, designed for working with beans. The package serves as the underlying medium for other functionality and is typically not used by developers. The next layer of abstraction is the `org.springframework.beans.factory.BeanFactory` interface which is the root interface for accessing the Spring IoC container. An implementation of `BeanFactory` enables you to access the objects that are instantiated and managed by the Spring IoC container.

The most commonly used `BeanFactory` definition is the `XmlBeanFactory` which loads beans based on definitions in an XML file, as shown in code listing below:

```
BeanFactory factory = new XMLBeanFactory(new FileInputSteam("beans.
xml"));
```

To retrieve a bean from BeanFactory you simply call the `getBean()` method: passing in the name of the bean you want to retrieve, as shown in listing below

```
OrderBean orderbean = (MyBean) factory.getBean("order");
```

Next we look at IoC concepts in action by taking an example of a Loan processing system. The following example should be sufficient to understand the concepts of IoC used in the context of the book.

Creating a Spring IoC application

We will take an example of a Loan Processing Application. For simplicity our Loan process system carries out three steps for approving or rejecting the loan. These steps include Customer Address verification, Credit verification, and Loan assessment.

We start by designing our application, and identifying the entity model of the system that would interact with the system. All of the entity can be modelled as POJO. We will define the following entity model for the Loan processing system:

- Address POJO—this contains address information
- Customer POJO—this contains customer information. The customer object holds a reference to the address object instance.
- Loan POJO—this contains Loan information and holds a reference to the address Customer object.

Each POJO provides a set of properties and corresponding `get`/`set` method to set the information. For instance `Customer` object provides the `setFirstname` and `getFirstName` methods to set and get the `firstName` property.

> The source code and build file of is available in the `ApacheCXFBook/springapp` folder of the source code distribution. Refer to the Appendix *Getting Ready with the Code examples* for detailed instructions on how to download the source code from the Packt web site.

Creating the entity model

We will now create the entity models. Let's start off by creating the Address model. We will name this implementation class as `Address`. The following is the code listing for `Address.java`:

```
package demo.spring;

public class Address {

    private String addressLine1;
```

```
    private String addressLine2;
    private String city;
    private String state;
    private String country;

    public String getAddressLine1() {
        return addressLine1;
    }
    public void setAddressLine1(String addressLine1) {
        this.addressLine1 = addressLine1;
    }
    public String getAddressLine2() {
        return addressLine2;
    }
    public void setAddressLine2(String addressLine2) {
        this.addressLine2 = addressLine2;
    }
    public String getCity() {
        return city;
    }
    public void setCity(String city) {
        this.city = city;
    }
    public String getState() {
        return state;
    }
    public void setState(String state) {
        this.state = state;
    }
    public String getCountry() {
        return country;
    }
    public void setCountry(String country) {
        this.country = country;
    }


}
```

As you see above the `Address` class is pretty straightforward and provides properties and methods to store address information, such as address line, city, state, and country.

Next we will create the Customer entity model. We will name this implementation class as `Customer`. The following is the code listing for `Customer.java`:

```
package demo.spring;

public class Customer {

    private String firstname;
    private String lastname;
    private String SSN;
    private String DOB;
    private Address address;
    public String getFirst name() {
        return firstname;
    }
    public void setFirstname(String firstname) {
        this.firstname = firstname;
    }
    public String getLastname() {
        return lastname;
    }
    public void setLastname(String lastname) {
        this.lastname = lastname;
    }
    public String getDOB() {
        return DOB;
    }
    public void setDOB(String dob) {
        DOB = dob;
    }
    public Address getAddress() {
        return address;
    }
    public void setAddress(Address address) {
        this.address = address;
    }
    public String getSSN() {
        return SSN;
    }
    public void setSSN(String ssn) {
        SSN = ssn;
    }

}
```

The `Customer` object contains a reference to `Address` information, which stores the address information for the customer.

Finally we create the Loan entity. We will name this implementation class as `Loan`. The Following is the code listing for `Loan.java`:

```
package demo.spring;

import java.util.Date;

public class Loan {

    private Customer customer;
    private String loanApplicationId;
    private Date loanApplyDate;
    private String loanStatus;
    public String getLoanStatus() {
        return loanStatus;
    }
    public void setLoanStatus(String loanStatus) {
        this.loanStatus = loanStatus;
    }
    public Customer getCustomer() {
        return customer;
    }
    public void setCustomer(Customer customer) {
        this.customer = customer;
    }
    public String getLoanApplicationId() {
        return loanApplicationId;
    }
    public void setLoanApplicationId(String loanApplicationId) {
        this.loanApplicationId = loanApplicationId;
    }
    public Date getLoanApplyDate() {
        return loanApplyDate;
    }
    public void setLoanApplyDate(Date loanApplyDate) {
        this.loanApplyDate = loanApplyDate;
    }

}
```

The `Loan` object contains a reference to `Customer` information, which stores the customer information. Clients interact with the Loan system by creating an instance of `Loan` object.

With the entity modelled, we now create the various services for the Loan processing application that will carry out the required Loan functions.

Creating services

As part of the Loan processing application, we will create three services—verify Address, verify Credit and Loan assessment. These services are also designed as POJO. We start off by creating the Address verification service which validates an address.

We create an interface and implementation for the Address verification service. We will name the interface as `VerifyAddress` and the implementation class as `VerifyAddressImpl`. The Following provides the code listing for `VerifyAddress.java`:

```
package demo.spring;
public interface VerifyAddress {

   public boolean verifyAddress(Address address);
}
```

`VerifyAddress` interface provides the method `verifyAddress` which takes `Address` object as input and returns `true` or `false` to denote a valid or an invalid address. The following provides the code listing for `VerifyAddressImpl.java`. As part of the implementation, we provide a dummy implementation, which returns `false` if address city is `null`.

```
package demo.spring;
public class VerifyAddressImpl implements VerifyAddress {
   public boolean verifyAddress(Address address) {
      System.out.println("verifyAddress called");
      if(address.getCity() == null){
         return false;
      }
      return true;
   }
}
```

Next we will create the Credit Verification service which provides credit verification about the customer. We create an interface and implementation for the Credit verification service. We will name the interface as `VerifyCredit` and the implementation class as `VerifyCreditImpl`. The following provides the code listing for `VerifyCredit.java`:

```
package demo.spring;
public interface VerifyCredit {
   public String GOOD_CREDIT ="GOOD";
   public String BAD_CREDIT ="BAD";
   public String verifyCredit(Customer customer);
}
```

`VerifyCredit` provides one method, `verifyCredit` which takes `Customer` object as input and returns String with value either `GOOD_CREDIT` or `BAD_CREDIT`. The following provides the code listing for `VerifyCreditImpl.java`. As part of the implementation, we provide a dummy implementation, which returns `GOOD_CREDIT` if customer SSN starts with `A`. In a real world implementation, you would probably use one of the various external credit rating services offered over the web.

```
package demo.spring;
public class VerifyCreditImpl implements VerifyCredit {
   public String verifyCredit(Customer customer) {
      System.out.println("verifyCredit called with SSN " +
      customer.getSSN());
      if(customer.getSSN().startsWith("A")){
         return GOOD_CREDIT;
      }else{
         return BAD_CREDIT;
      }
   }
}
```

Next we will create the `LoanAssessment` service which provides loan assessment, taking into account the loan and customer details. We create an interface and implementation for the Loan Assessment service. We will name the interface as `LoanAssessment` and implementation class as `LoanAssessmentImpl`. The following provides the code listing for `LoanAssessment.java`:

```
package demo.spring;
public interface LoanAssessment {

   public String LOAN_APPROVED ="APPROVED";
   public String LOAN_REJECTED ="REJECTED";
```

```
    public Loan assessLoan(Loan loan);
}
```

`LoanAssessment` provides one method, `assessLoan` which takes the `Loan` object as input and returns the `Loan` object as output with the loan status as `APPROVED` or `REJECTED`. The following provides the code listing for `LoanAssessmentImpl.java`. As part of the implementation, we provide a dummy implementation, which sets the loan as approved if Customer SSN starts with "A".

```
package demo.spring;
import java.util.Date;
public class LoanAssessmentImpl implements LoanAssessment {
    public Loan assessLoan(Loan loan) {
        //Assign a unique id.
        loan.setLoanApplicationId(loan.getCustomer().getSSN() +
        System.currentTimeMillis());
        System.out.println("assessLoan loan id generated is "+
        loan.getLoanApplicationId());
        //Dummy implementation
        if(loan.getCustomer().getSSN().startsWith("A")){
            loan.setLoanStatus(LOAN_APPROVED);
        }else{
            loan.setLoanStatus(LOAN_REJECTED);
        }
        return loan;
    }
}
```

Creating the application and wiring POJO

So far we have created the loosely coupled POJO components as part of the Loan Processing application. From the implementation of the service and entity models, you can see the simplicity associated with POJO implementation and these POJO can be tested without the need for any external container dependency. The other feature is that these objects can be reused across the system and not just with Loan processing applications. For instance, address verification service and credit rating can be used wherever there is need for address and credit verification. Next we will assemble the services to realize the Loan Processing application. We will create an interface and implementation for the `LoanProcess` application. We name the interface as `LoanProcess` and implementation class as `LoanProcessImpl`. The following provides the code listing for `LoanProcess.java`:

```
package demo.spring;
public interface LoanProcess {
   public Loan applyLoan(Loan loan);
   public VerifyAddress getVerifyAddress();
   public void setVerifyAddress(VerifyAddress verifyAddress);
   public VerifyCredit getVerifyCredit();
   public void setVerifyCredit(VerifyCredit verifyCredit);
   public LoanAssessment getLoanAssessment();
   public void setLoanAssessment(LoanAssessment loanAssessment);
}
```

`LoanProcess` provides the `get/set` method to access the services, `VerifyAddresss`, `VerifyCredit`, and `LoanAssessment`, along with a method `applyLoan()`, which the client would call for applying the loan. The following shows the implementation for `LoanProcessImpl.java`:

```
package demo.spring;
public class LoanProcessImpl implements LoanProcess {
   private VerifyAddress verifyAddress;
   private VerifyCredit verifyCredit;
   private LoanAssessment loanAssessment;
   public VerifyAddress getVerifyAddress() {
      return verifyAddress;
   }
   public void setVerifyAddress(VerifyAddress verifyAddress) {
      this.verifyAddress = verifyAddress;
   }
   public VerifyCredit getVerifyCredit() {
      return verifyCredit;
   }
   public void setVerifyCredit(VerifyCredit verifyCredit) {
      this.verifyCredit = verifyCredit;
   }
   public LoanAssessment getLoanAssessment() {
      return loanAssessment;
   }
   public void setLoanAssessment(LoanAssessment loanAssessment) {
      this.loanAssessment = loanAssessment;
   }
   public Loan applyLoan(Loan loan) {
      //Step one - verify address
```

```
        boolean validAddress = getVerifyAddress().
        verifyAddress(loan.getCustomer().getAddress());
        if(!validAddress){
           throw new RuntimeException("Address for Customer SSN "+
           loan.getCustomer().getSSN() + " is not valid");
        }
        //Step two -verify credit
        String status = getVerifyCredit().
        verifyCredit(loan.getCustomer());
        if(status.equalsIgnoreCase(VerifyCredit.BAD_CREDIT)){
           //If bad credit, disapprove Loan
           loan.setLoanStatus(LoanAssessment.LOAN_REJECTED);
           return loan;
        }else {
           return getLoanAssessment().assessLoan(loan);
        }
   }

 }
```

As you see above, `LoanProcessImpl` provides `get/set` method implementations for various services, `getVerifyCredit()`, `setVerifyCredit()`, and so on , along with a dummy implementation for the `applyLoan()` method. `applyLoan()` calls the various services as part of load processing. First it calls `getVerifyAddress().verifyAddress()` to verify the address, next it calls the `getVerifyCredit().verifyCredit()` method to verify the credit and finally `getLoanAssessment().assessLoan()`, which approves or rejects the loan.

As you see, nowhere in the code have we created an instance of a service object that is `VerifyAddress`, `VerifyCredit` or `LoanAssessment`. So how does `LoanProcessImpl` get the services instance at runtime? All these dependencies are injected by the Spring IoC container using a configuration file. The configuration file tells the Spring ICO container how to instantiate, configure and wire the dependency in your application. In the Loan processing application, the setter methods for the services are called by Spring IoC framework reading the configuration file. The `applyLoan()` method will then use the service references to carry out the implementation.

The following is the listing of the Spring configuration file for the Loan processing application. We name the configuration file as `loanprocess.xml`.

```
<?xml version="1.0" encoding="UTF-8"?>
<beans xmlns="http://www.springframework.org/schema/beans"
      xmlns:xsi="http://www.w3.org/2001/XMLSchema-instance"
```

```
        xsi:schemaLocation="http://www.springframework.org/schema/beans
        http://www.springframework.org/schema/beans/spring-beans-
  2.0.xsd">

     <bean id="loanProcess" class="demo.spring.LoanProcessImpl">
        <property name="verifyAddress">
           <ref bean="verifyAddress" />
        </property>
        <property name="verifyCredit">
           <ref bean="verifyCredit" />
        </property>
        <property name="loanAssessment">
           <ref bean="loanAssessment" />
        </property>
     </bean>

     <bean id="verifyAddress" class="demo.spring.VerifyAddressImpl">
         <!--  wire dependency-->
      </bean>


      <bean id="verifyCredit" class="demo.spring.VerifyCreditImpl">
         <!--  wire dependency-->
      </bean>

      <bean id="loanAssessment" class="demo.spring.LoanAssessmentImpl">
         <!--  wire dependency-->
      </bean>

  </beans>
```

Let's analyze the `loanprocess.xml` code listing. We start off with the `<beans>` tag which defines the XML Schema for Spring beans framework. These are standard definitions for Spring , which you would find in any Spring configuration file. Next we define the beans used in our Loan Process application using the `<bean>` tag. The bean tag defines information on how to create the bean and defines a unique id, class definition, property, references, and various other properties. For a list of properties associated with bean definition, refer to Spring documentation. For instance, the `demo.spring.LoanAssessmentImpl` bean definition looks like the following:

```
<bean id="loanAssessment" class="demo.spring.LoanAssessmentImpl">
       <!--  wire dependency-->
</bean>
```

To wire the `loanAssessment` dependency to the `LoanProcessImpl` bean definition, you use the setter-based dependency injection and use the `ref bean` definition to wire the `loanAssessment` bean with the `loanAssessment` property.

Note that the `LoanProcessImpl` object provides `getter` and `setter` methods for the `loanAssesment` property and the following definition provides the wiring.

```
<bean id="loanProcess" class="demo.spring.LoanProcessImpl">
      <property name="loanAssessment">
         <ref bean="loanAssessment" />
      </property>
   </bean>
```

Similarly the `verifyAddress` and `verifyCredit` bean is defined and injected to the `loanProcess` bean. We have thus assembled our Loan processing application.

The same concepts of dependency injection have been applied throughout the book where we have used Spring configuration. CXF also provides its own schema and bean definition that you can use to configure CXF components, like the `<jaxws:client>` definition which lets you create JAXWS clients, rather than writing code to create the clients. All of the CXF components can be wired through Spring configurations and can leverage various features offered by Spring framework.

Creating the standalone client

We will now create the standalone client which will invoke the Loan processing application. We will name this implementation class as `LoanProcessClient`. The following provides the code listing for `LoanProcessClient.java`:

```
package demo.spring.client;
import java.util.Date;
import org.springframework.context.support.
ClassPathXmlApplicationContext;
import demo.spring.Address;
import demo.spring.Customer;
import demo.spring.Loan;
import demo.spring.LoanProcess;
public class LoanProcessClient {

   public static void main(String[] args){
      try
       {
      System.out.println("LoanProcessClient started");
```

```
        ClassPathXmlApplicationContext appContext =
        new ClassPathXmlApplicationContext(new String[] {
            "/demo/spring/loanprocess.xml"
        });

       System.out.println("Spring configuration file loaded");

       Customer customer = new Customer();
       customer.setFirstname("Naveen");
       customer.setLastname("Balani");
       customer.setSSN("A0989999999");

       //Address
       Address address = new Address();
       address.setAddressLine1("Stree one");
       address.setCity("Mumbai");
       address.setCountry("India");

       customer.setAddress(address);

       Loan loan = new Loan();
       loan.setCustomer(customer);
       loan.setLoanApplyDate(new Date());


       LoanProcess loanProcess = (LoanProcess)
       appContext.getBean("loanProcess");

       Loan loanResponse =loanProcess.applyLoan(loan);

       System.out.println("Loan status for customer with SSN " +
       loan.getCustomer().getSSN() + " is " +
       loanResponse.getLoanStatus());

        }
       catch(Exception e){
          e.printStackTrace();
       }
       }

}
```

`LoanProcessClient` creates the `Customer`, `Address`, and `Loan` object, and populates it with some data. `LoanProcessClient` also loads the Spring configuration files through `ClassPathXmlApplicationContext` as shown below:

```
ClassPathXmlApplicationContext appContext =
new ClassPathXmlApplicationContext(new String[] {
      "/demo/spring/loanprocess.xml"
   });
```

After the Spring configuration file is loaded, all the beans defined will be instantiated and the references will be wired. You can then access the bean, for instance `LoanProcess` POJO, through the `getBean()` method as shown below:

```
LoanProcess loanProcess = (LoanProcess)
      appContext.getBean("loanProcess");
```

Once the client gets a reference to `LoanProcess` object, it then executes the `applyLoan()` process on it and get backs the `LoanResponse` object and prints the status of loan on the console.

Running the program

Before running the program, we will organize the code so far developed in the appropriate folder structure. You can create the folder structure as shown below and put the components in the respective sub folders.

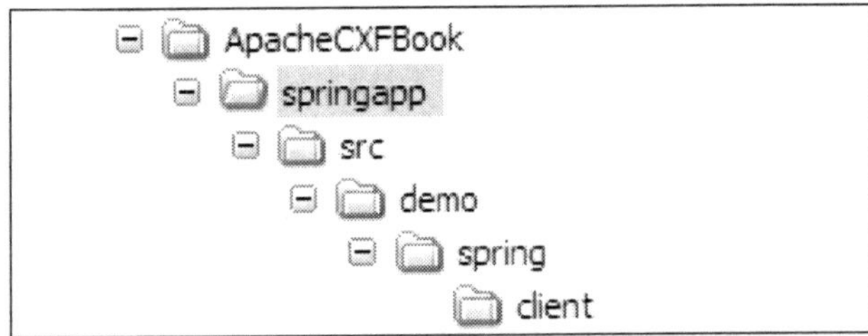

- As you see in the figure above, `springapp` is the project folder for this appendix chapter. `springapp/src` is the location of our source code. Place the Java code into the respective package folders in the `springapp/src` folder. Place `loanprocess.xml` in the `src/demo/spring` folder.
- Once the code is organized, we will go about building and executing the code.

Building the code

To build the code we will use the Maven tool. To set up the Maven environment, refer to Appendix A *Getting Ready with the Code examples*. The `pom.xml` file for this example is provided in `springapp` folder. The code below illustrates the `pom.xml` file:

```
<project xmlns="http://maven.apache.org/POM/4.0.0" xmlns:xsi=
"http://www.w3.org/2001/XMLSchema-instance"
  xsi:schemaLocation="http://maven.apache.org/POM/4.0.0
  http://maven.apache.org/maven-v4_0_0.xsd">
<modelVersion>4.0.0</modelVersion>
<groupId>packt</groupId>
<artifactId>springloanapp</artifactId>
<packaging>jar</packaging>
<version>1.0-SNAPSHOT</version>
<name>springloanapp</name>
<url>http://maven.apache.org</url>
<build>
      <!--Source Directory -->
      <sourceDirectory>src</sourceDirectory>
      <resources>
         <resource>
            <directory>src</directory>
            <includes>
               <include>**/*.properties</include>
               <include>**/*.xml</include>
            </includes>
         </resource>
      </resources>
      <plugins>
         <plugin>
            <artifactId>maven-compiler-plugin</artifactId>
            <configuration>
               <source>1.5</source>
               <target>1.5</target>
            </configuration>
         </plugin>
         </plugins>
</build>
<properties>
   <!-- Set the latest Spring version here -->
   <spring-version>2.5</spring-version>
   </properties>
<dependencies>
   <dependency>
```

```
        <groupId>org.springframework</groupId>
        <artifactId>spring</artifactId>
        <version>${spring-version}</version>
        </dependency>
    </dependencies>
    </project>
```

Open the command prompt window, go to the `springapp` folder and run the command `mvn clean install`. It will build the source code and put the class files under the target folder. The following screenshot shows the output generated on running the `mvn clean install` command:

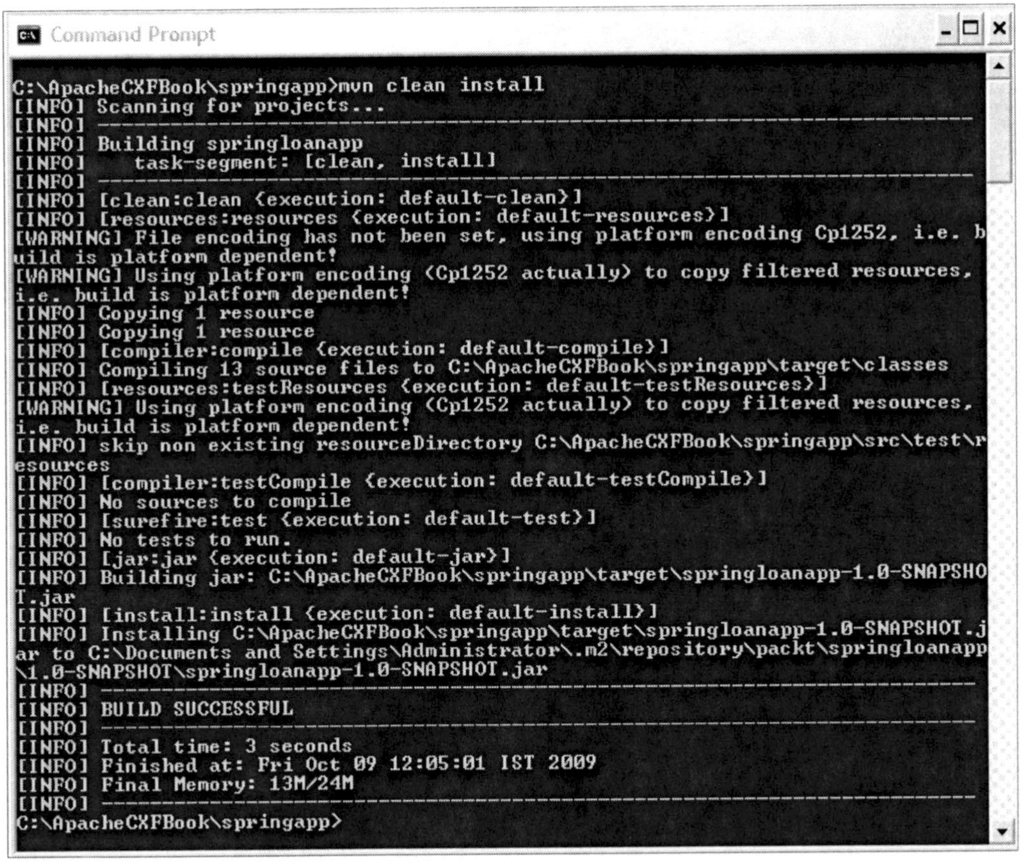

```
Command Prompt
C:\ApacheCXFBook\springapp>mvn clean install
[INFO] Scanning for projects...
[INFO] ------------------------------------------------------------------------
[INFO] Building springloanapp
[INFO]    task-segment: [clean, install]
[INFO] ------------------------------------------------------------------------
[INFO] [clean:clean {execution: default-clean}]
[INFO] [resources:resources {execution: default-resources}]
[WARNING] File encoding has not been set, using platform encoding Cp1252, i.e. b
uild is platform dependent!
[WARNING] Using platform encoding (Cp1252 actually) to copy filtered resources,
i.e. build is platform dependent!
[INFO] Copying 1 resource
[INFO] Copying 1 resource
[INFO] [compiler:compile {execution: default-compile}]
[INFO] Compiling 13 source files to C:\ApacheCXFBook\springapp\target\classes
[INFO] [resources:testResources {execution: default-testResources}]
[WARNING] Using platform encoding (Cp1252 actually) to copy filtered resources,
i.e. build is platform dependent!
[INFO] skip non existing resourceDirectory C:\ApacheCXFBook\springapp\src\test\r
esources
[INFO] [compiler:testCompile {execution: default-testCompile}]
[INFO] No sources to compile
[INFO] [surefire:test {execution: default-test}]
[INFO] No tests to run.
[INFO] [jar:jar {execution: default-jar}]
[INFO] Building jar: C:\ApacheCXFBook\springapp\target\springloanapp-1.0-SNAPSHO
T.jar
[INFO] [install:install {execution: default-install}]
[INFO] Installing C:\ApacheCXFBook\springapp\target\springloanapp-1.0-SNAPSHOT.j
ar to C:\Documents and Settings\Administrator\.m2\repository\packt\springloanapp
\1.0-SNAPSHOT\springloanapp-1.0-SNAPSHOT.jar
[INFO] ------------------------------------------------------------------------
[INFO] BUILD SUCCESSFUL
[INFO] ------------------------------------------------------------------------
[INFO] Total time: 3 seconds
[INFO] Finished at: Fri Oct 09 12:05:01 IST 2009
[INFO] Final Memory: 13M/24M
[INFO] ------------------------------------------------------------------------
C:\ApacheCXFBook\springapp>
```

Executing the code

You execute the Java client program `LoanProcessClient` by giving the following command on the command prompt window:

```
mvn exec:java -Dexec.mainClass=demo.spring.client.LoanProcessClient
```

Upon executing this command, the following output as shown in the screenshot below will be displayed. If you look at the **INFO**: log event highlighted in the output below, you see the beans—**loanProcess**, **verifyAddress**, **verifyCredit,** and **loanAssessment** being loaded by the Spring container based on the **loanprocess.xml** file.

You will then see that the output of the POJO methods being printed at the console, "**verifyAddress called**", "**verifyCredit called with SSN A0989999999**", "**assessLoan loan id generated is A09899999991255071849921**", and "**Loan status for customer with SSN A0989999999 is APPROVED**"

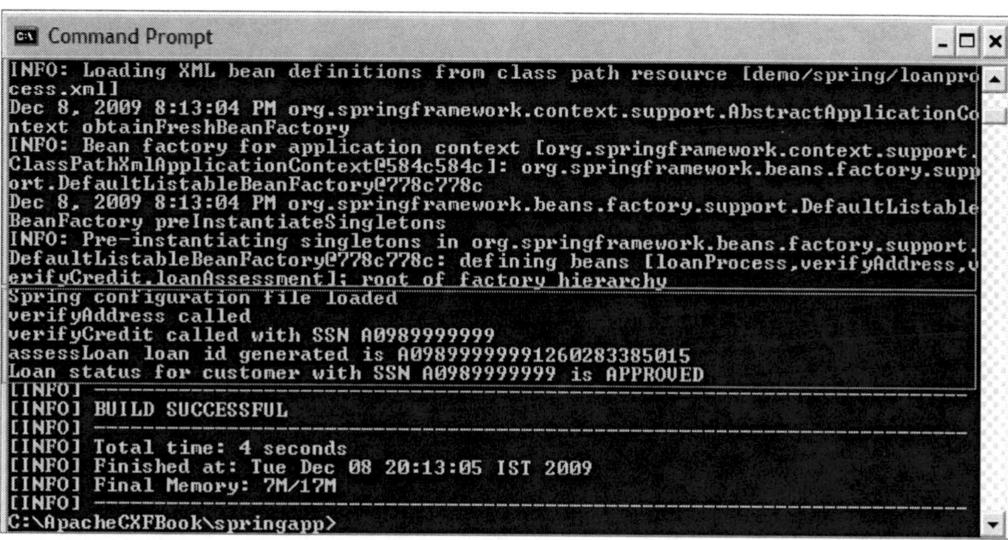

Command Prompt
INFO: Loading XML bean definitions from class path resource [demo/spring/loanprocess.xml]
Dec 8, 2009 8:13:04 PM org.springframework.context.support.AbstractApplicationContext obtainFreshBeanFactory
INFO: Bean factory for application context [org.springframework.context.support.ClassPathXmlApplicationContext@584c584c]: org.springframework.beans.factory.support.DefaultListableBeanFactory@778c778c
Dec 8, 2009 8:13:04 PM org.springframework.beans.factory.support.DefaultListableBeanFactory preInstantiateSingletons
INFO: Pre-instantiating singletons in org.springframework.beans.factory.support.DefaultListableBeanFactory@778c778c: defining beans [loanProcess,verifyAddress,verifyCredit,loanAssessment]; root of factory hierarchy
Spring configuration file loaded
verifyAddress called
verifyCredit called with SSN A0989999999
assessLoan loan id generated is A09899999991260283385015
Loan status for customer with SSN A0989999999 is APPROVED
[INFO] --
[INFO] BUILD SUCCESSFUL
[INFO] --
[INFO] Total time: 4 seconds
[INFO] Finished at: Tue Dec 08 20:13:05 IST 2009
[INFO] Final Memory: 7M/17M
[INFO] --
C:\ApacheCXFBook\springapp>

We have thus successfully assembled and executed our Loan Processing application using Spring IoC container features.

Summary

In this appendix chapter we looked at the concept of POJO development, IoC, and AOP. We then looked at features provided by Spring framework and executed a sample Loan processing application which demonstrated IoC principles using Spring IoC container. Going through the entire Spring framework and features is a vast topic in itself, and in this appendix chapter our intention was to provide you with just enough details to understand the concepts around dependency injection and Spring integration that we have used in the context of CXF web services development in this book.

Index

Symbols

A

B

C

D

I

J

L

M

N

O

P

R

S

T

U

W

X

Packt Open Source Project Royalties

When we sell a book written on an Open Source project, we pay a royalty directly to that project. Therefore by purchasing Apache CXF Web Service Development, Packt will have given some of the money received to the Apache Sowftware Foundation project.

In the long term, we see ourselves and you—customers and readers of our books—as part of the Open Source ecosystem, providing sustainable revenue for the projects we publish on. Our aim at Packt is to establish publishing royalties as an essential part of the service and support a business model that sustains Open Source.

If you're working with an Open Source project that you would like us to publish on, and subsequently pay royalties to, please get in touch with us.

Writing for Packt

We welcome all inquiries from people who are interested in authoring. Book proposals should be sent to `author@packtpub.com`. If your book idea is still at an early stage and you would like to discuss it first before writing a formal book proposal, contact us; one of our commissioning editors will get in touch with you.

We're not just looking for published authors; if you have strong technical skills but no writing experience, our experienced editors can help you develop a writing career, or simply get some additional reward for your expertise.

About Packt Publishing

Packt, pronounced 'packed', published its first book "Mastering phpMyAdmin for Effective MySQL Management" in April 2004 and subsequently continued to specialize in publishing highly focused books on specific technologies and solutions.

Our books and publications share the experiences of your fellow IT professionals in adapting and customizing today's systems, applications, and frameworks. Our solution-based books give you the knowledge and power to customize the software and technologies you're using to get the job done. Packt books are more specific and less general than the IT books you have seen in the past. Our unique business model allows us to bring you more focused information, giving you more of what you need to know, and less of what you don't.

Packt is a modern, yet unique publishing company, which focuses on producing quality, cutting-edge books for communities of developers, administrators, and newbies alike. For more information, please visit our website: `www.PacktPub.com`.

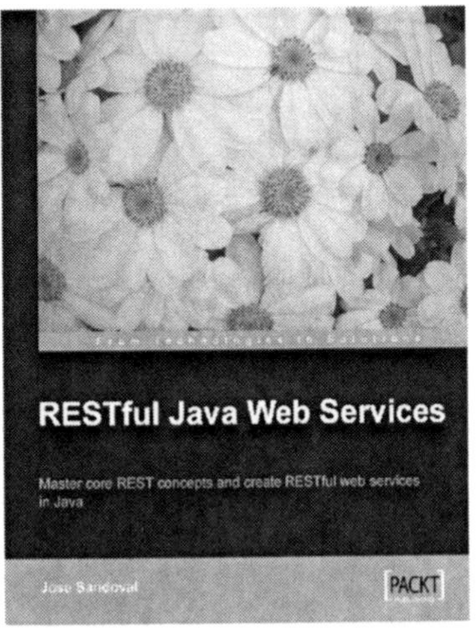

RESTful Java Web Services

ISBN: 978-1-847196-46-0 Paperback: 256 pages

Master core REST concepts and create RESTful web services in Java

1. Build powerful and flexible RESTful web services in Java using the most popular Java RESTful frameworks to date (Restlet, JAX-RS based frameworks Jersey and RESTEasy, and Struts 2)
2. Master the concepts to help you design and implement RESTful web services
3. Plenty of screenshots and clear explanations to facilitate learning

---

Spring Persistence with Hibernate

ISBN: 978-1-849510-56-1 Paperback: 460 pages

Build robust and reliable persistence solutions for your enterprise Java application

1. Get to grips with Hibernate and its configuration manager, mappings, types, session APIs, queries, and much more
2. Integrate Hibernate and Spring as part of your enterprise Java stack development
3. Work with Spring IoC (Inversion of Control), Spring AOP, transaction management, web development, and unit testing considerations and features

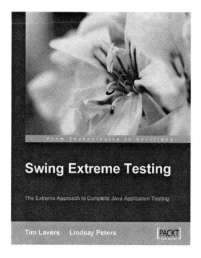

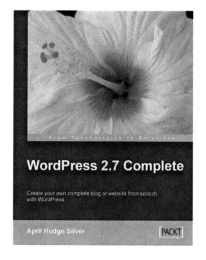

CPSIA information can be obtained at www.ICGtesting.com
229506LV00003B/62/P

9 781847 195401